JOHN FOX

A Painter in Venice | Un peintre à Venise

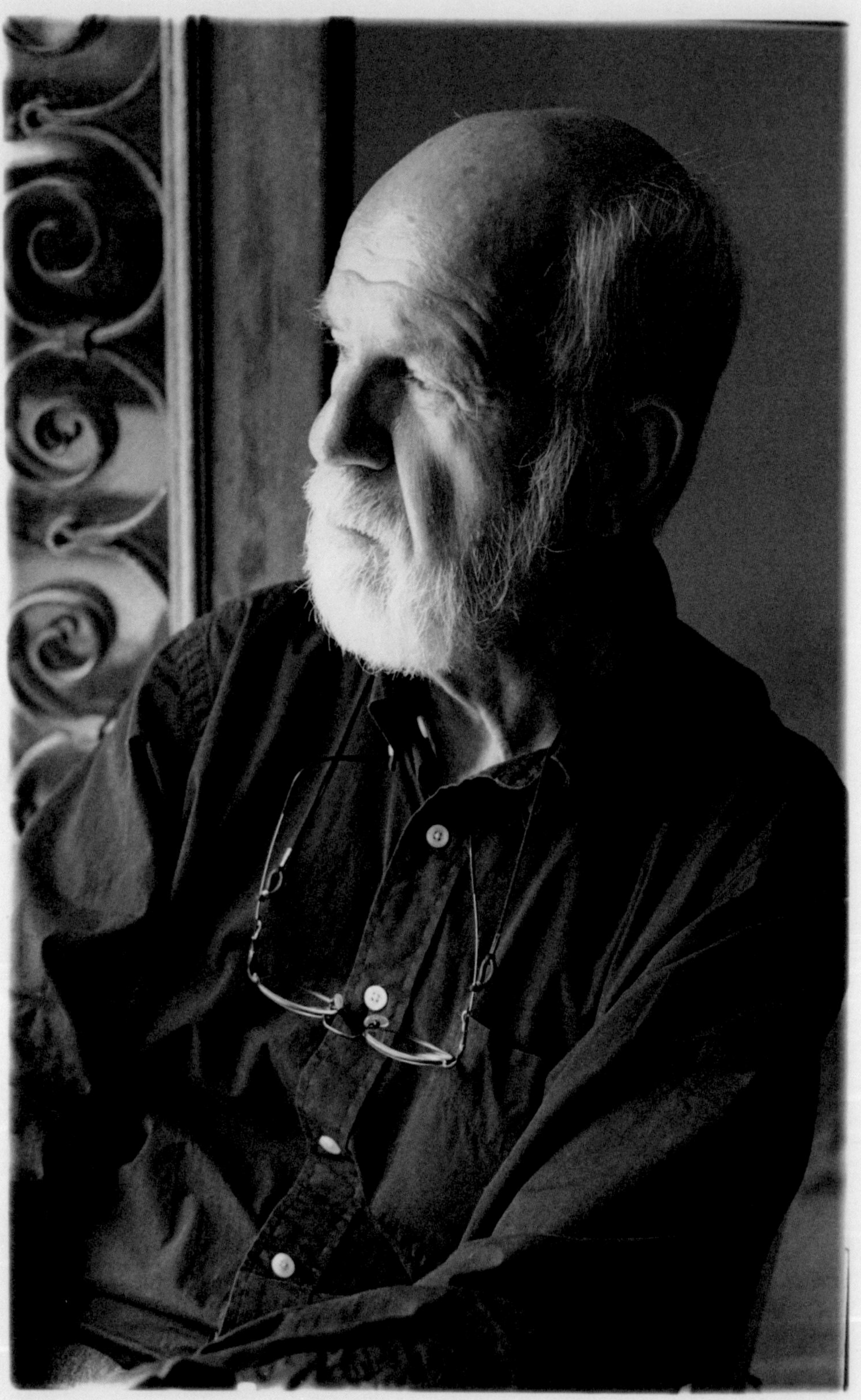

JOHN FOX

A Painter in Venice | Un peintre à Venise

VICTORIA LEBLANC, JOHN LEROUX, SANDRA PAIKOWSKY

Beaverbrook Art Gallery | Musée des beaux-arts Beaverbrook

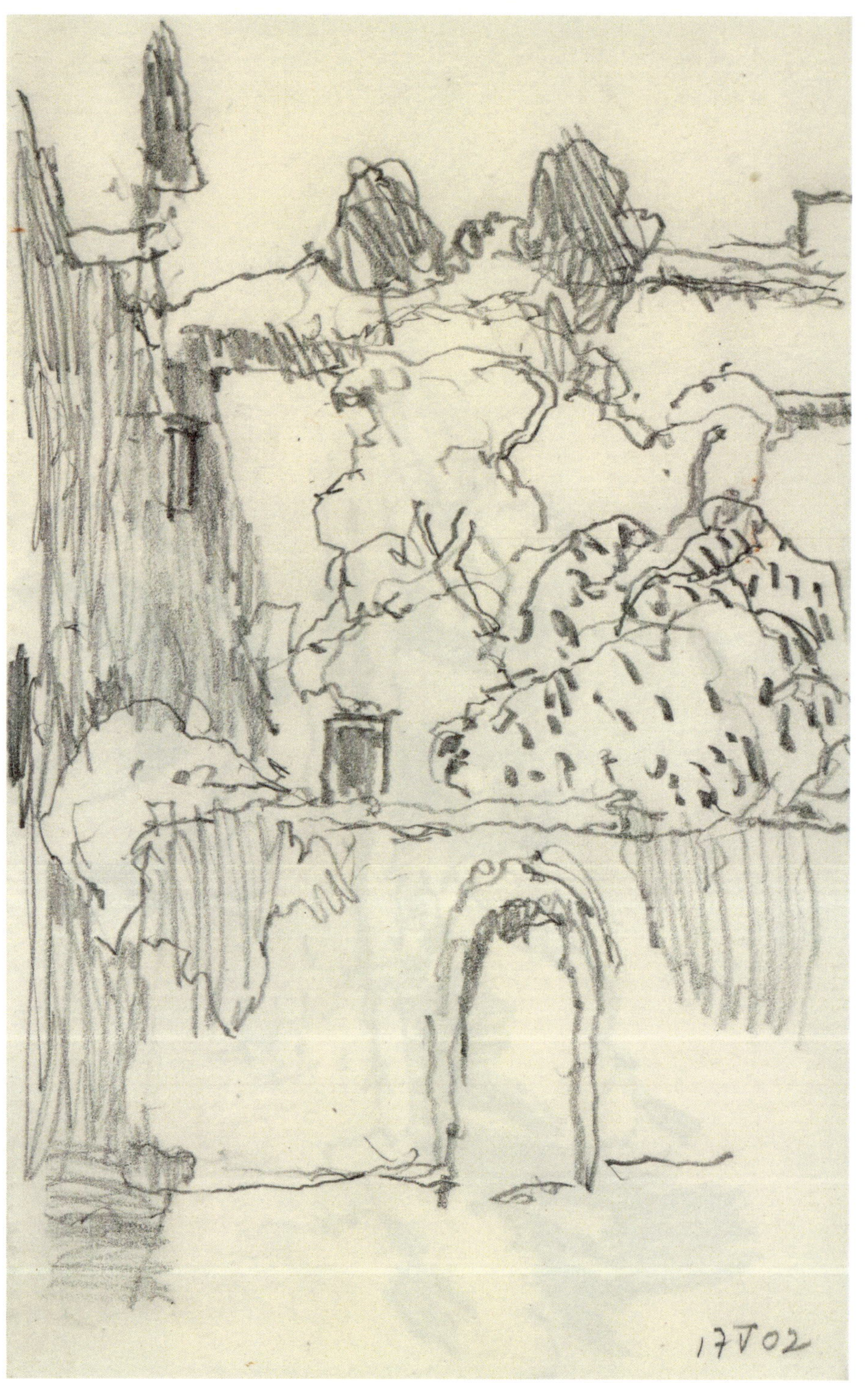

1. *Campiello della Madonna*,
17 May 2002 | 17 mai 2002

Contents | Table des matières

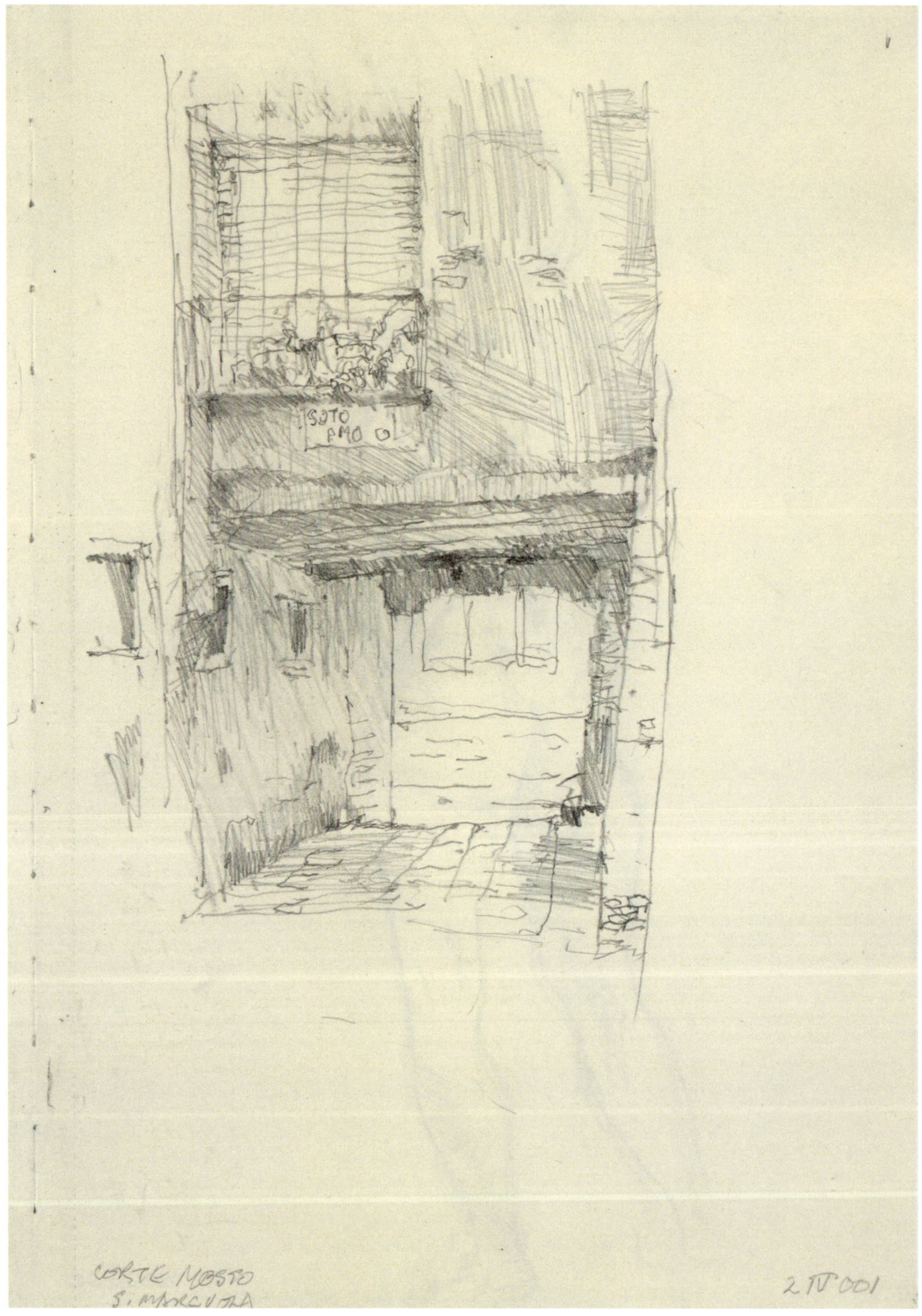

2. *Corte Mosto S. Marcuola (Sottoportego Mosto)*, 2 April 2001 | 2 avril 2001

Drawing Venice

JOHN LEROUX

At 21 years old, I was living a dream. I spent the better part of 1992 in Venice, studying architecture at the renowned Iuav (Istituto Universitario di Architettura di Venezia) as an international exchange student. But things didn't go quite as planned; and in retrospect, that was much more valuable.

After a week of lectures in Italian, the foolish assumption that my fluent French would serve me well in Venetian academia crashed to the ground. I could barely understand the lectures, and there was no question that by the time I absorbed the language, the term would be over. But as a humble student, I had three things in my possession: this extraordinary city, loads of time, and an empty sketchbook. I took to the winding canalled streets of Venice (the *calli*, *fondamente*, *rive*, and *rami*) with pen in hand and inexhaustible curiosity. By fervently sketching the city, I learned more in the ensuing months than I ever thought possible.

An artist can only absorb the exceptional qualities of a place through looking—unencumbered and with patience. My Venetian sketching outings were surrounded by peach and yellow stuccoed walls, noble Istrian stone, worn red brick, and canals of seafoam green. They not only taught me to see, they became potent gifts of memory that are forever etched in my mind. I remember making every sketch I ever drew in Venice and what I felt at those moments, as I'm sure John Fox did in his dozens of sketchbooks. They are time machines that become more meaningful with every passing year.

There is no better way to connect with a place than to draw or paint it. This requires a commitment of time, a rigour of pushing through a pictorial creation that may not turn out as planned, and a humility in knowing that you are but one in a long line of artists attempting to exalt this place; but you try your hardest. This is why I am so drawn to John Fox's Venice work. He loved this city as an extension of his very being. He consummated that relationship through a devotional routine of drawing and painting every single day he was in the Most Serene Republic of Venice.

Perusing John Fox's sketchbooks and watercolours of his beloved adopted city is to get as close to the insights and immediacy of an artist as one can. Tourists in Venice tend to keep moving, other than to shop and eat. There's simply so much to see that a three-day package tour leaves one spent. This is where John's work is a revelation. He lived in the city for long periods of time, so he could meander at his own pace. He returned to unusual corners countless times, easily moving through lesser-known *campi* (squares) (fig. 1) and *sottoporteghi* (passageways) (fig. 2) just as a local would. His was the Venice of the Venetians (fig. 3). Getting far past the tourist distractions of Piazza San Marco and the trinkets on the Rialto Bridge, and into the living, worn areas of the floating city was John's modus operandi. Recording place and time was his way of acknowledging a deeply personal journey. He delighted in the aged walls, shuttered windows (fig. 4), and organic growth (fig. 5) in lesser-known parts of Venice. He knew intrinsically that they had as much character and gravitas as the gold mosaic-encrusted interior of the thousand-year-old Basilica di San Marco.

An avowed explorer of the city, John had his favourite spots which he would often return to over and over again (figs. 6, 7). He was fascinated by the subtle changes of light or slight shifts in perspective that would occur when he revisited a specific locale at different times of the day or the season (figs. 8, 9), or when he moved his point of view a few metres here or there (figs. 10, 11). His multiple depictions of such lesser-known places as the Sottoportego Mosto (figs. 12, 13) or the Campiello de la Chiesa San Francesco della Vigna (figs. 14, 15) tell us in no uncertain terms that John is urging us to go back and look again, as there is always something more to see and be astounded by.

Spending time in Venice is an exceptional privilege. The anthropomorphic qualities of the aged buildings, leaning and almost groaning through their weathered facades, are treasures to an artist who has the wherewithal to give of themselves to this intimate relationship. With pencil or brush in hand over a blank page, one can immortalize a particular spot forever. John Fox's artworks of Venice are humanistic gifts that speak to a lifetime's work. He did not capture the city: he opened his heart and hand to it, and shared with us the joys of being alive in a place of incomparable beauty.

3. *Campo San Giacomo dell' Orio*, 2000

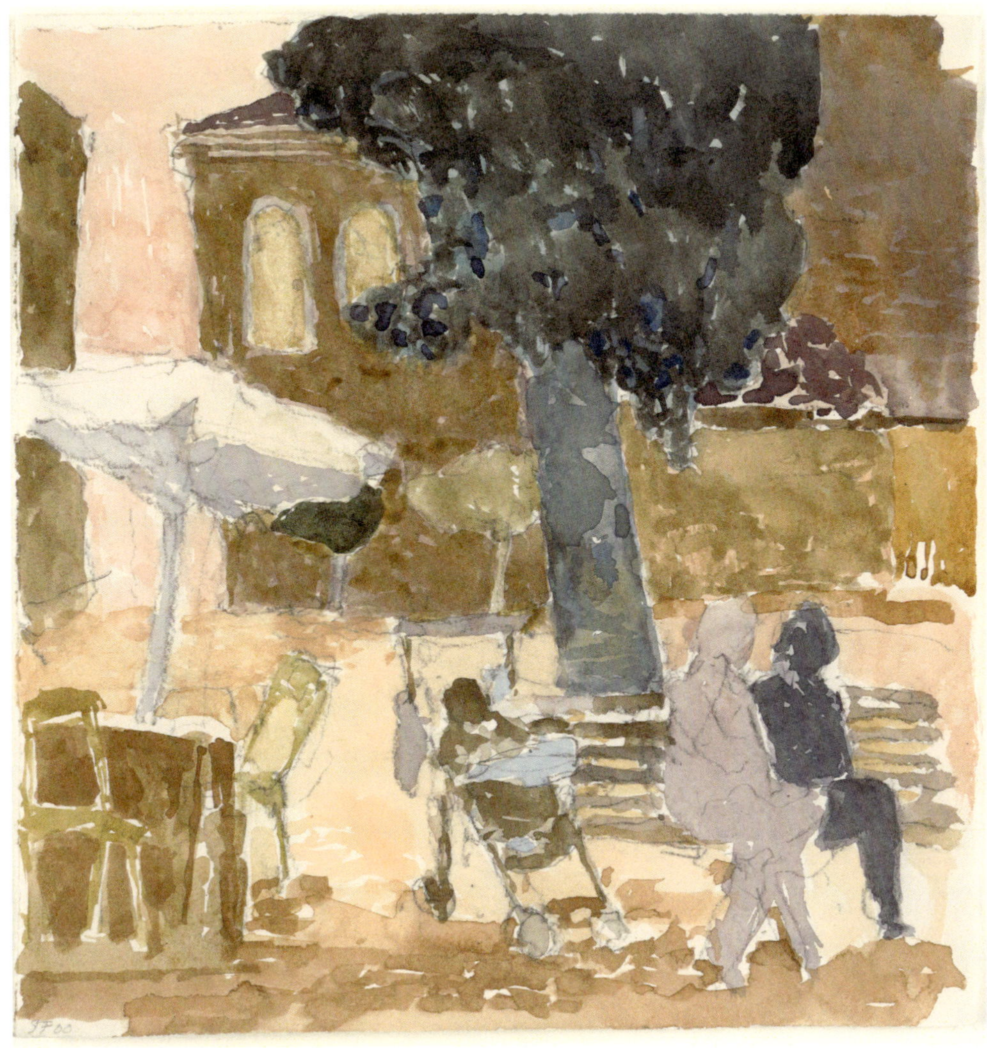

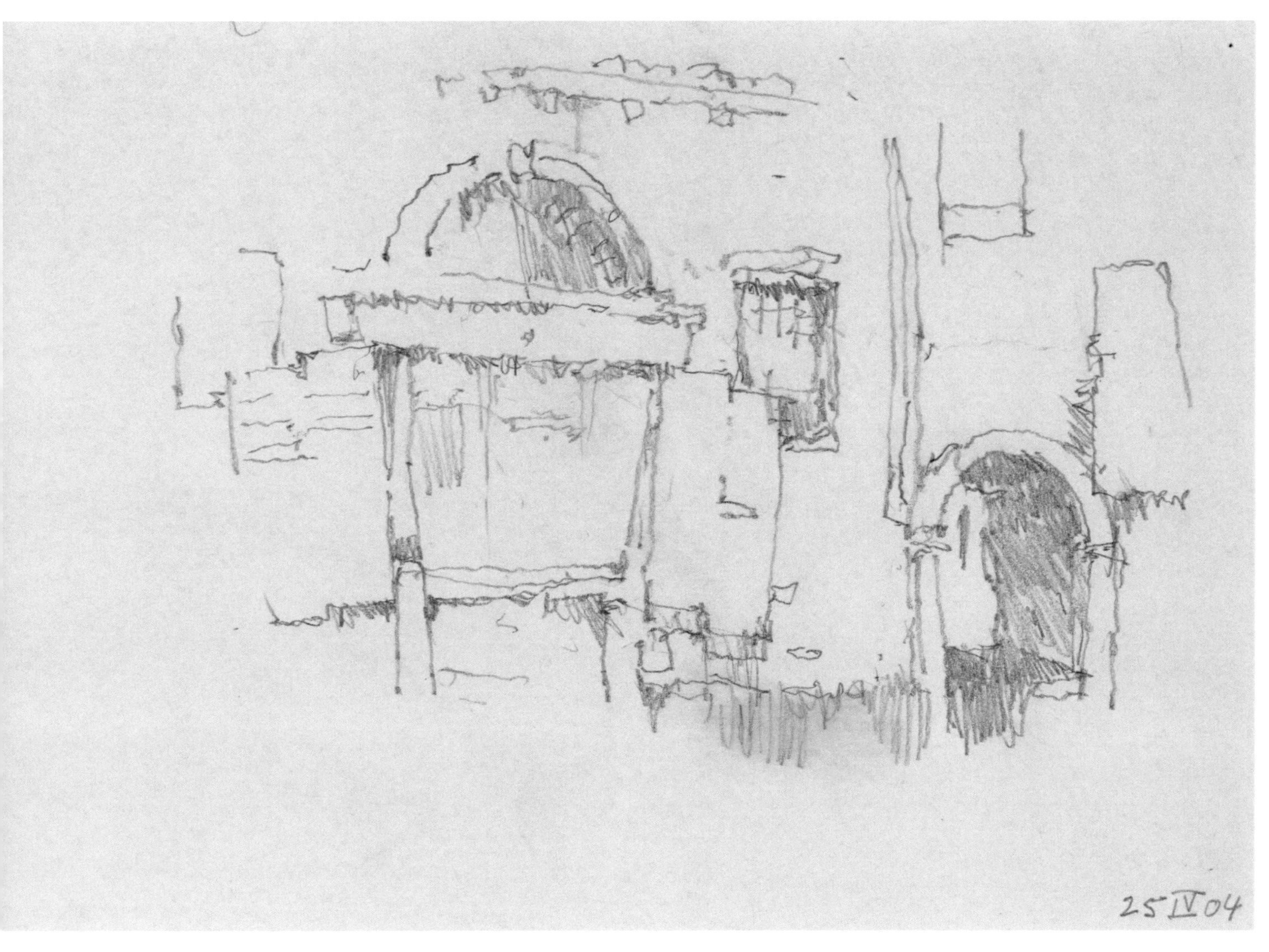

4. *Window and Sottoportego, Rio Madonna dell' Orto*, 25 April 2004 | 25 avril 2004

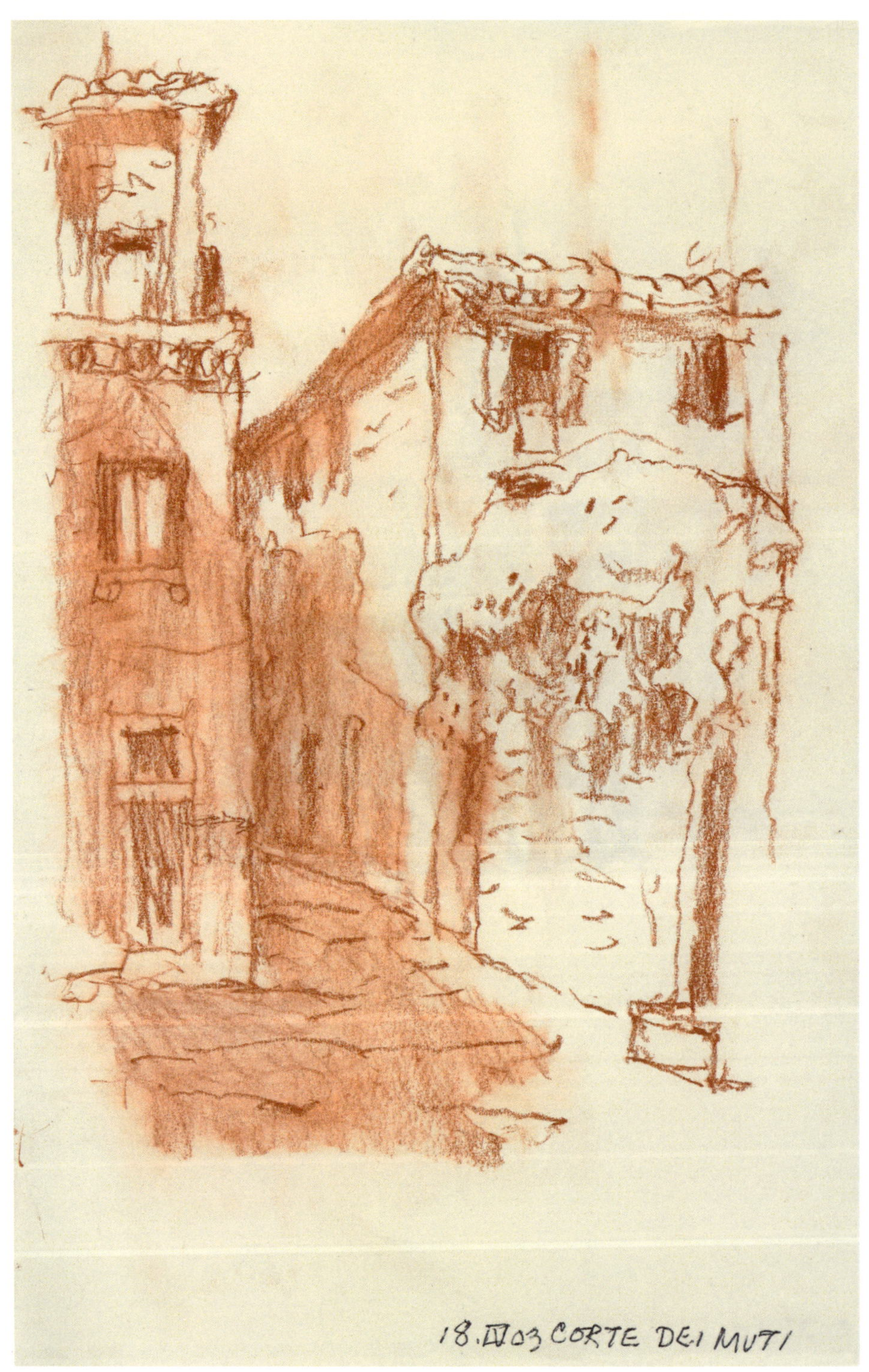

5. *Corte dei Muti*, 18 April 2003 | 18 avril 2003

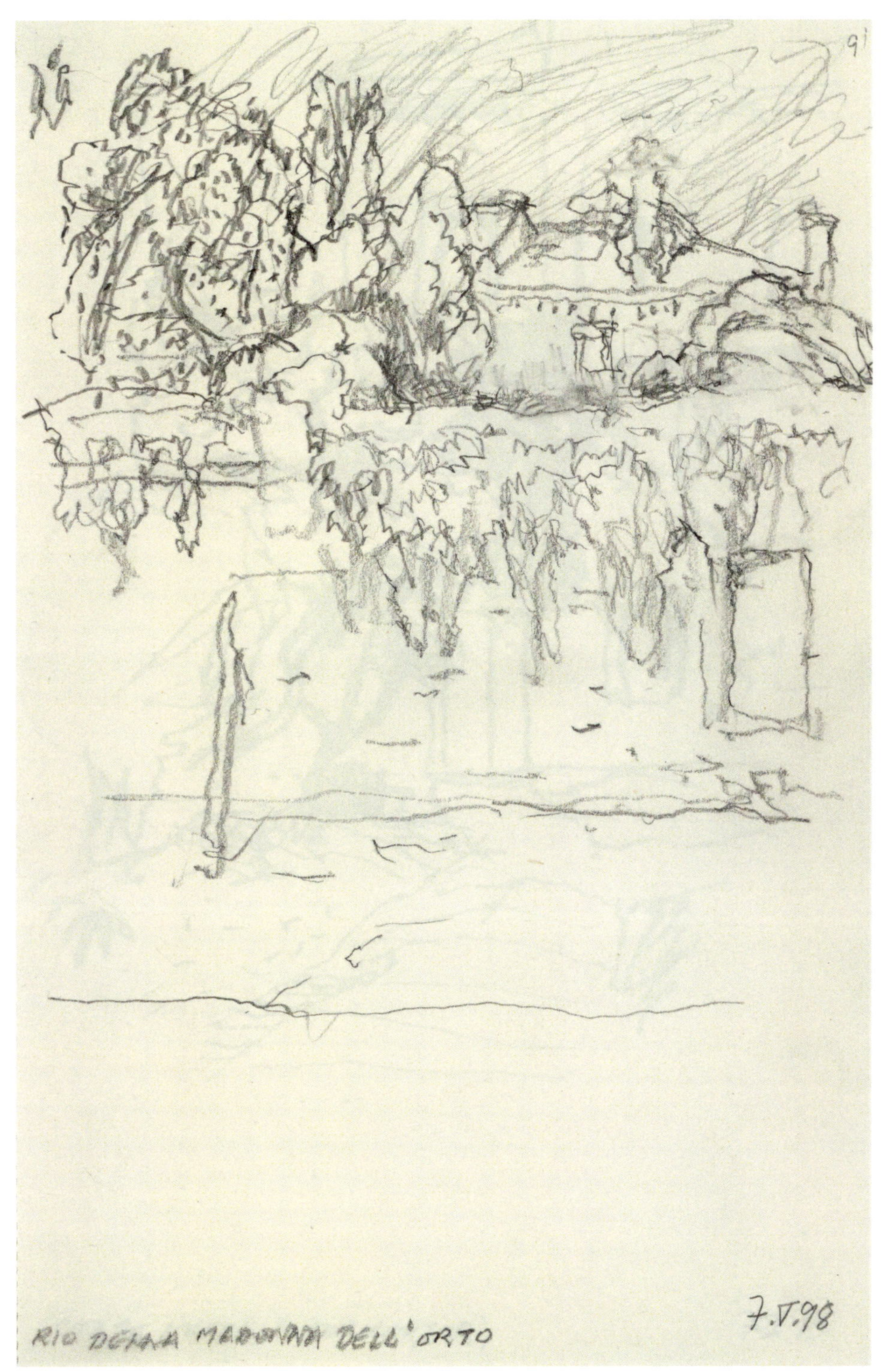

6. *Rio della Madonna dell' Orto*,
7 May 1998 | 7 mai 1998

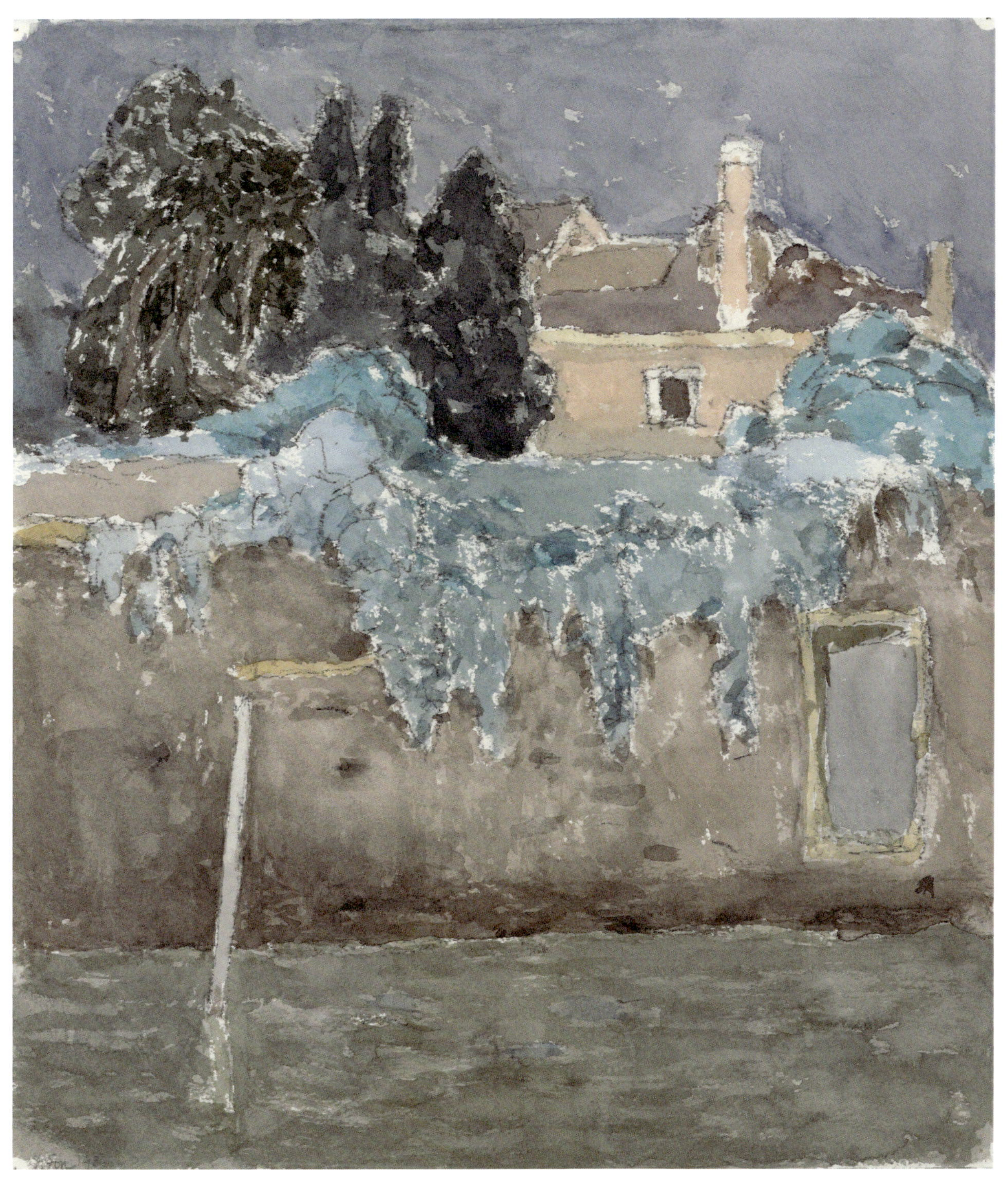

7. *Rio della Madonna dell' Orto*, 1993

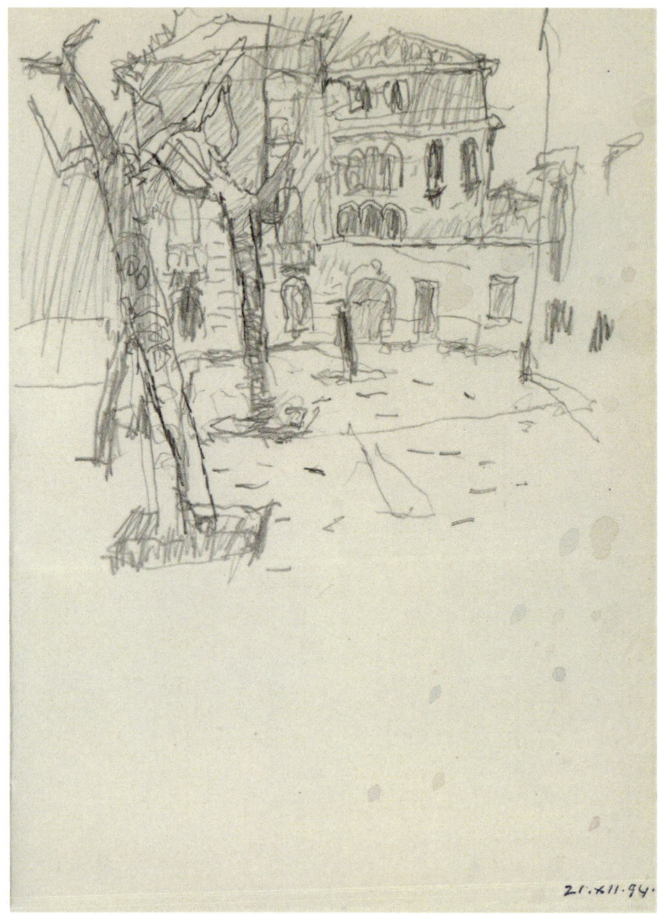

(above | ci-dessus)

8. *Campo dei Gesuiti*, 21 December 1994 | 21 décembre 1994

(right | à droite)

9. *Campo dei Gesuiti*, 3 May 1998 | 3 mai 1998

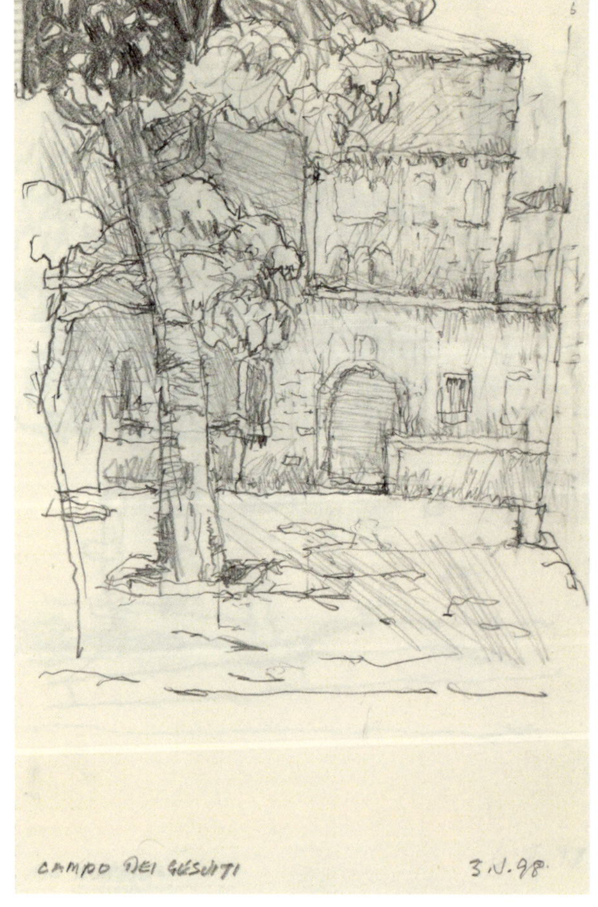

Dessiner Venise

JOHN LEROUX

Nous sommes en 1992, j'ai 21 ans, je vis un rêve. Je passerai l'essentiel de l'année à Venise, étudiant l'architecture au fameux Istituto Universitario di Architettura di Venezia (IUAV), dans le cadre d'un échange international. Sauf que tout ne se passera pas comme prévu. Tant mieux !

Après une semaine de classe, je constate en effet que, contrairement à ce que je m'étais imaginé, ma maîtrise du français ne m'est d'aucun secours pour bien comprendre l'italien… et le trimestre se sera envolé bien avant que je puisse remédier à la situation. Heureusement, l'humble étudiant que je suis a trois richesses : une ville splendide à ma portée, du temps à revendre et un carnet de croquis vide. En quelques mois, j'apprendrai bien davantage que ce que j'aurais cru en sillonnant les rues et les canaux (*calli*, *fondamente*, *rive* et *rami*) de Venise, armé de mes crayons et d'une insatiable curiosité.

L'artiste ne peut saisir la beauté d'un lieu qu'en l'observant en pleine liberté, avec patience. Mes escapades vénitiennes furent riches de tous ces murs de stuc pêche et crème, de ces nobles pierres d'Istrie, de ces vieilles briques rouges, de canaux verts comme l'écume de mer. Elles ne m'ont pas seulement appris à regarder : elles m'ont légué des souvenirs impérissables. En effet, j'ai encore gravé dans ma mémoire chaque lieu dessiné et ce que j'y ai vécu. Comme John Fox et ses dizaines de carnets de croquis, j'en suis convaincu. Ces dessins sont des machines à voyager dans le temps, qui gagnent en valeur d'année en année.

Rien de mieux, pour faire corps avec une ville, que de la dessiner (ou de la peindre). Il faut toutefois accepter d'y mettre le temps et de travailler avec discipline pour un résultat parfois inattendu — sans compter l'humilité de savoir que l'on n'est qu'un parmi tant d'autres qui ont cherché à exalter ses charmes. Mais on essaie quand même. C'est ce que j'aime chez John Fox : il chérissait cette ville au point de se fondre en elle, assez pour consacrer chacune de ses journées à dessiner et à peindre sa passion pour la Sérénissime.

Les esquisses et les aquarelles de John Fox nous ouvrent une porte privilégiée sur le regard intime et personnel dont il embrassait sa ville bien aimée. Les touristes, à Venise, ne savent pas s'arrêter, sauf pour manger ou acheter. Or on n'aura jamais assez d'un forfait de trois jours pour découvrir une ville aussi foisonnante. C'est là que nous attend John Fox, lui qui a longtemps habité la ville et qui a donc eu tout le temps voulu pour flâner et nous la faire découvrir. Cent fois il est retourné dans les mêmes recoins perdus, déambulant entre les places, ou *campi* (fig. 1) et leurs passages couverts, ou *sottoporteghi* (fig. 2), comme un simple Vénitien — ce qu'il était devenu, d'ailleurs, d'un certain point de vue (fig. 3). Loin des distractions touristiques de la Piazza San Marco et des babioles du pont Rialto, il s'engouffrait dans les secteurs vivants et patinés de la cité flottante. En notant les dates et les lieux, il tissait la trame d'un itinéraire foncièrement personnel. Il ne se lassait pas des vieux murs, des fenêtres closes (fig. 4) ou des excroissances végétales (fig. 5) des coins secrets de la ville. D'instinct, il leur accordait autant de grandeur et de noblesse qu'aux mosaïques sur fond d'or de la basilique millénaire de San Marco.

Découvreur invétéré, John Fox n'hésitait donc pas à revenir encore et encore aux mêmes endroits (fig. 6 et 7), fasciné par les subtiles variations de lumière ou de perspective selon l'heure du jour, le moment de l'année (fig. 8 et 9) ou le point de vue, qu'il suffit de déplacer de quelques mètres (fig. 10 et 11). Ses variantes de divers endroits peu connus de la ville, que ce soit le *sottoportego* Mosto (fig. 12 et 13) ou le campiello de l'église San Francesco della Vigna (fig. 14 et 15), nous adressent un message sans équivoque : n'ayez pas peur de revenir en un même lieu, qui saura toujours vous révéler de nouvelles splendeurs.

Séjourner à Venise, c'est un privilège. En voyant ces vieux édifices aux façades usées se pencher sur vous presque en gémissant, on jurerait qu'ils sont vivants. L'artiste de talent qui croque ces lieux en se laissant inspirer par ce rapport intime participe de son immortalité. C'est ce que John Fox a fait en se promenant dans la ville, carnet d'une main et crayon ou pinceau de l'autre. Il n'a pas mis la ville en boîte : il lui a ouvert son cœur et ses mains, créant ainsi une œuvre humaniste qui trouve écho dans le travail de toute une vie. Par lui, nous pouvons goûter la joie d'être vivant dans un lieu d'une beauté aussi incomparable.

10. *Bridge on the Rio Santa Fosca*,
1 April 2003 | 1er avril 2003

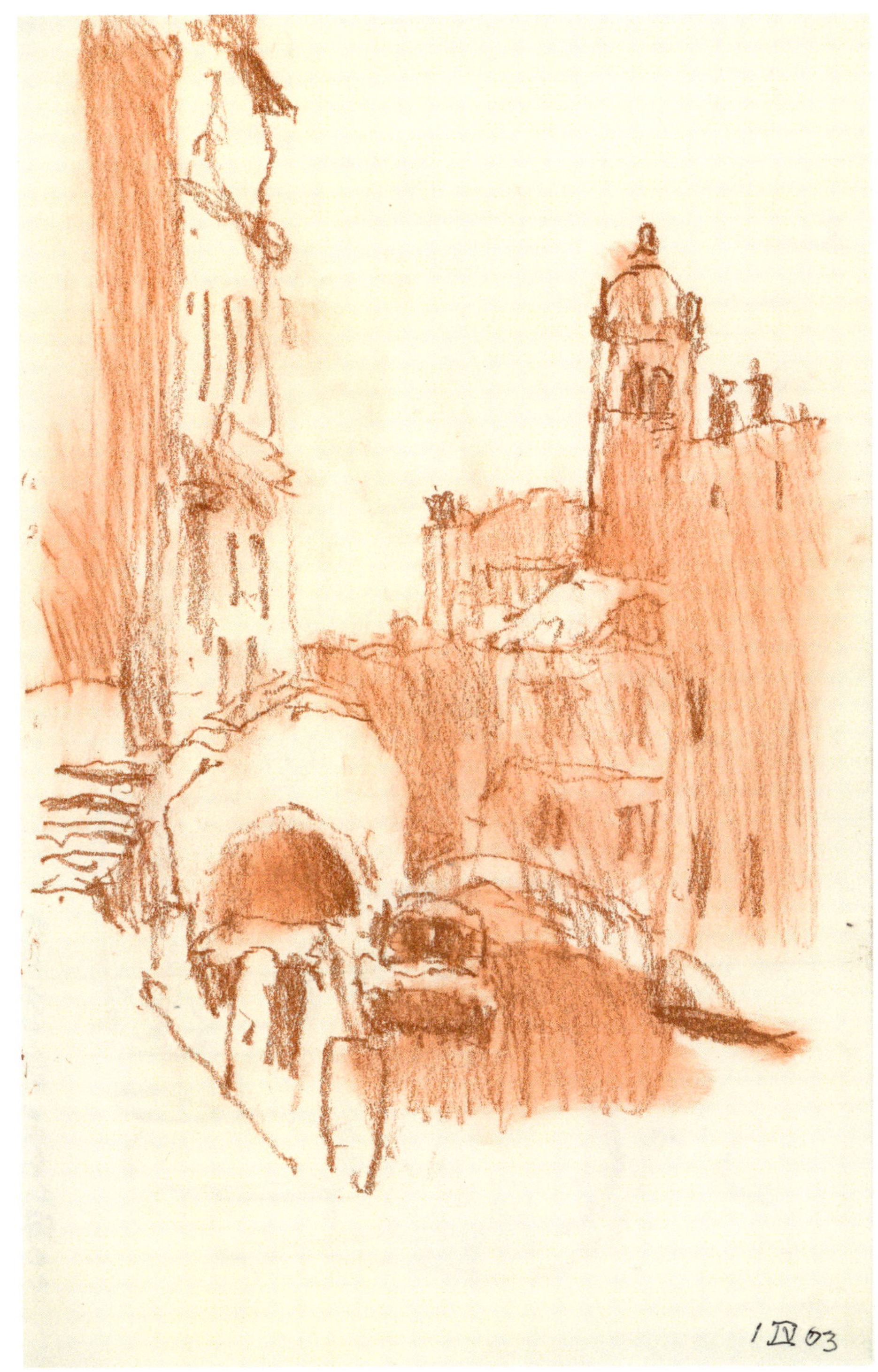

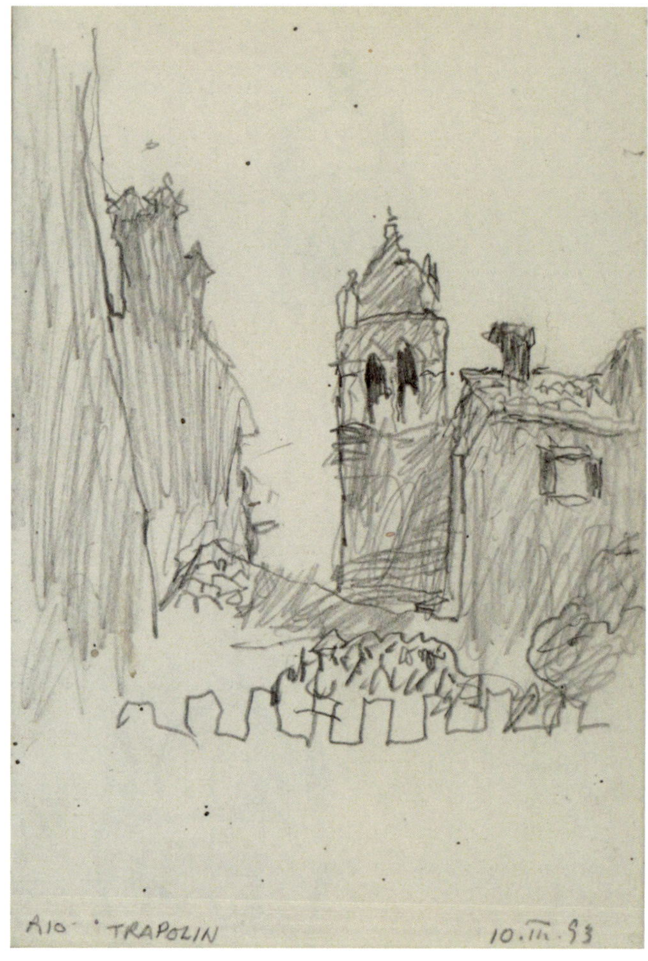

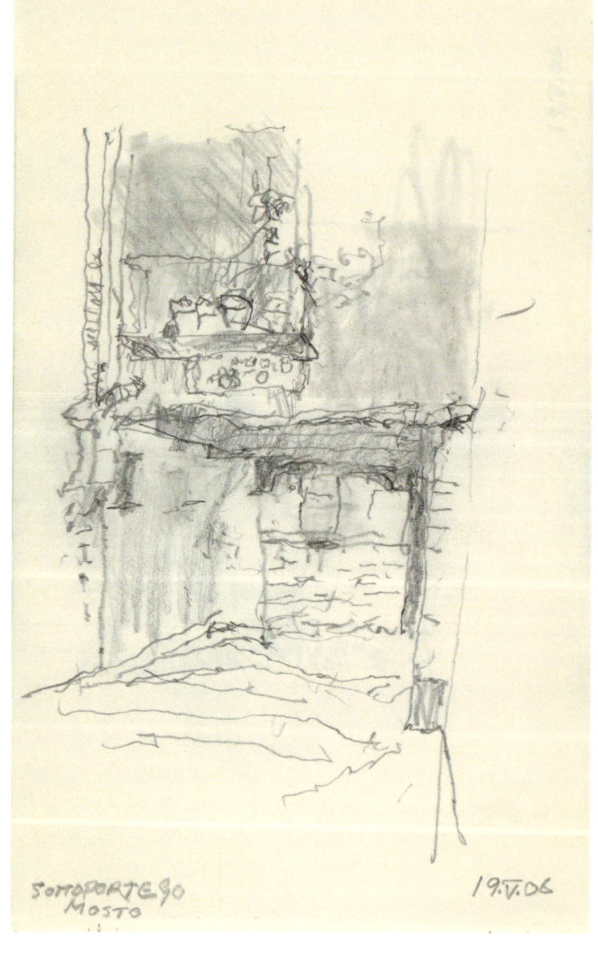

(above | ci-dessus)
11. *Rio Trapolin (at Santa Fosca Church)*, 10 March 1993 |10 mars 1993

(right | à droite)
12. *Sottoportego Mosto*, 19 May 2006 | 19 mai 2006

(opposite | ci-contre)
13. *Sottoportego Mosto*, 2003

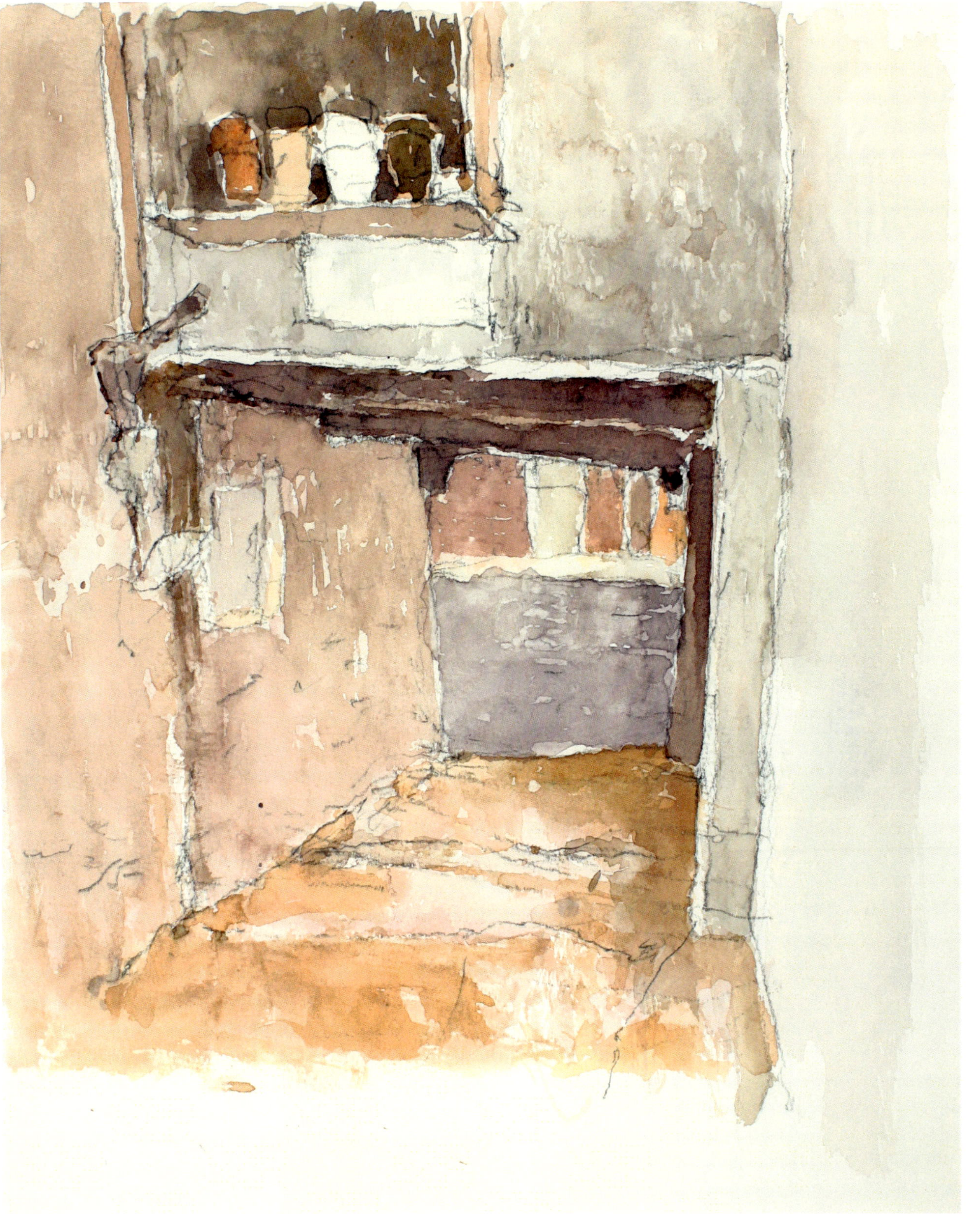

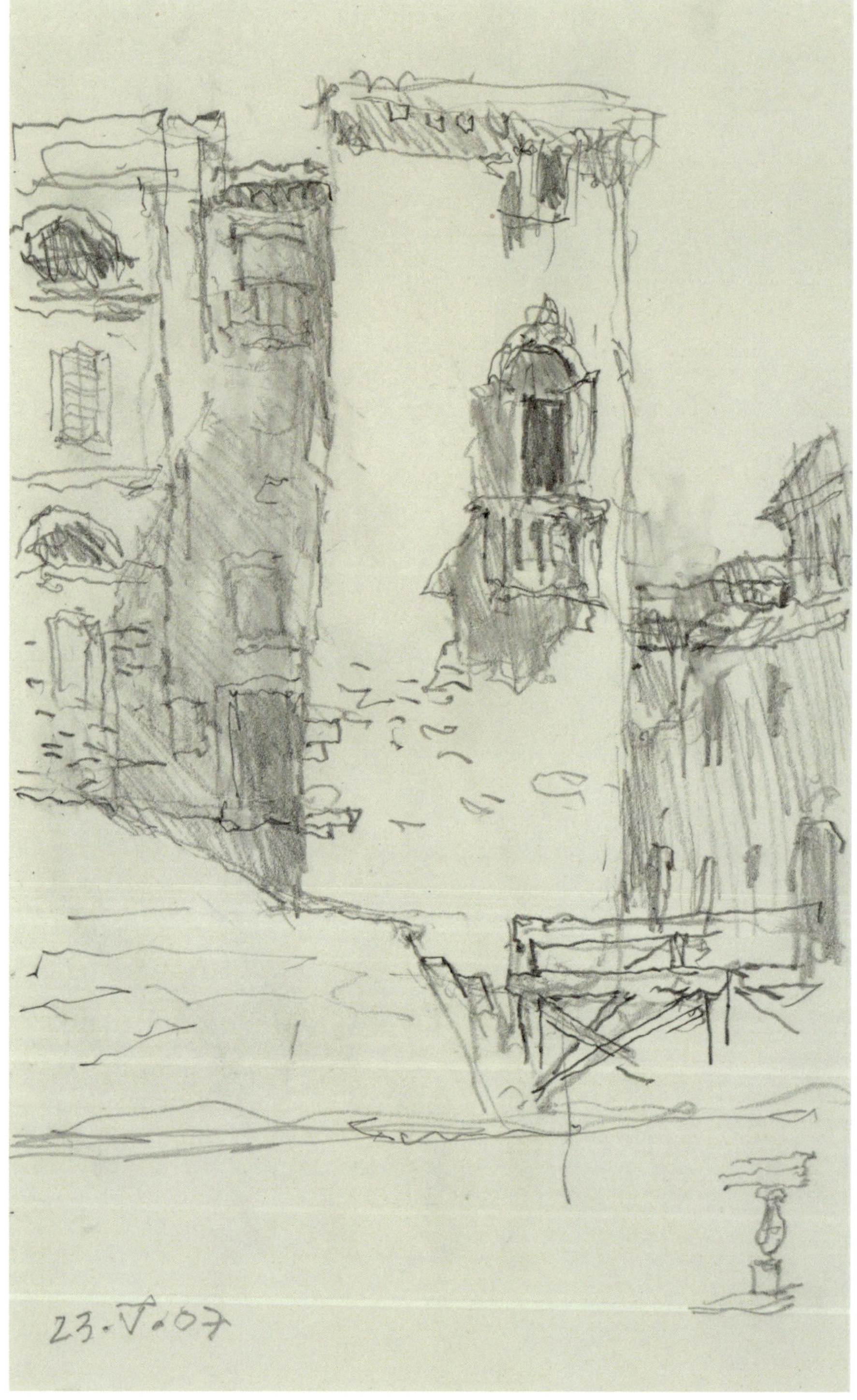

14. *Campiello San Francesco della Vigna*, 23 May 2007 | 23 mai 2007

(opposite | ci-contre)
15. *Campiello San Francesco della Vigna*, 2007

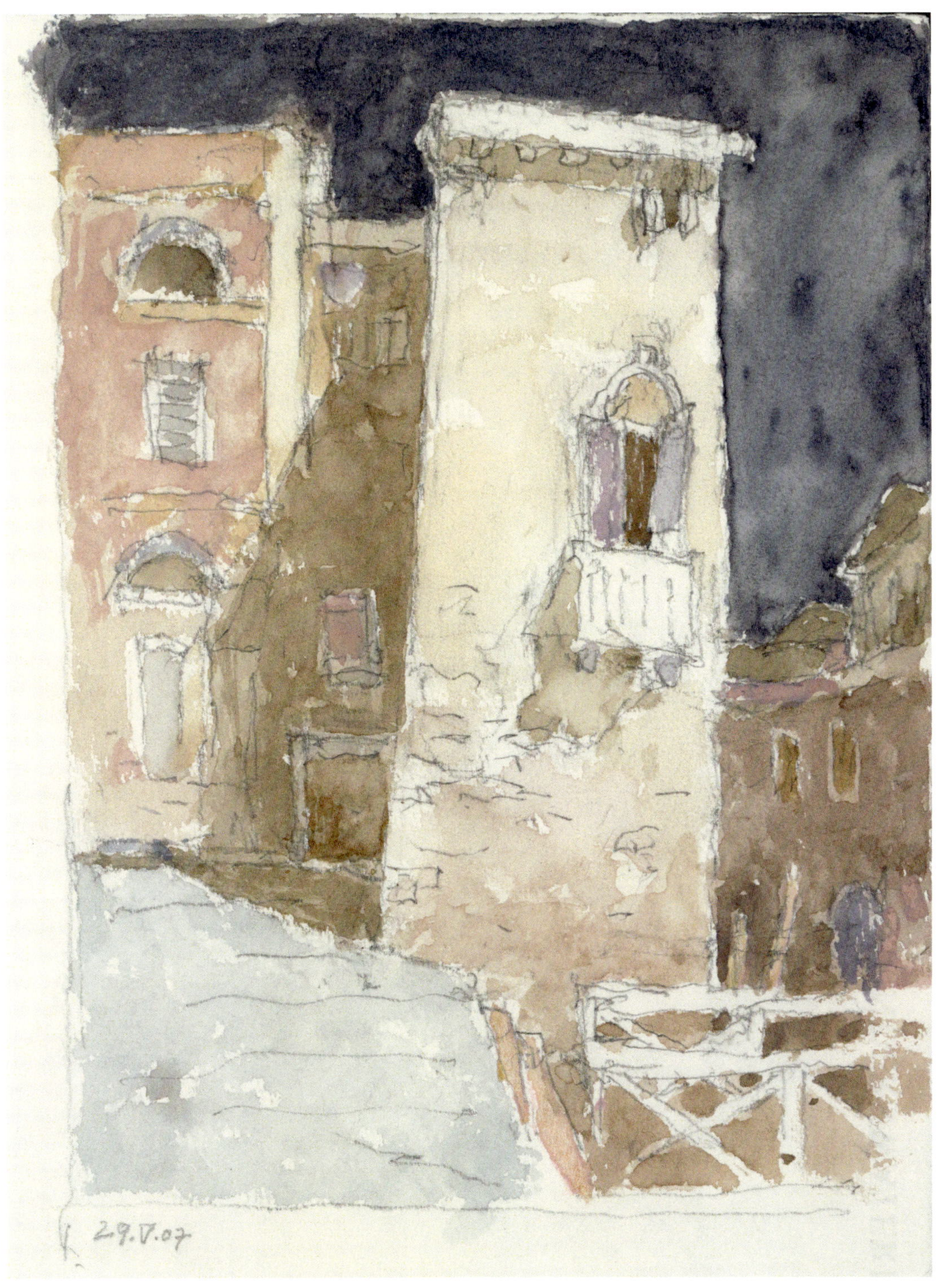
29.V.07

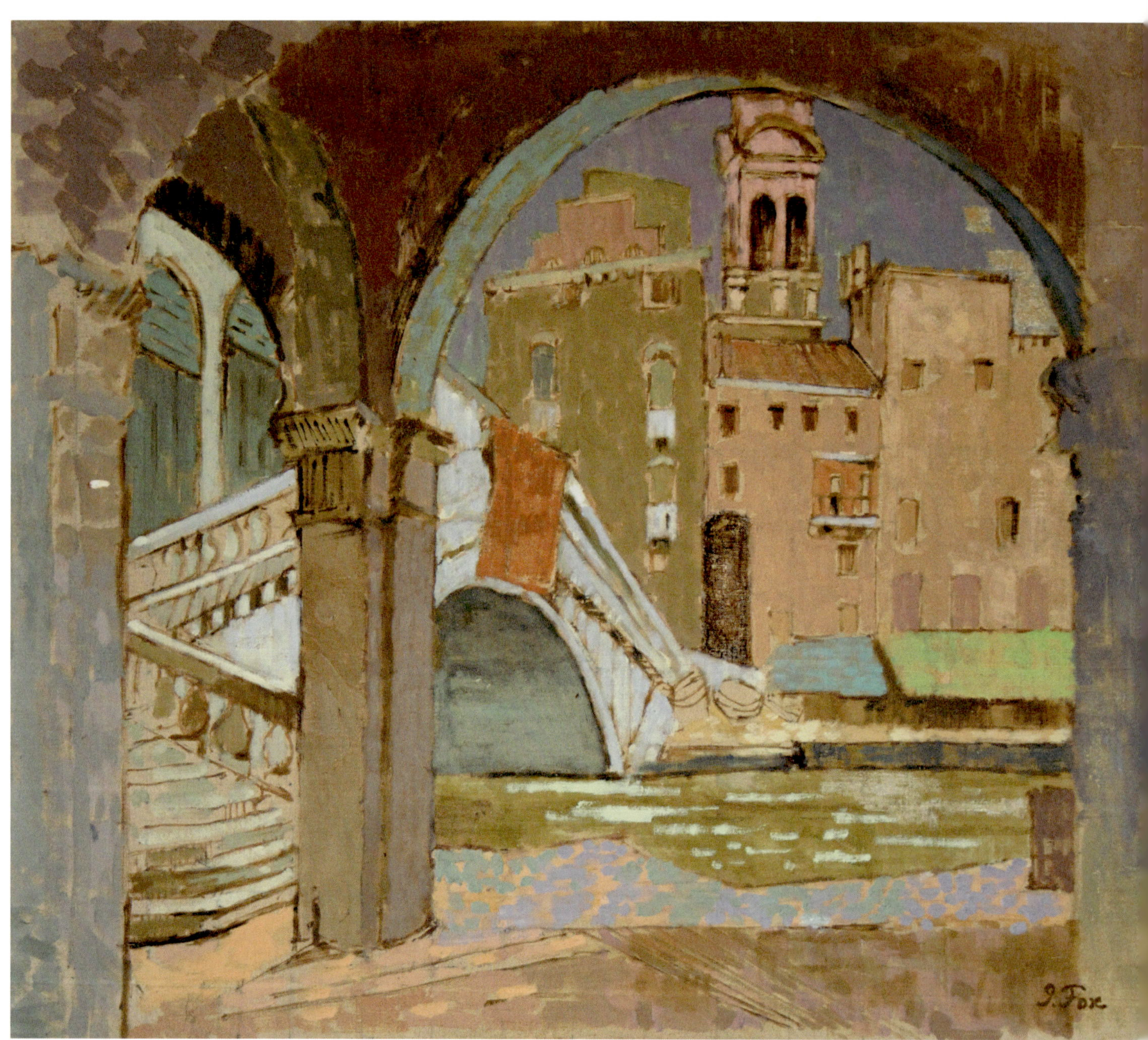

John Fox
Images of Venice

SANDRA PAIKOWSKY

John Fox's passion for Venice began before his first visit to the city. A student at the Slade School of Fine Art in London, England, he spent six weeks in 1952 in the British National Gallery copying Titian's *Venus and Adonis*. He kept the copy for the rest of his life. It is first a homage to Titian and his transformation of paint into light and colour, which underlies all of John's painting, and secondly, it is a sign of his own lifelong love of Venice.

On his first trip to Venice in August the following year, John was overwhelmed by Titian's last painting, *The Pietà*, in the Accademia museum, and it forever remained his touchstone of what painting is and what it can achieve. John's earliest Venetian images are panoramic, as though he were trying to encapsulate everything he saw as he walked the city (fig. 16). A parallel desire to absorb the paintings by Venetian sixteenth- to eighteenth-century artists in churches, museums, and confraternities[1] would continue for the next fifty years. A second trip to Venice in July 1956, in between months spent in Florence and Paris, began a new way of John's drawing and painting the city as a moment in time, witnessed by his images of quiet corners of public squares (fig. 17) or church interiors (fig. 18). A trip from Montreal in the mid-1960s continued his interest in well-known subjects like the *Grand Canal* (fig. 75) and the Rialto market (fig. 19), but he saw the ancient city with contemporary eyes (fig. 20), much like his aesthetic mentor, the Canadian painter James Wilson Morrice (1865–1924), had accomplished in his own Venetian pictures decades earlier.

In March 1977 and for many years to come, John and I began what would become over thirty years of annual trips; we had become partners the previous year, and were married in Venice at the City Hall in 1982. For a long time, our visits were from early December to early January, working around our teaching schedules in the Faculty of Fine

16. *Rialto Bridge*, 1956

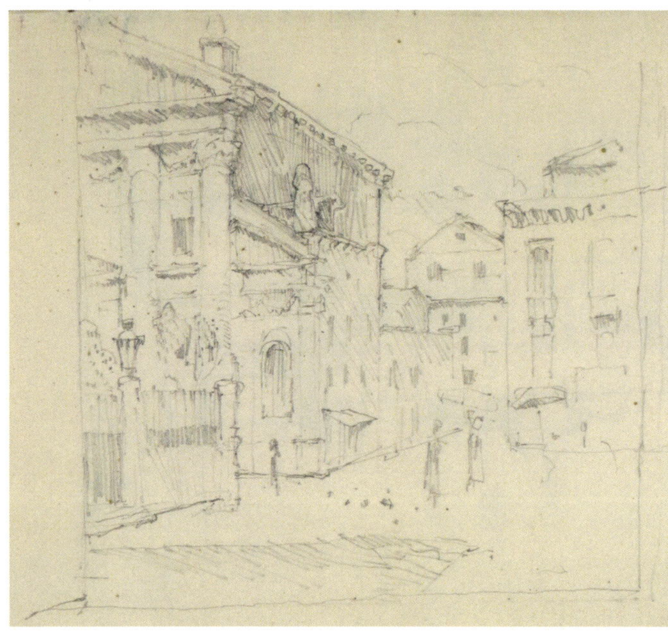

17. *San Vidal Church and Campo Morosini,* 1956

(opposite | ci-contre)
18. *Interior, Church of the Salute,* 1956

Arts at Concordia University. Occasionally we would also manage a month in the spring or summer in the same year. A week-long stay in November 1990 to see the *Titian, Prince of Painters* exhibition at the Ducal Palace was as necessary as breathing. In the late fall of 1992, we spent two months on the nearby island of Burano (fig. 21). A December move to Venice through March made this our longest stay yet, as John and I were on sabbaticals. From early 1993 onwards, we usually stayed near the ancient Jewish Ghetto in the north-west corner of Venice, in the borough or *sestiere* of Cannaregio.

We then returned to month-long winter trips and a rare summer visit, partially because John did not have a place in Venice to work on canvas, and he missed his own studio space, his regular drawing from models, his art supplies, and his books. He would rent a small workspace in spring 2004 (fig. 22), but it wasn't home. From around 2000 until John's death in Venice in 2008, we spent two months in the city, usually in the late spring and early summer.[2] Seeing the city in both winter and summer was akin to visiting two different places—each with its distinctive light, air, and colour—but always that "Paradise of Cities."[3]

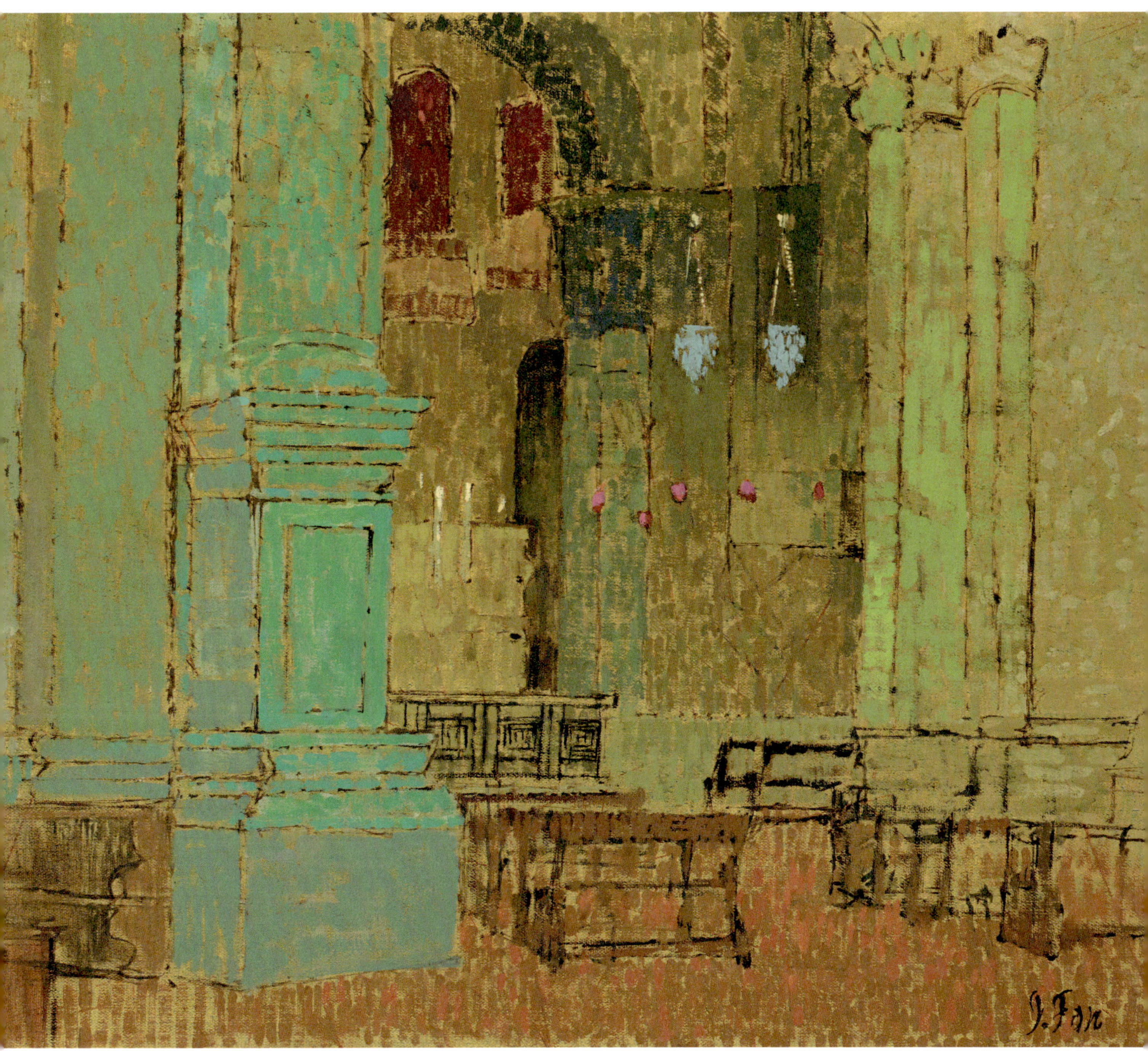

19. *Rialto Fish Market,* 1964

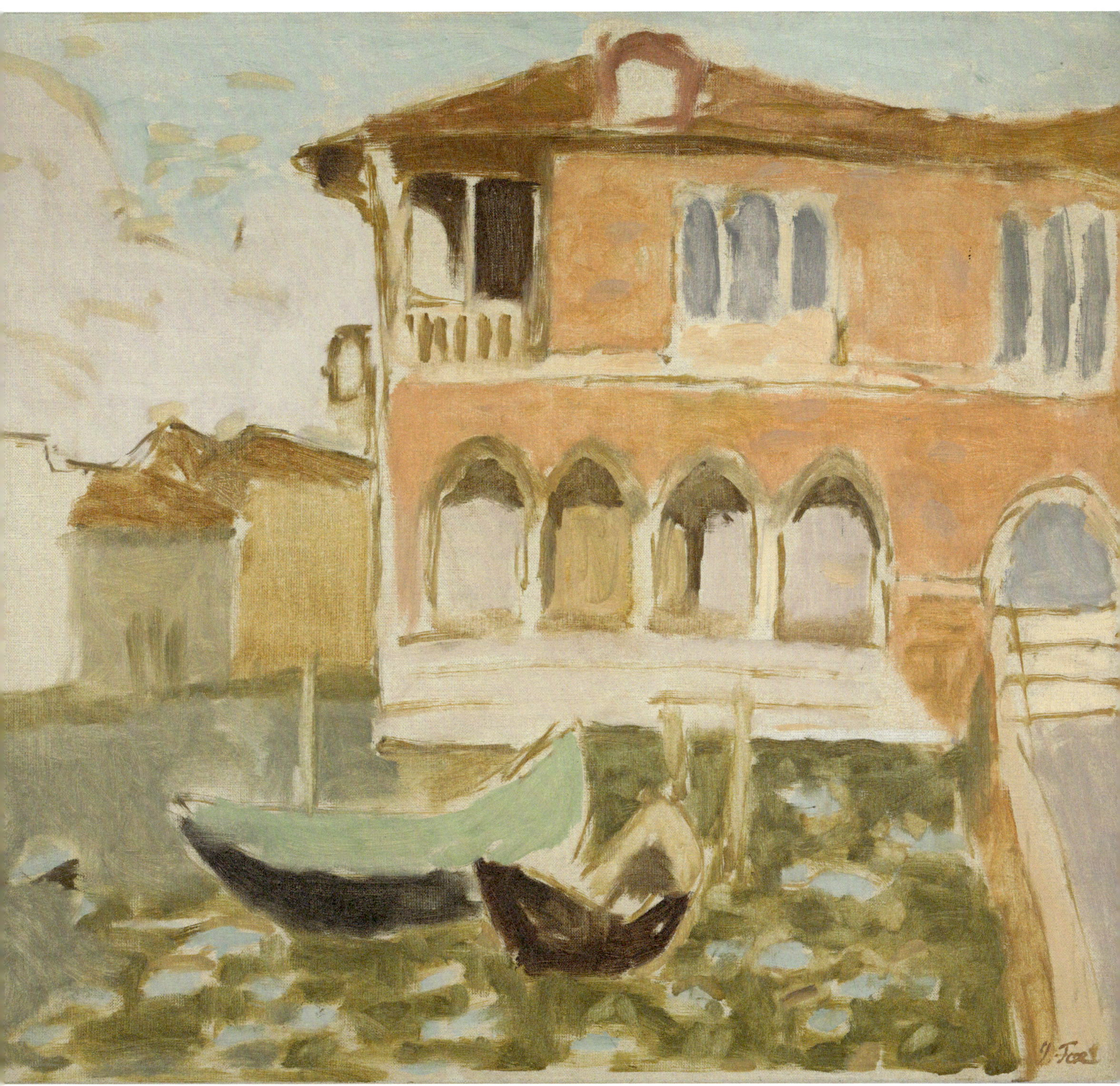

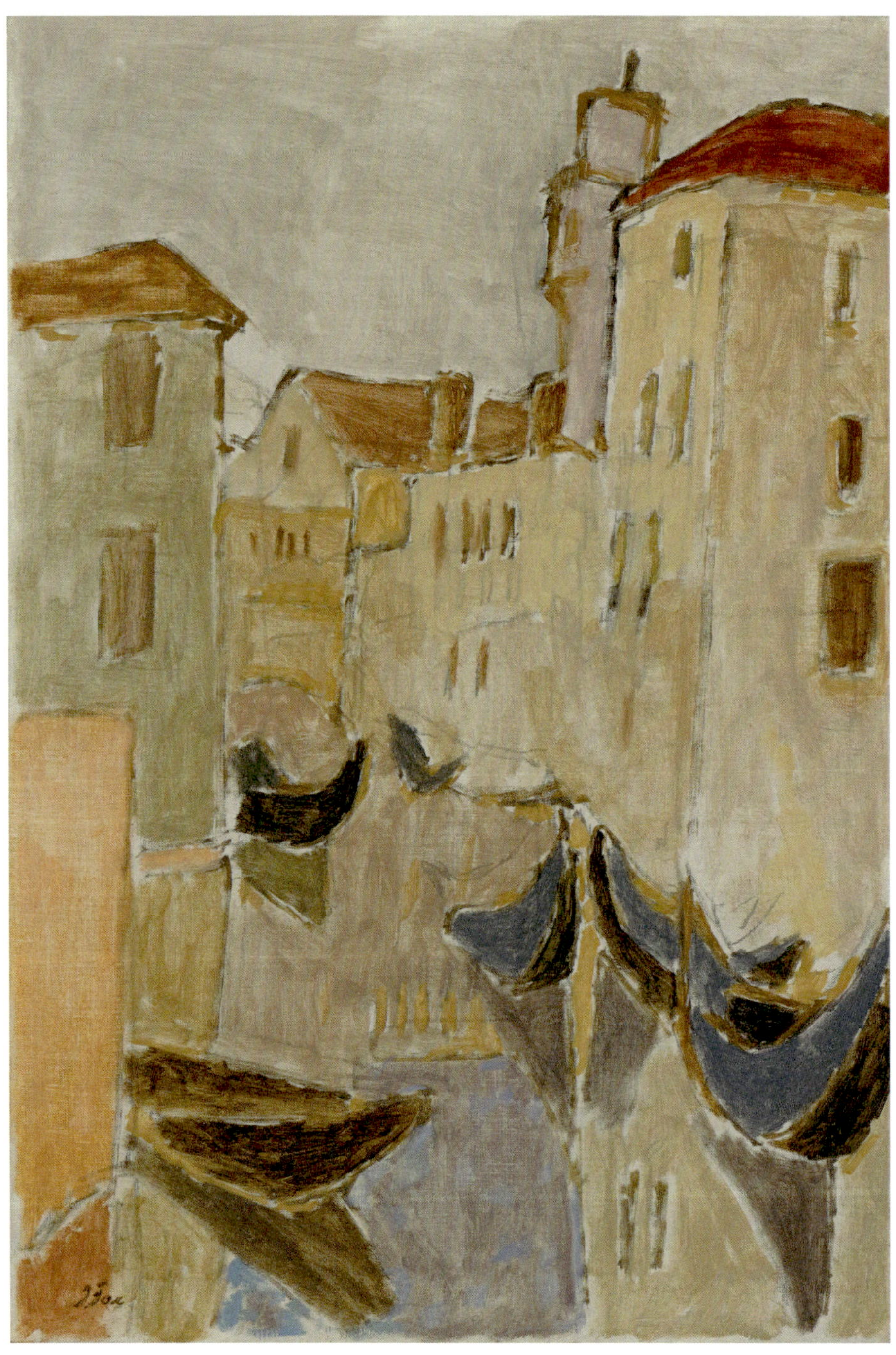

(opposite | ci-contre)
20. *Canal, Venice [Rio Sant' Angelo]*, 1964

(below | ci-dessous)
21. *Burano*, 1992

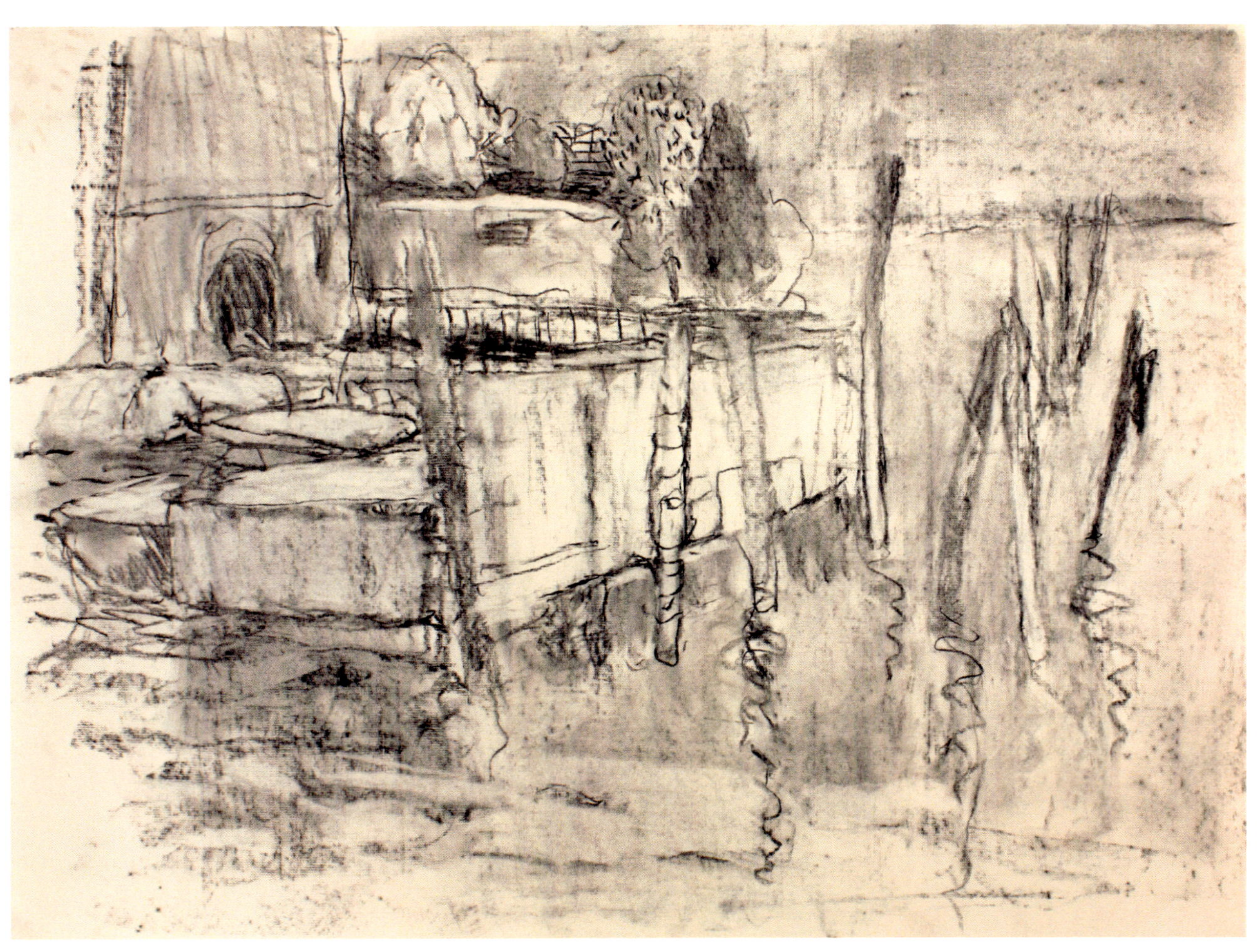

22. *Venice Studio*, 2004

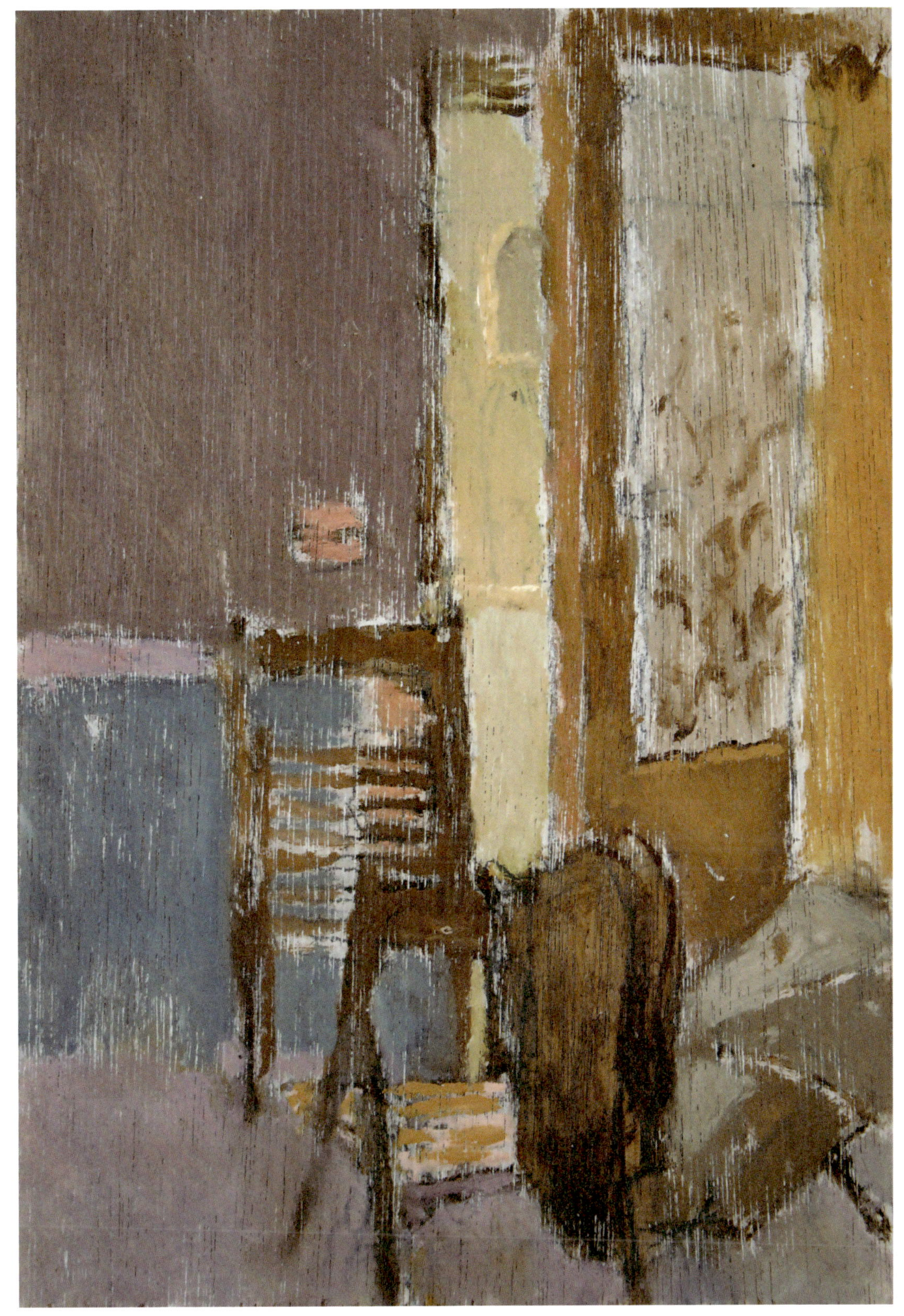

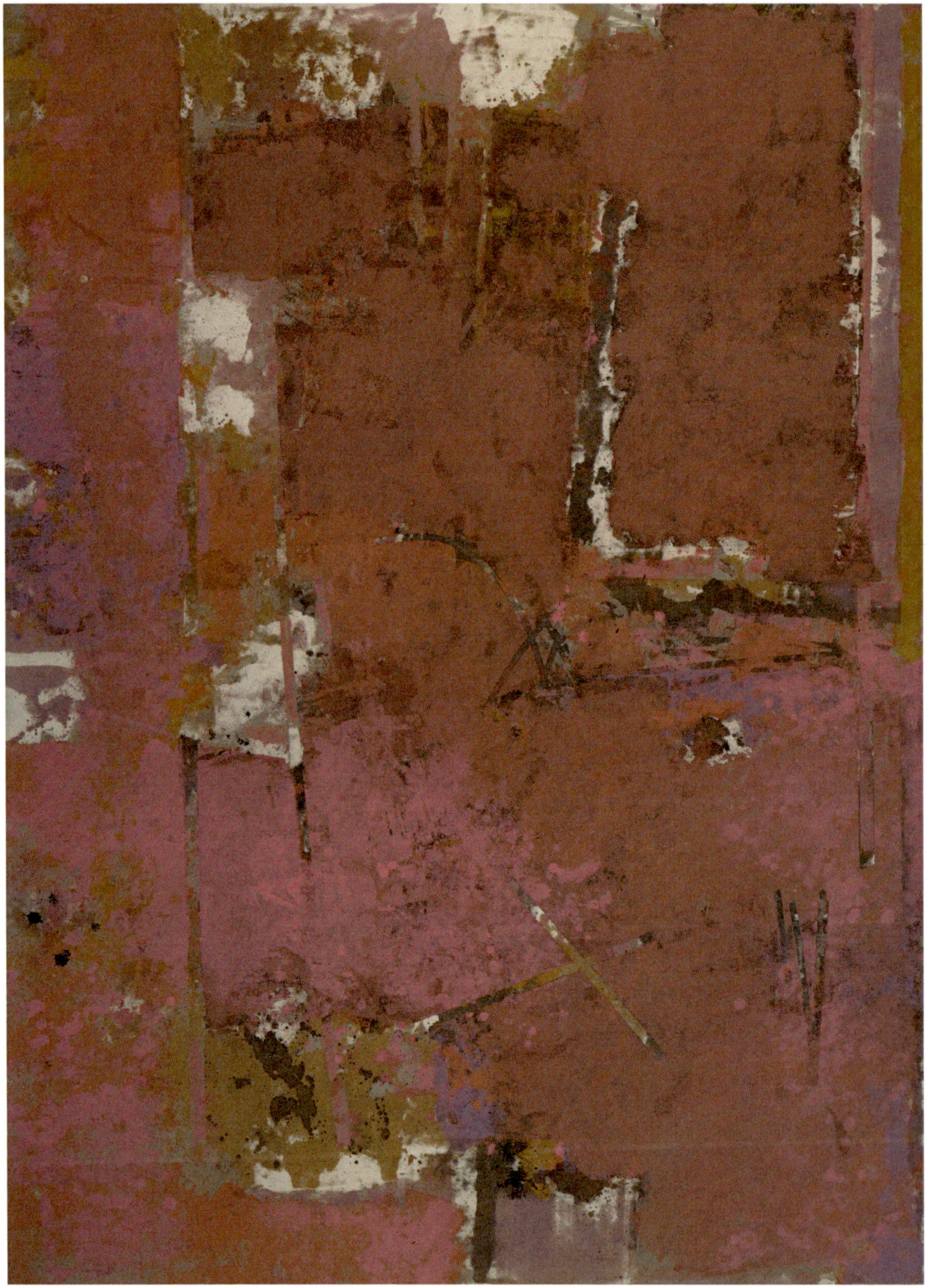

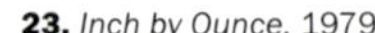

23. *Inch by Ounce*, 1979

Ways of Working in Venice

From John's student days and throughout his fifty-year career, drawing was his primary way of thinking and working. Even when he made abstract images from the early 1970s to the mid-1980s (figs. 23, 24), he continued to draw people, places and things (fig. 25).[4] In Venice, sketchbook drawing became a daily habit and it was the only way he worked out of doors. Along with a few pencils, sometimes some red chalk or charcoal, and always his trusty eraser, John would carry one or two notebooks whenever and wherever he was in Venice. The drawings in most sketchbooks span a couple of years; none is entirely devoted to Venice. His Moleskine sketchbooks were purchased there or brought to Venice from Montreal. From the mid-1990s on, he regularly bought Daler hardback *quaderni per schizzi* in a stationary shop near the large square, Campo San Giacomo dell' Orio (fig. 3). His sketchbooks were his prized possessions. Unlike many artists, John used his sketchbooks only for drawing, without notes to other things. He left behind over eighty sketchbooks, and forty per cent contain images of Venice, although the number of Venetian drawings vary from one book to another. His drawings were the basis for his Venice watercolours and references for his canvasses. A few sketchbooks or portfolios of paper are likely missing because there are Venetian paintings with no extant drawings.

Throughout our decades of annual trips, John made drawings during late morning strolls, and sometimes again in the afternoon. He walked until he found the right place—or until it found him. In the mornings, I usually went with him and a stop for brioche and espresso was part of the deal (fig. 26). We typically set off with no destination in mind, sometimes for only a short distance, depending on what caught his eye. We often returned for a second or third look to a site he had drawn earlier. In the afternoon, he was on his own but his routes were still random. He also drew and painted interiors of places where we were living (fig. 27), and the occasional view from the window (figs. 32, 35). During our earliest visits we stayed a little too close to San Marco, surrounded by elaborate *palazzi* and frazzled tourists, so we walked further afield to sites more evocative of the timeless authenticity of Venice and its way of life, defined as *venezianità*. On one trip in the early 1990s, John did life drawing at the studio of a Venice acquaintance, but he was not used to working with unfamiliar models in someone else's atelier. Perhaps John's sketchbook drawings of saintly sculptures in Venetian churches were a stand-in for his working from the live model in Montreal (fig. 33).

In later years when we were living further away from the Piazza San Marco and surroundings, John felt more at home in places best known to local residents. He drew while sitting on a public bench, or leaning up against a wall or a bridge, wanting to keep the moment as private as possible and drawing little attention to himself. An endearing exception occurred when he was working in a secluded street, where a gentleman living in the narrow *calle* had noticed him earlier on. Much to John's surprise and appreciation, the *veneziano* approached him with a small chair that he had carried down from his apartment. With a minimum of words, he assured John that he could leave the chair by the main doorway when he was finished, and wished him a pleasant day.

Wherever we were, John saw Venetian buildings and their surroundings for their design, rather than their history (fig. 34). His notebooks show that he drew many of the same places over several years because of his empathy with the composition of the site, and the *rapprochement* between its natural and built elements (figs. 1, 8). But each image differed; some were drawn from decidedly different angles (figs. 36, 37), others with just a slight turning of his head, many as a direct view—like the variations in his drawings from a model. Occasionally, he drew a site as both a vertical and a horizontal, on the same walk or at different times. He might also draw different versions of a subject on a single outing or two: as a rapid sketch and a more exact copy, and sometimes adding details of one or two elements from the site (figs. 8, 9). He often returned the next day to see if he got it right. While John usually dated the images in his sketchbooks, other dates remain as good guesses. Only rarely did he give the name of the site. It is easy to identify subjects when they were his favourite places. Other times, it is a mystery to me, especially when a place is the same unidentified subject in an untitled drawing and watercolour (figs. 38, 39).

Perhaps as a reflection of his love of paperworks by the eighteenth-century Venetian painter Giambattista Tiepolo, John's pencil and chalk drawings are both notational and dynamic, and his hand is equally flexible and controlling. At the same time, John wanted to find his own way to model form that was more sensitive than descriptive lines. He joyously believed that he had finally succeeded in 2007, at nearly eighty years old, when he drew the buildings, bridge, and canal of the small square beside the church of San

Francesco della Vigna (fig. 14). Using fewer lines and more shading, his pencil marks are like individual brushstrokes, and the dark and light patches like paint on paper (fig. 15).

Drawings were done for their own sake, and while many became watercolours, others did not for no obvious reason. Sometimes John painted watercolours of the same site on different visits to Venice, others only once. Watercolour was always John's favourite medium and I feel that his interest in watercolours of Venice goes hand in hand with his return to figuration in the mid-1980s, after almost fifteen years of making non-representational images (fig. 23). While the facts of the subject remained true, he chose the colours—sometimes close to real appearances, but mostly determined by his imagination. Years of abstract work gave John the authority to inscribe Venice with his own colour and light, without disturbing the site's authenticity (figs. 40, 41).

John's watercolours were painted indoors, usually in the afternoon and in Venetian kitchens with a mix of artificial and natural light that was not dissimilar from the lighting in his Montreal studio. The one exception was in spring 1996 when we stayed in a *casinò*, a small *palazzo* once owned by a line of the Habsburg dynasty, and now a centre for French Romantic music. Because of its high walls and private forecourt, John could draw and paint directly out of doors, with no one watching except the sculptures of chubby *putti* that lined the property's raised Renaissance garden and its massive medlar trees (figs. 42, 43). Wherever he was, John worked his watercolours with his sketchbook nearby, looking at a drawing he had made that day and possibly those of a few days or weeks earlier (figs. 44, 46). Although he did not bring older sketchbooks with him to Venice, his prodigious memory could easily recall his drawings of a similar place.

He might make more than one watercolour in an afternoon, and work on them again over the next few days. He also looked at those he had done earlier that visit, and made what he believed were obvious revisions. While the Venice watercolours show a range of colour, about one-fifth were painted in tones of red conté, and many have some pencil drawing (fig. 45). He occasionally made two or more versions of the same subject, in distinctly different colours (figs. 47, 48), or in subtler or stronger tones of the same colour. In the first years of our trips, he bought sheets of watercolour and drawing paper from a state-owned store that sold Fabriano products (figs. 25, 34). But with its closing and the continual demise of professional art supply shops in Venice, John carried his own paper and his Winsor & Newton watercolour tubes from Montreal.

An evening or two before we returned to Montreal, John would take out his watercolour paintings and examine each with a more than critical eye. He would then carefully rip up those that disappointed him and told me that more might go when he was back in his studio. I cannot hazard a guess at how many watercolours did not make the return trip because I would leave the apartment in disbelief (and exasperation) until he completed the process (fig. 55). The survivors were secured in a handmade portfolio and carried onto the airplane.

Painting with oils is a cumbersome process and working on small wood panels called *pochades*, rather than on canvas, proved less taxing. Because of the panel's intimate size, John could see and set down everything at once—not unlike drawing in a sketchbook—and he worked from the centre outward, playing shapes and tonalities against each other. John had painted pochades during his earlier trips to Venice (fig. 75), and then again in spring 2004 when he rented a small studio for two months along the wide Cannaregio Canal, close to our apartment in the Ghetto Nuovissimo (frontispiece). The studio, which took several weeks to dry out from the constant flooding caused by the canal, was his main subject (fig. 22), along with drawings and watercolours for the panels. Equally important, he continued to paint on panel when he came back to Montreal that summer, but now the subject was mainly figures.

John's canvases of Venice were done in Montreal and fall into three categories. The first group derives directly from his Venetian drawings and watercolours. There is, however, an important difference between his early and his late works. In those from his first trips, the architecture shapes the space; in later paintings, the space shapes the architecture (figs. 51, 56). While preserving the exactitude of the Venice site, the image is transformed by the tonal richness of layering oil on linen, and the sensations created by reinventing colour and light back in Montreal. His 1997 canvas of the *Habsburg Garden*, for example (fig. 43), has luscious blues and greens not found in his several watercolours painted at the site. In his own workspace, away from Venice, he could freely concentrate on ways of painting rather than ways of seeing. The second group of Venetian canvases are inspired by the city but really come from his imagination (fig. 68). While these oils may reference John's sketchbook drawings and watercolours, they were prompted more by his memories of Venice in concert with his own inventiveness. A third and more elusive category are his non-representational canvases in acrylic or oil stimulated by the sights and sensations of Venice, such as the Beaverbrook Art

Gallery's *Inch by Ounce* from 1979 (fig. 23). The pictures allude to Venetian buildings with their worn stonework and peeling stucco. Lines and shapes suggest bits of ancient architecture and contemporary graffiti as John maps the watery city (fig. 24). These images referencing Venice in the abstract were also a means for John to reimagine the city when he returned to figuration.

John's interest in printmaking began as a student at the Slade in London. Decades later in Montreal and in tandem with his move back to representation from abstraction, he pulled a few etchings and monoprints based on his Venetian sketchbook drawings. As a way to keep his hand in practice while in Venice, John signed up for a weekly etching class at the Bottega del Tintoretto in 2007, on the Sensa Canal adjacent to Tintoretto's house and near our apartment. Because the art school was open to anyone, the etching materials were far from professional and John made no prints to show. On the positive side, he worked with a master printer from France, experimenting with papers, inks and wiping, and the different ways of calibrating an etching press. Congenial late afternoon breaks, fuelled by local wine and pastry with students and staff, were also a way to practise his excellent Italian.

24. *Untitled No.8308,* 1983

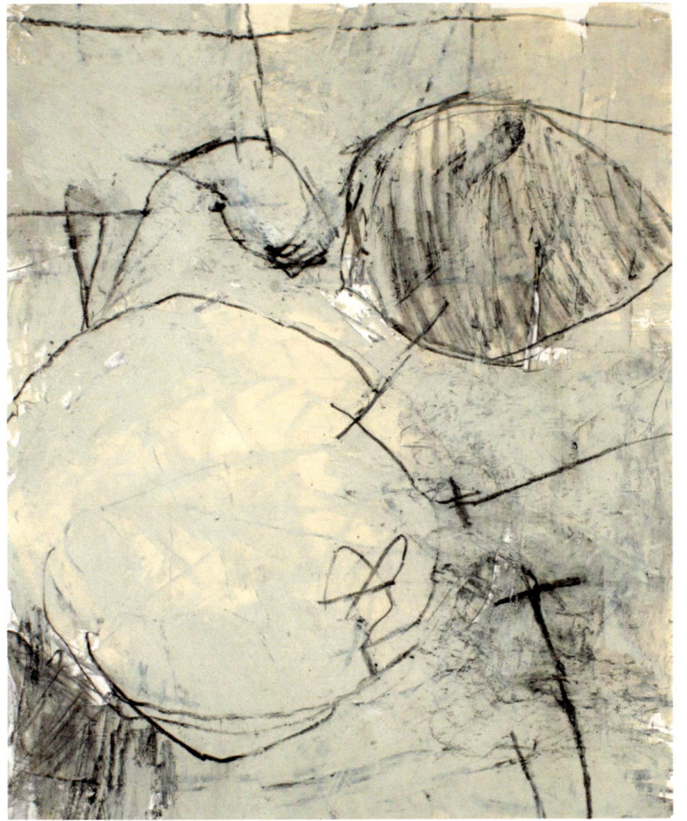

During most trips to Venice, John also took photographs, using a Leica M3 as well as a Minolta box camera; the images were taken for his own pleasure. His subjects, usually architectural, are not directly linked to his Venetian drawings or paintings, and he used only black and white film (fig. 49). He processed his film in a makeshift darkroom at home in Montreal long after he had taken the photographs. A 1982 exhibition of photography by painters was the only time John showed his images. His black and white view of the Hotel La Residenza on the Campo Bragora to the east of St. Mark's Square was reproduced and praised in Montreal newspapers. (fig. 50).

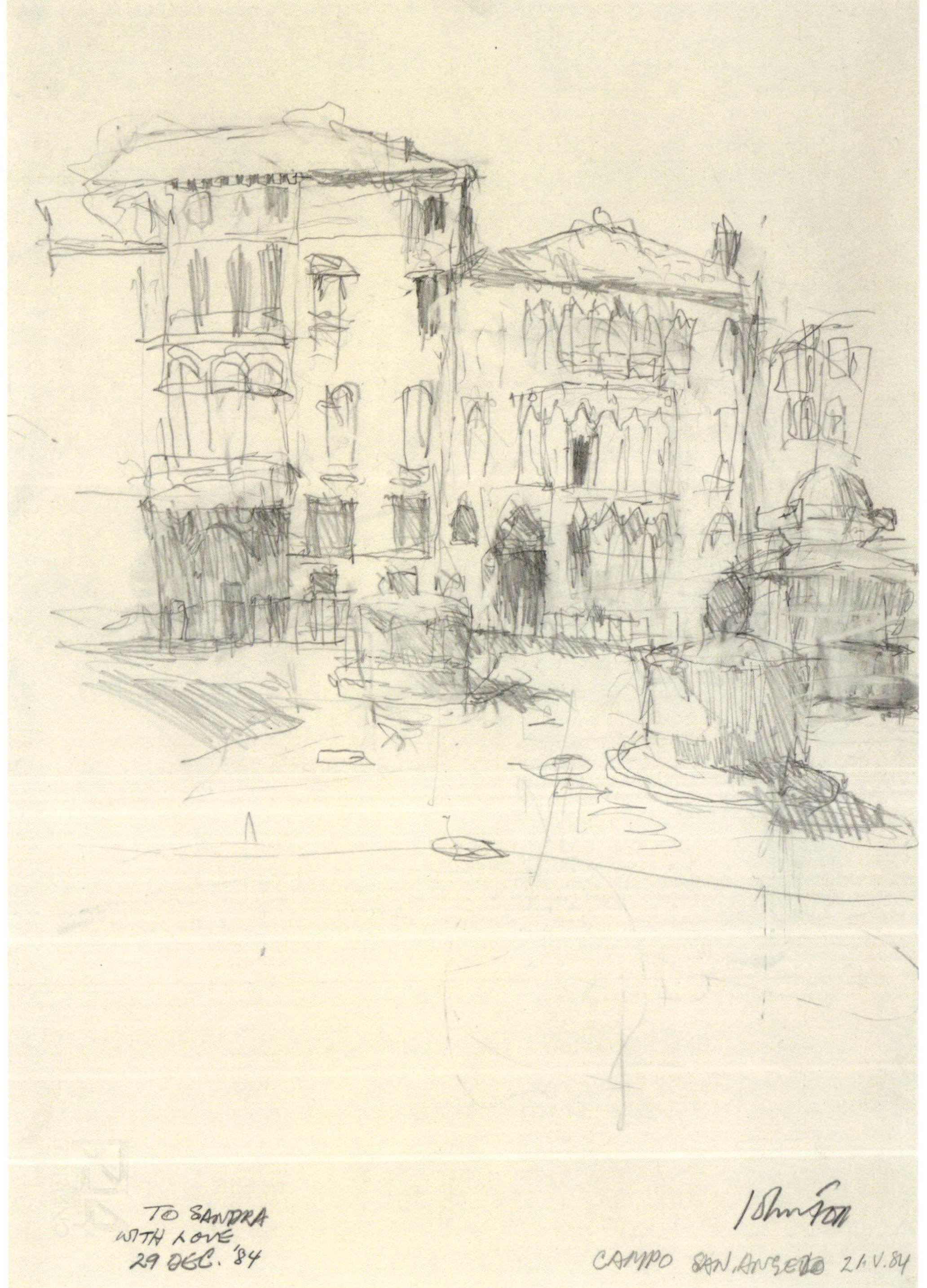

25. *Campo San Angelo*, 1984

(opposite | ci-contre)
26. *Caffè Tartaruga*, 2008

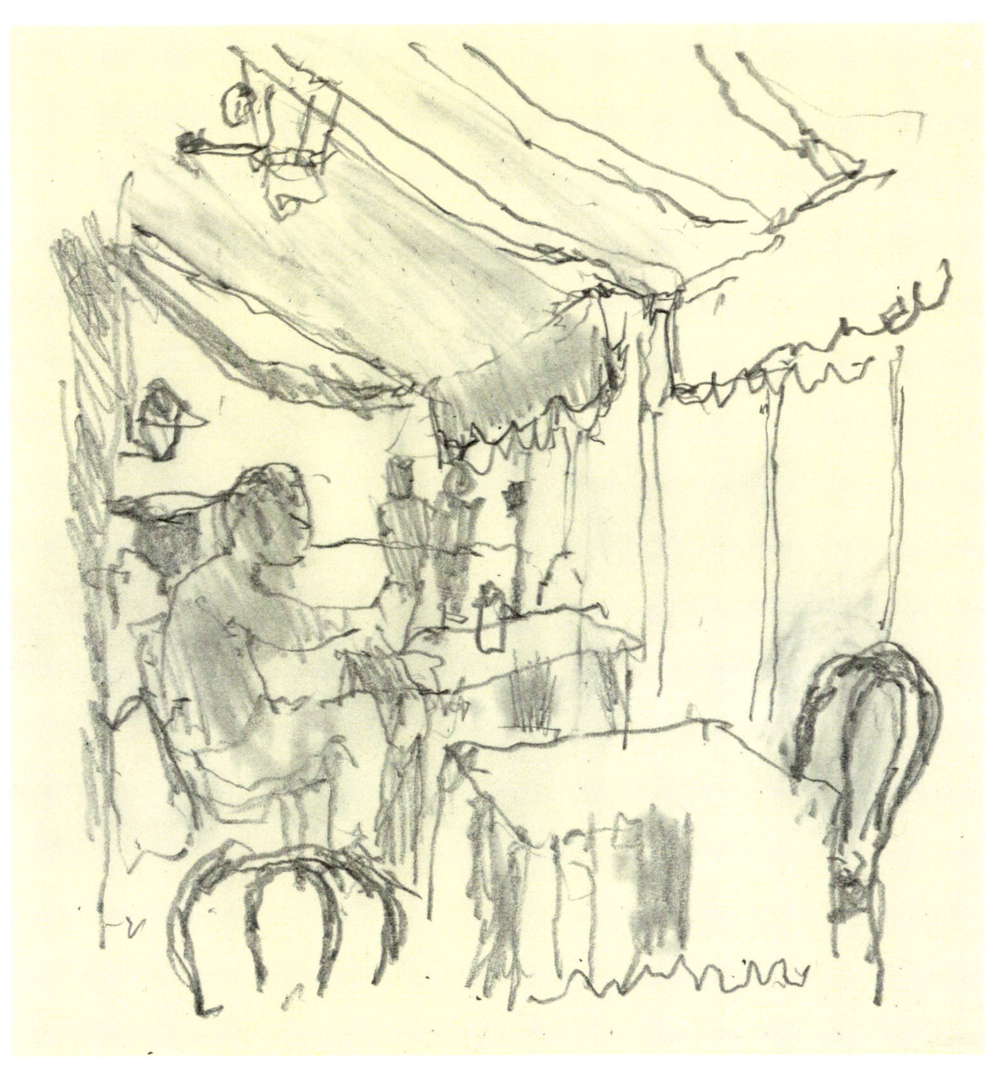

Ways of Seeing Venice

Venice is a city of contradictions: centuries of architectural styles jostle for the same space, lapping water erupts into shipping channels, canals and walkways with no obvious route secretly map the city's seventeen-hundred-year-old history. Venice is also a visual object, shaped by direct and reflected light, clear and muffled colour, geometric and organic forms, open and closed spaces. As James McNeill Whistler wrote in a spring letter to his mother, "This amazing city (is) created . . . especially for the painter."[5]

The sestiere of Cannaregio never lost its attraction for John because of canals that rimmed residential streets, and hidden gardens that spewed foliage over high walls. Latterly, he drew remote parts of the borough of Castello by wandering its backstreets. Santa Croce and San Polo sestieri also enticed John, even after we had lived there. Some of our walks to places well away from San Marco were prompted by my search for buildings occupied by confraternities when I was teaching courses on art patronage in Renaissance Venice. Such outings gave us a very different way to see the city. Our excursions usually included visits to the numerous churches that held more paintings and sculptures than Venetian museums. Cima, Titian, Tintoretto, Veronese, Lotto, Tiepolo, and Piazzetta are only a few of the Venetian painters that captured John's imagination. Equally important were sculptures by the Lombardo family, Sansovino, Rizzi, and those unknown carvers whose work enhanced Venetian buildings, inside and out. John's admiration for the city's full and relief sculpture was also infused by his reading and rereading of Adrian Stokes' classic *Venice: An Aspect of Art.*

27. *Interior of the Palazzo Barbaro*, 1991

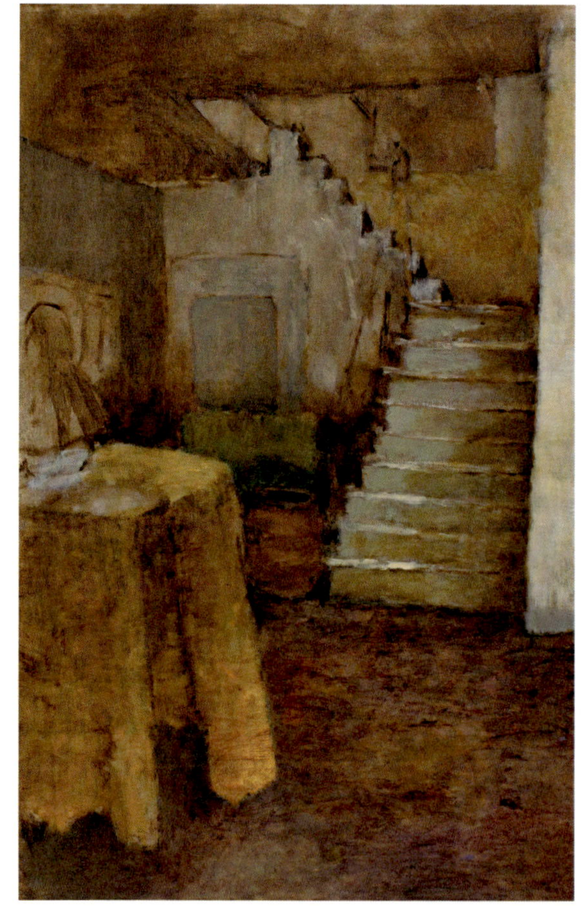

From the time of his earliest trips and ever after, John made drawings and watercolours that I call canalscapes. During his first visits, he was taken with Venice's great waterways: two panels and a canvas show the Grand Canal from the Accademia Bridge in the direction of the Piazza San Marco (fig. 75). In a view from his room in the Pensione

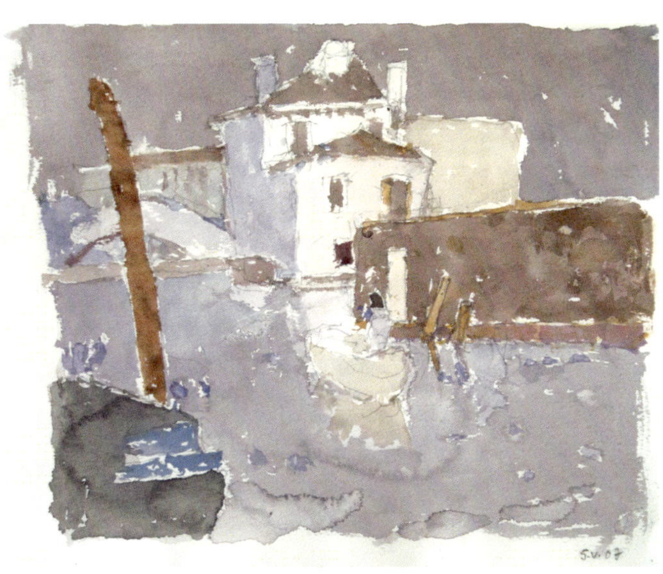

28. *Rio Madonna dell' Orto Towards the Scuola Misericordia*, 2007

La Calcina in 1964, a panel and canvases show the Zattere promenade, the Giudecca Canal, and the Redentore church (fig. 35). But John was more intrigued by the network of about one hundred and seventy-five inner canals, each one called a *rio*. He was especially taken by how they seem to determine the flow of the architecture, and how water modulated the colour of the buildings by reflecting light from the sky back onto their façades. Some of his canalscapes are bound on both sides by buildings as in two canvases, the 1957 painting of the Rio della Verona (fig. 51) and the Beaverbrook Art Gallery's canvas of the Rio Sant' Angelo (fig. 20) from his 1963 trip. Their geometry is absent from the curvaceous 2007 watercolour of the *Rio San Daniele* (fig. 60), but John's tilting shapes go back to the Beaverbrook's painting of boats in a canal. From the same year, a drawing and watercolour of the *Rio Madonna dell' Orto* (figs. 28, 52), a canal not far from our apartment, unusually includes a boat, the workhorse *sandolo.* Both watercolours are wrapped in the sensuous warmth and clear air of early summer that made our living on the Misericordia Canal so extraordinary.

In Venice, a street that runs alongside a canal is called a *fondamenta*, and often along only one side of the rio. Walking along those close to our apartment, John did many drawings from the fondamenta, showing the canal and the brick or stone walls with water-doors that enclose buildings with a few trees or a garden on the opposite side. In his 1998 *Rio Sant' Alvise* (fig. 57), one of his favourite places, the canal and architecture have his usual angularity but the pavement locates his place in the picture. The pavement disappears in *Rio della Madonna dell' Orto* (figs. 6, 7) from the same year, and the view is more intimate. That sensation is also there in a 2002 red conté of a garden and favourite restaurant seen from a narrow street across the Rio della Sensa (fig. 59). John had earlier used the motif of water and walls in his 1992 large drawing and watercolour of a dock in Burano on a side of the island away from Venice (fig. 21). Because there wasn't much to do in Burano during our two-month stay, John made many, many drawings. The ramshackle setting here is the opposite of the picturesque streets usually associated with Burano. A Venetian counterpart is his 1993 *Canal Grande* (fig. 53) with its view of the Palazzo Balbi and where its placidity, compared to most of Venice, is implicit in the stillness of John's watercolour brush.

He also drew buildings from across a canal without showing the water or indicating his physical distance from the subject. This explains the intimacy of his 1993 watercolour of the Rio Trapolin, and the wall, garden and bell tower belonging to Santa Fosca church (fig. 78). His numerous drawings of the site (fig. 11) were part of our regular walks that included a stop at the only *caffè* along the canal. A watercolour of two shops near Santa Fosca, along the Rio Terra della Maddalena, is a rare subject for John (fig. 30). He disliked the wide street and took long routes to avoid its crowds. But he gives no clue to the identity of the site, and the dark patch at the foot of the water steps is all that indicates an unusual curving canal. The view is actually from the campo of the Maddalena church across the canal, and John concealed how much he had compressed the space.

Returning to the Rio Madonna dell' Orto, John's 2004 watercolour of a dilapidated window (now remodelled) and the arched walkway (*sottoportego*) turns the humble subject into a dignified portrait (figs. 4, 29). His empathy to the site's *venezianità* is evident in its gorgeous colour and joyous light. Among John's last watercolours (figs. 41, 58) are differently toned images of the Rio di Ca' Moro, at the western end of our canal in Cannaregio. Along with a third paperwork, John's repetition of exactly the same view evokes the Italian artist Giorgio Morandi's still-lifes of bottles and bowls, and how repetition can identify an artist's ways of painting. While different light and colour make each Ca' Moro watercolour independent, they are at once figurative and abstract paintings, which John believed were much the same thing.

From his first trip onwards, John was seduced by the squares or *campi* dotted across Venice. These greatly extended church forecourts are also social spaces lined with housing, cafés, and shops—like the market in the 2004 *Campo Santa Margherita* (fig. 45) near our special lunch spot. Campi come in all shapes and sizes, but John was most attracted to the few with benches and plots of trees like little oases, where he could sit undisturbed and draw whatever caught his eye. Early on, we became habitués of *Campo San Giacomo dell' Orio* (fig. 3), sort of near the Rialto market, unfrequented by tourists but filled with Venetians of every age. Once we moved to Cannaregio on the other side of the Grand Canal, John spent much time, alone or with me, drawing in the

29. *Window and Sottoportego, Rio Madonna dell' Orto*, 2004

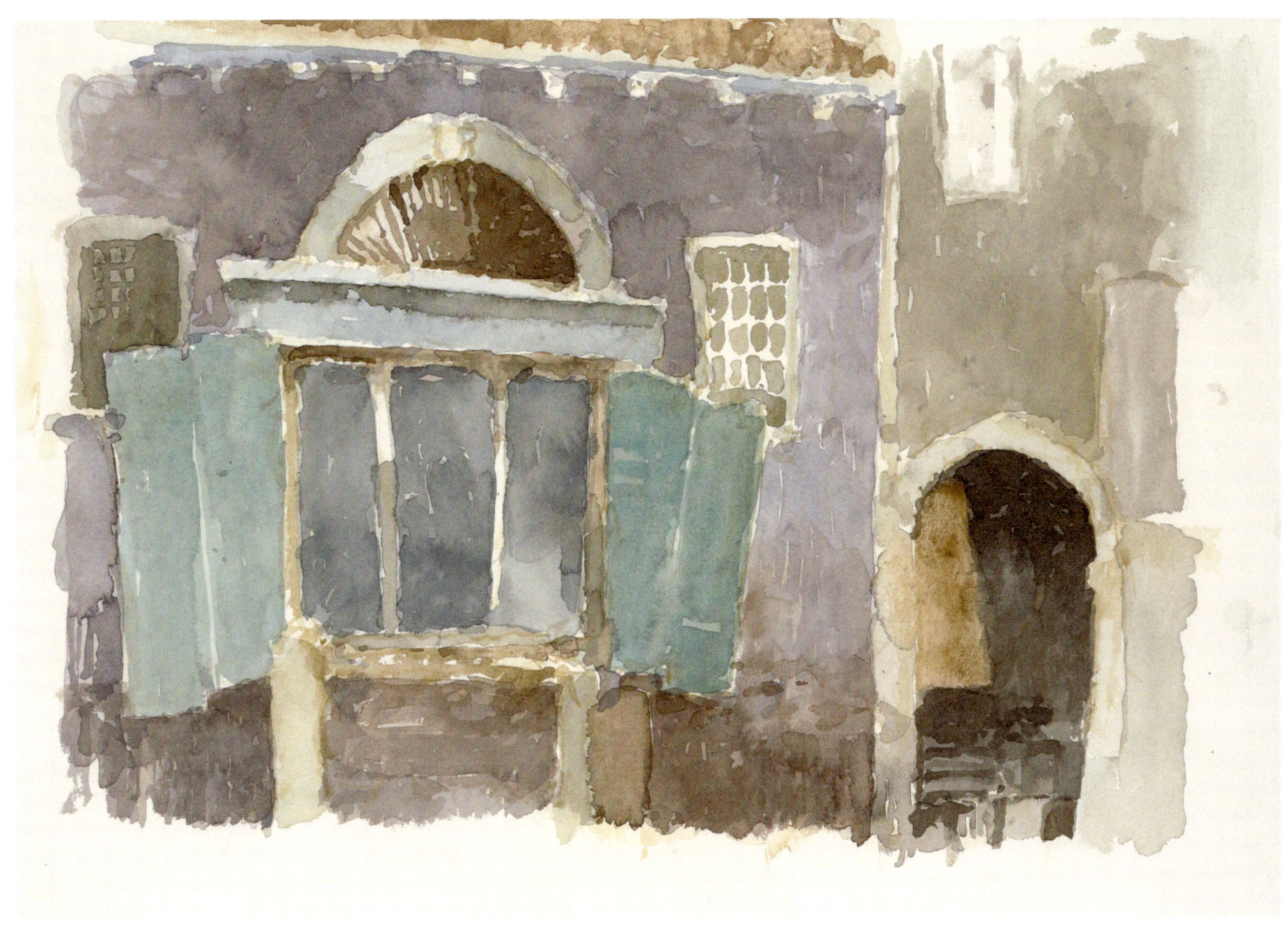

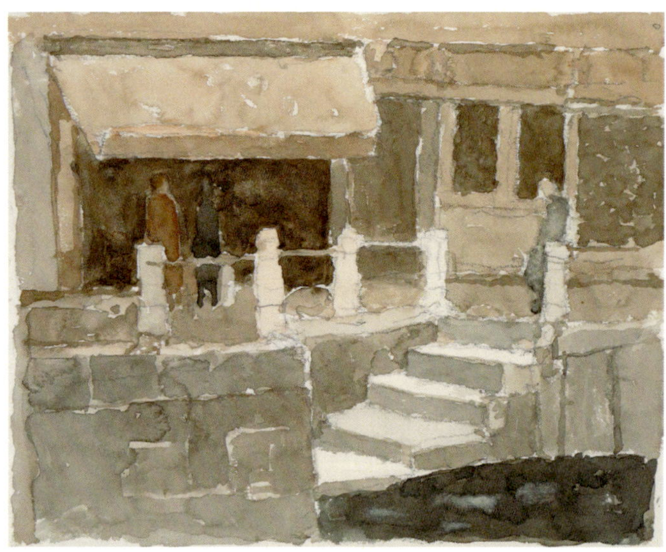

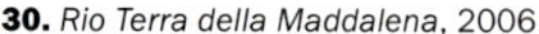

30. *Rio Terra della Maddalena*, 2006

Campo dei Gesuiti near the northern lagoon (figs. 8, 9). The campo's few trees at its narrow southern end, alongside its red benches, were the antithesis of the palazzi on the opposite side of a hidden canal, seen in other watercolours (fig. 79). Differences in his Gesuiti paintings might start with his choice of a bench, and then the light of midwinter or early summer determined their colour and character.

While John made many images of the Sant' Alvise Canal, he adored its adjacent campo for its *venezianità*. The peace and pleasure of the place is the real subject of his late watercolour and drawing of a slice of the Sant' Alvise church, the convent directly in front of his bench, and the tall residential building on the other side of the canal (figs. 72, 73). There are also drawings and a gentle watercolour of the Ghetto Nuovo (figs. 44, 46), close to our Cannaregio living space. His enjoyment of routes rarely taken by tourists was intrinsic to the pleasure he took from living in Venice. Walking through Campo Santa Ternità in eastern Castello, John discovered the entranceway and garden of the Palazzo Soranzo.

A 2003 canvas (fig. 62) and numerous watercolours (fig. 61) and drawings from two consecutive years trace how he was compelled by the building's shapes and surfaces, unmatched by anything in this most ordinary square. Another canvas of the same date, *Campiello della Madonna* (fig. 63), a small square halfway between our apartment and the Rialto, also derived from many drawings (fig. 1) and similarly red-toned watercolours. In both the campo and campiello images, John reverses the ratio of the scale of the buildings to their surroundings, so that they become his own sites.

Venice has four hundred bridges and each square usually has at least two bridges across adjacent canals. Although the Campo dei Gesuiti was a favourite subject, the steps of its major bridge are often only implied in his watercolours and drawings. But it comes into its own in a 2002 watercolour (fig. 40) in a view from the opposite side of the square where he usually worked. John was standing near the wall of the Gesuiti church's ancient monastery, and the watercolour closely follows a sketchbook drawing. The differences, as always, are those between pencil and paint. A smaller bridge, seen in the 2004 watercolour along the Fondamenta Moro (fig. 69), heads towards the Convent of the Servi from the Campo San Marziale, also not far from where we were living. (Nothing in Venice is very far away.) The angles of the bridge, the walls, and the door come from John's leaning against the unseen fondamenta wall rather than the site itself. Before living in the Ghetto Nuovissimo, we had stayed a couple of times along the Campiello Albrizzi, near the Rialto market. In winter 1998–99 he painted two watercolours of the Ponte delle Tette (figs. 47, 48), once notorious for its prostitutes, behind the Palazzo Albrizzi. They are based particularly on a sketchbook drawing with a frame line (fig. 31), suggesting John had immediately seen its potential as a painting. His repetition of the same subject affirms how changes in scale, colour, and light make for insistently different images, as Giorgio Morandi had already made clear.

31. *Ponte delle Tette*, 22 December 1998 | 22 décembre 1998

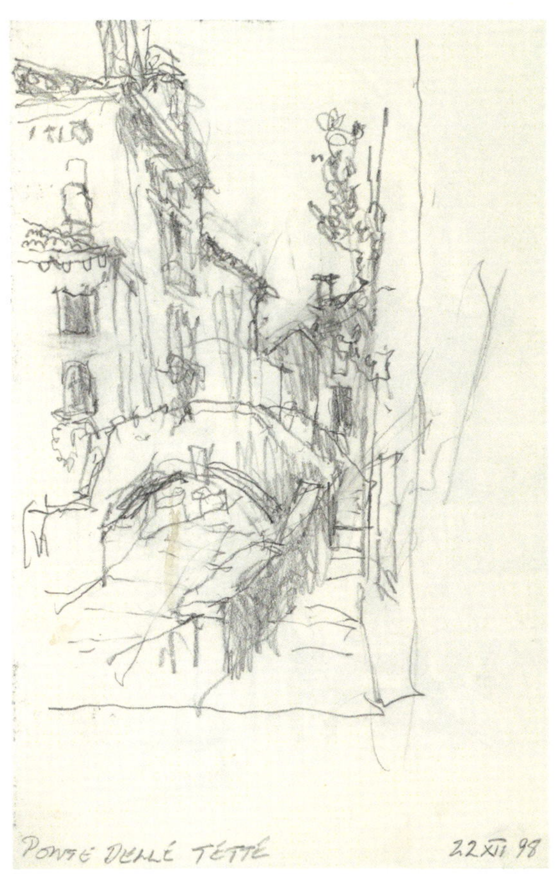

John rarely drew the exterior of Venice's almost one hundred and forty churches, but he did go inside specifically to draw. The added benefit to their art and architectural wonders was that he could get warm in the winter and cool in the summer thanks to the thick stone walls. Equally important, he could amble through the church or sit in a pew to draw without being disturbed or even noticed. Considering his dislike of ornate Venetian buildings, John was surprisingly lured by the most famous of them all, the Basilica San Marco (fig. 70). Seated on the aisle near the north transept, he drew several views looking towards the high altar, intrigued by the intertwined sculpture and architecture that made their own arabesques. A small 2004 panel of the Carmini church (figs. 64, 67) gives an inkling of the size of the vast building, while a small drawing for an unfinished canvas focuses on one of the Carmini's winding pulpit staircases and a side altar (fig. 65). John's sketchbooks were filled with images of the architectural details of church interiors and often its sculpture. Drawings of small religious objects, such as the censer and candelabra in a corner of the Gesuiti church, easily became 1993 still lifes of shapes and spaces (fig. 66).

Although John made many sketches of the interiors of places where we lived in Venice, they were mainly a way to draw for his own pleasure. Other interiors were of the small studio he rented in spring 2004. In a panel with its iron grill door open to the Cannaregio Canal, he arranged the architecture and furniture like a geometric abstract painting (fig. 22). While the studio's dampness from floods made life uniquely Venetian, but unconducive to work, it gave John time to read the art books and exhibition catalogues left behind by others. A watercolour of the enclosed cloister of the San Pietro di Castello church should also be seen as an interior. Predating San Marco as the first basilica of Venice, its small ancient cloister becomes a domestic space with a clothesline hanging from the apartments above the arched walkway in his 2007 drawing and watercolour (fig. 71).

Venetian street names have their own vocabulary depending on their width, length, and place. John's walks through the city also measured his fascination with where a *calle* (street) might take him, where a *ramo* (small side street) might lead. Turning a corner near the Rio della Sensa took John to the Ramo dei Muti that led to one of the last gondola-making boatyards (*squero*) in Venice. He made numerous pencil and red chalk drawings of the narrow street over several years, standing on the squero's bridge or leaning against a wall. In his 2003 works (figs. 5, 56), the Muti's architecture has been reduced to simplified skewed shapes, verging on the abstract. Unusual for his Venice pictures, a young girl stands almost at the center as unobtrusive and watchful of her surroundings as was John. Any pedestrian space in Venice could lead to a *sottoportego*, those ancient flat or arched passageways under a building that end in a street, a campo, or as here in the various *Sottoportego Mosto* (figs. 2, 12, 13) at the Grand Canal at San Marcuola church near the Ghetto. John's angled view animates the scruffy space, just as it had earlier turned the canal, bench, and buildings alongside the remote church of San Nicolò dei Mendicoli into a lively geometric jigsaw puzzle (fig. 74). His tilted shapes reappear in the *Campo delle Gorne* canvas, beside the thirteenth-century Arsenale where Venice built her warships (fig. 54).

Some of John's Montreal paintings on linen canvas reconstruct Venice almost entirely from his imagination and his memories. *Worksite* (fig. 68), from 1994, was his homage to the labourers who were constantly repairing and restoring Venice, even if the only direct reference to the city is the white surround of the window at the upper right. John's last painting to leave the studio was *Palazzo da Silva* (fig. 76), painted in 2007 to mark our twenty-fifth wedding anniversary. Set loosely in the living room of the Ghetto Nuovissimo apartment, the window and furniture are accurate, but the muted red wall is an allusion to the colour of Venice—its architecture and its art. John portrayed himself as a young and an old man, inscribing his first and what unknowingly had been his penultimate visit to Venice. The direct gaze between us reflects a life ineffably enhanced by our experience of that Paradise of Cities and wrapped in the unbridled glow of Venice.

NOTES

1 A confraternity or *scuola* was a charitable association of lay Venetians that ensured the social, material and religious well-being of their members. Scuole included guilds, groups of non-Venetian residents, and those devoted to various Catholic rites and saints. While most scuole met in small rooms, some owned buildings with artworks, and were often architecturally important, like the six Scuole Grande.

2 John's ashes were interred in the Cimitero di San Michele, Venice. I have continued to travel to Venice almost annually since 2008. Many trips were devoted to researching and writing my book *James Wilson Morrice. Paintings and Drawings of Venice* (Stuttgart: arnoldsche Art Publishers), published in late 2023.

3 The descriptor derives from the May 6, 1841 diary entry of the British critic John Ruskin: "Thank God I am here; it is the paradise of cities." For a discussion on John Fox's later Venetian painting in the context of his Montreal artwork, see Sandra Paikowsky et al, *Refiguration* (Montreal: Visual Arts Centre, McClure Gallery, 2010).

4 John's non-figurative work is the subject of Liz Wylie et al, *John Fox. Abstractions* (Montreal: Battat Contemporary, 2012) and Sandra Paikowsky, *John Fox Abstractions* (Bloomfield, ON: Oeno Gallery, 2015).

5 Letter from James McNeill Whistler to Anna Matilda Whistler, March/May 1880. Charles Lang Freer Papers, Freer Gallery of Art and Arthur M. Sackler Gallery Archives, Smithsonian Institution, Washington, D.C.

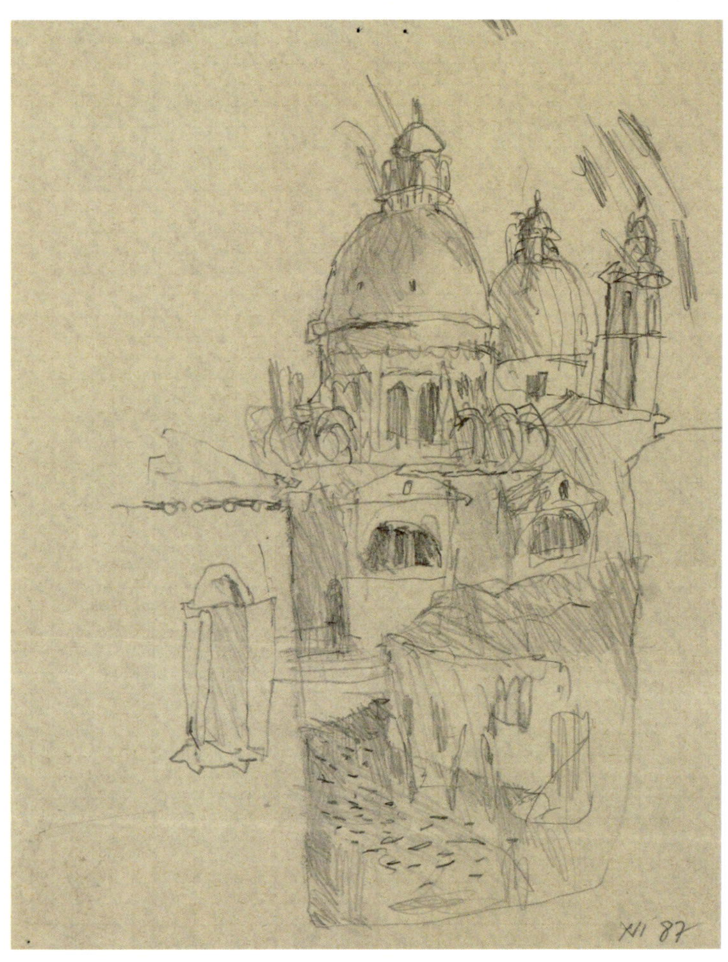

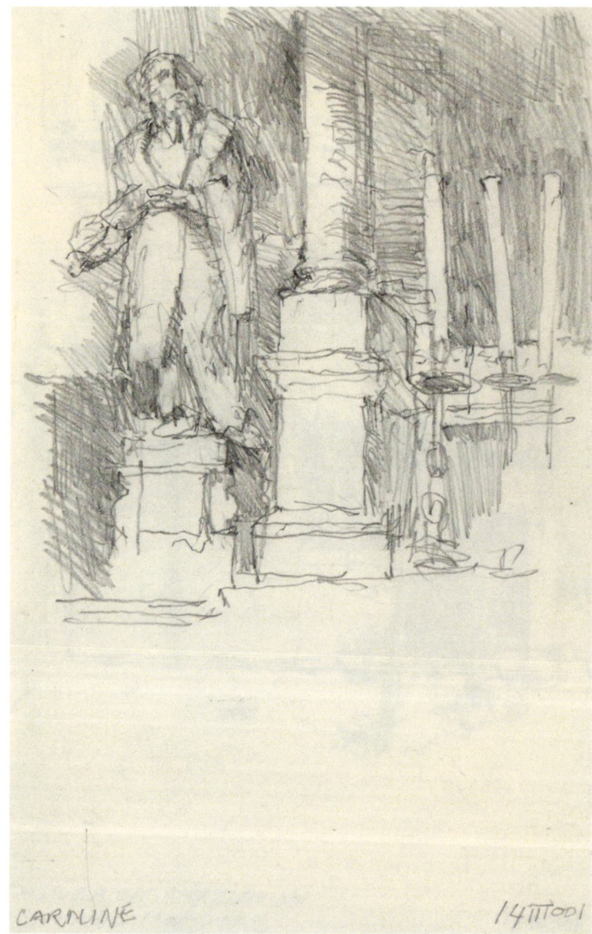

(from left | à partir de la gauche)
32. *Church of the Salute*, 1987
33. *Carmine (Sculpture, Carmine Church)*, 14 March 2001 | 14 mars 2001

34. *Rialto Fish Market*, c. 1980 |
vers 1980

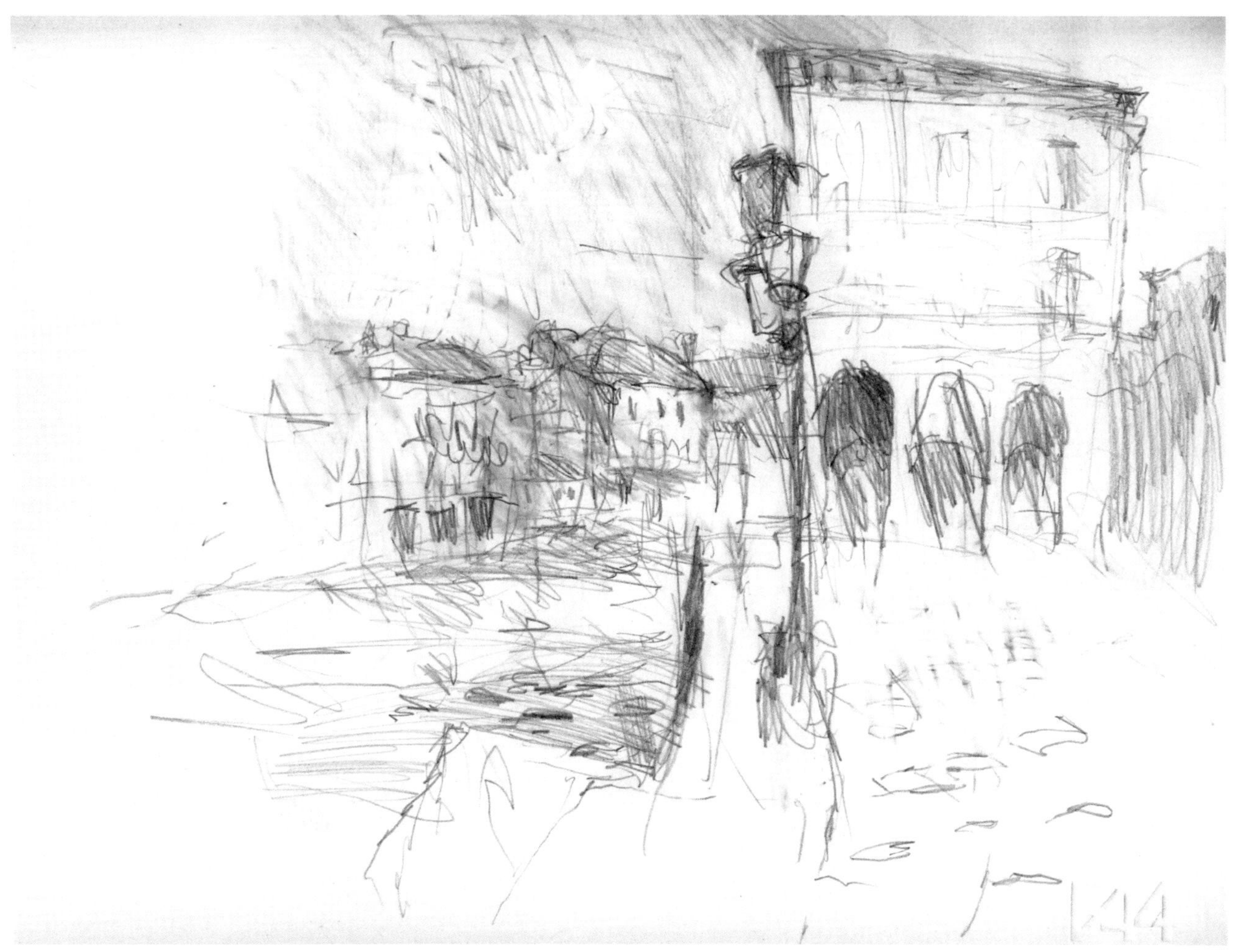

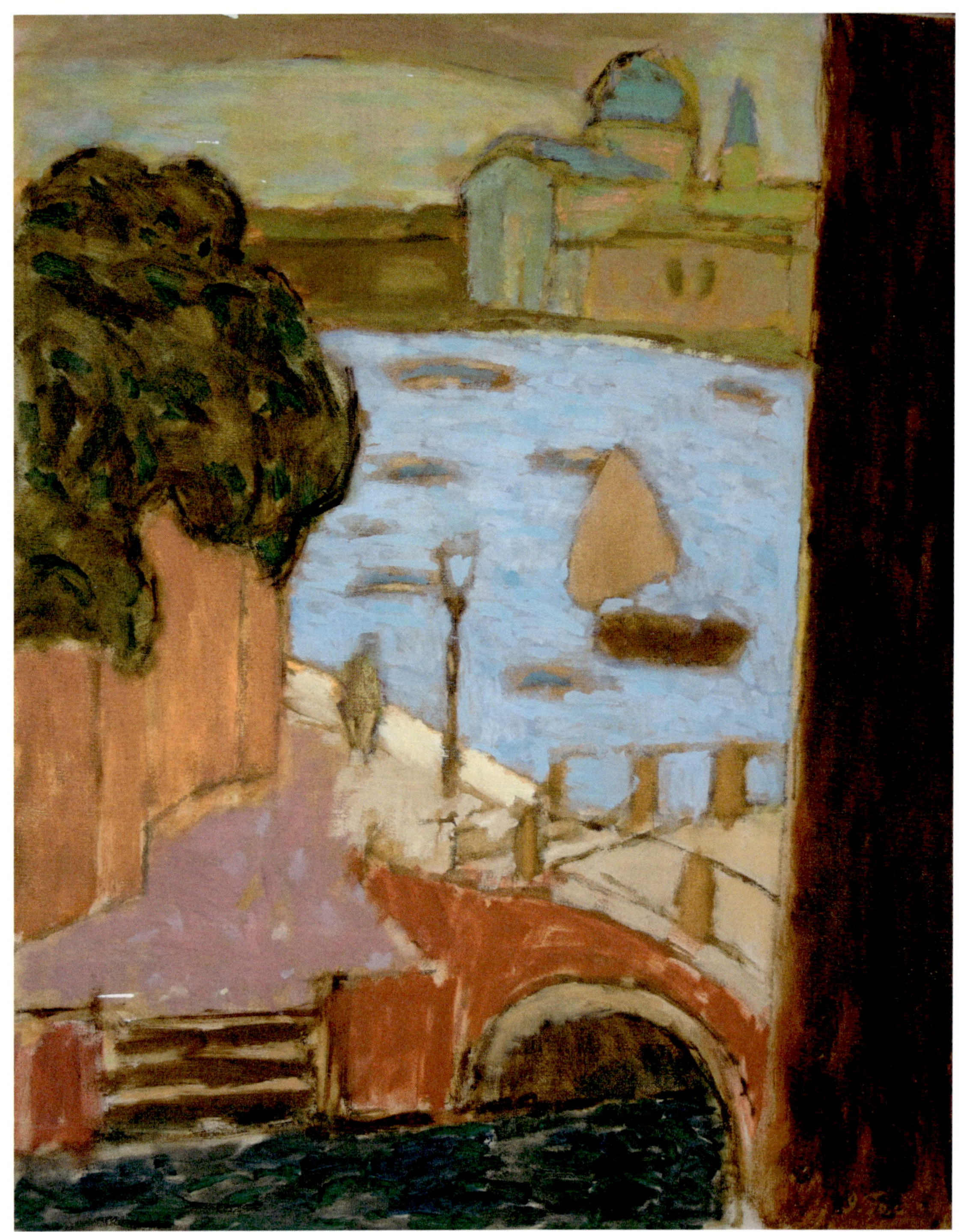

 35. *View of the Zattere and Church of the Redentore*, 1964

John Fox
Images de Venise

SANDRA PAIKOWSKY

John Fox s'est épris de Venise avant même d'y aller. C'était en 1952, pendant ses études à la Slade School of Fine Art de Londres et les six semaines passées à copier *Vénus et Adonis* de Titien à la National Gallery britannique. Jamais il ne s'est départi de sa toile : c'était d'abord un hommage à Titien et à son habileté à transmuer la peinture en lumière et en couleurs, un art dont John fera le fondement de sa propre manière. C'était aussi un présage de l'amour à vie de John pour Venise.

Quand il s'y rend la première fois, en août 1953, John est subjugué par *La Pietà*, dernière œuvre de Titien, qu'il voit à l'Accademia et qui restera à jamais pour lui la référence de ce qu'est et peut faire la peinture. Ses premières représentations de la cité lagunaire sont panoramiques (fig. 16), comme s'il essayait de tout résumer tandis qu'il la parcourt. Parallèlement, il veut s'imprégner de l'œuvre des artistes vénitiens du XVIe au XVIIIe siècle, qu'il découvre dans les églises, les musées et les confréries[1]. Il y consacrera 50 ans. Un deuxième séjour, en juillet 1956, entre quelques mois à Florence et à Paris, marque le début d'une nouvelle manière de dessiner et peindre Venise, soit comme autant de moments saisis dans quelque coin tranquille d'une place (fig. 17) ou d'une église (fig. 18). Quand il y retourne depuis Montréal, au milieu des années 1960, il éprouve un intérêt renouvelé pour des sujets classiques comme le Grand Canal (fig. 75) et le marché du Rialto (fig. 19), tout en jetant sur la ville ancienne un œil contemporain (fig. 20), comme l'avait fait, un demi-siècle plus tôt, son mentor, le peintre canadien James Wilson Morrice (1865–1924), dont l'esthétique l'aura tellement inspiré.

En mars 1977, John et moi avons fait le premier voyage annuel d'une série de 31 dans la lagune. Nous étions en couple depuis un an, et nous nous sommes mariés à l'hôtel de ville de Venise en 1982. Pendant longtemps, nos séjours dans la Sérénissime, en décembre et en janvier, ont été rythmés par notre calendrier d'enseignement à la

Faculté des beaux-arts de l'Université Concordia. Il nous est aussi arrivé d'y passer un mois au printemps ou à l'été. En novembre 1990, ce fut une escapade d'une semaine pour voir, au Palais des doges, *Titian: Prince of Painters* (*Titien, le prince des peintres*), une exposition qui nous semblait absolument incontournable. À la fin de l'automne 1992, un congé sabbatique nous a permis de passer deux mois sur l'île de Burano (fig. 21) avant de retourner à Venise, de décembre à mars, pour notre plus long séjour jusque-là. À partir de mars 1993, et pendant plus d'une décennie, nous avons logé à proximité de l'ancien ghetto juif de Cannaregio, un *sestiere* (quartier) du nord-ouest de Venise.

Nous avons ensuite repris nos séjours hivernaux d'un mois, plus quelques visites estivales. John n'arrivait pas à trouver l'espace nécessaire pour peindre sur toile, et le dessin d'après modèle, son atelier, ses fournitures et ses livres lui manquaient. À compter de 2004, il a loué un petit local à part, pour travailler (fig. 22), mais il ne s'y sentait pas chez lui. De 2000, environ, jusqu'à sa mort sur place, en 2008, nous avons passé deux mois par année à Venise, en général entre le printemps et l'été[2]. Venise n'est pas du tout la même l'hiver et l'été : l'air, la lumière et les couleurs, tout y est très différent. Elle reste cependant toujours « le paradis des villes[3] ».

Des manières de travailler à Venise

Pendant ses études et ses 50 ans de carrière, le dessin restera pour John le moyen privilégié de réfléchir et de travailler. Même après avoir abordé l'abstraction, du début des années 1970 au milieu des années 1980 (fig. 23 et 24), il continue de dessiner des personnages, des lieux et des objets (fig. 25)[4]. À Venise, le dessin dans des carnets de croquis faisait partie du quotidien ; c'était d'ailleurs son seul travail en extérieur. À tout moment et en tout lieu, il emportait ses crayons, parfois quelques bâtons de sanguine ou de fusain et, toujours, sa fidèle gomme à effacer, plus un ou deux carnets. Chaque carnet couvre environ deux ans, mais aucun n'est entièrement consacré à Venise. John achetait ses Moleskine sur place ou les apportait de Montréal. Vers le milieu des années 1990, il est passé aux cahiers cartonnés Daler (*quaderni per schizzi*), que vendait une papeterie à proximité du grand square appelé *campo* San Giacomo dell' Orio (fig. 3). Il tenait à ses carnets comme à la prunelle de ses yeux. À la différence d'autres artistes, il ne s'en servait que pour dessiner, sans rien y noter. Il en a laissé plus de 80, dont 40 % contiennent des images de Venise, qui ne sont toutefois pas réparties également dans l'ensemble. On y trouve des dessins préparatoires aux aquarelles ou des références pour les toiles qui allaient suivre. Il manque vraisemblablement un petit nombre de ces carnets ou portfolios, puisque certains tableaux ne semblent correspondre à aucun dessin préliminaire.

Chaque année, pendant des décennies, John a déambulé dans Venise en fin de matinée et parfois de nouveau en après-midi, jusqu'à trouver l'endroit propice. Ou peut-être est-ce l'endroit qui le trouvait ? Je l'accompagnais souvent le matin, à condition que la promenade passe par une brioche et un espresso à la table d'un café (fig. 26). Nous partions sans but, quelques fois pour peu de temps, selon ce qui retenait son attention. Il nous arrivait fréquemment de retourner deux ou trois fois dans un lieu qu'il avait déjà dessiné. Après dîner, il sortait seul, sans préparer davantage son itinéraire. Il a également dessiné ou peint le décor de nos appartements de location (fig. 27) et quelques vues depuis nos fenêtres (fig. 32 et 35). Au début, nous habitions trop près de San Marco, de ses *palazzi* richement ornementés et de ses touristes accablés de fatigue, mais nous avons vite préféré des lieux plus évocateurs de la *venezianità,* cette authenticité intemporelle de la ville et de son mode de vie. Au début des années 1990, John a dessiné sur le vif dans l'atelier d'une connaissance, à Venise, mais il n'aimait pas travailler ailleurs que chez lui avec des modèles peu connus. Qui sait si les sculptures des églises vénitiennes ne lui ont pas tenu lieu de modèles, à défaut de ceux, plus familiers, de Montréal (fig. 33) ?

Plus tard, quand nous nous sommes éloignés de Piazza San Marco au profit de lieux privilégiés des Vénitiens, John s'est senti nettement plus à l'aise. Il s'asseyait volontiers sur un banc public, ou s'adossait à un mur ou à un pont, pour dessiner sans attirer l'attention et préserver l'intimité du moment. Touchante exception, par contre, que cet homme venu un jour lui offrir une petite chaise depuis son appartement situé dans l'étroite et discrète *calle* où John avait travaillé quelques fois déjà, lui expliquant brièvement qu'il lui suffisait de la laisser près de la porte principale au terme de la séance. Surpris et ravi, John a remercié le *veneziano*, qui l'a quitté en lui souhaitant bonne journée.

Peu importe où nous étions, John était séduit par les formes plus que par l'histoire des bâtiments et du décor (fig. 34). Ses carnets contiennent nombre de croquis des mêmes endroits, dessinés au fil des ans, preuve de sa sensibilité à la composition formelle d'un lieu et au rapprochement entre ses éléments naturels et bâtis (fig. 1 et 8). Chaque fois, pourtant, il en livrait une vue différente. Dans certains cas, il a changé d'angle (fig. 36 et 37), et dans d'autres, il a tout au plus tourné la tête ; enfin, beaucoup de sujets ont été croqués de face. Autant de variations emblématiques de ses dessins d'après modèle. Il lui est arrivé, coup sur coup ou en des jours différents, de dessiner une même scène à la verticale et à l'horizontale, ou différentes versions d'un même sujet : d'abord un croquis rapide, par exemple, puis un dessin plus précis, enrichi de quelques détails (fig. 8 et 9). Il retournait souvent le lendemain s'assurer que le dessin était bien ce qu'il voulait qu'il soit. John avait l'habitude de dater les images de son carnet, mais dans certains cas, il faut se contenter de conjectures. De même, je reconnais aisément ses lieux favoris, mais parfois le mystère reste entier, parce que les lieux sont rarement identifiés et que les œuvres ne sont pas toutes titrées (fig. 38 et 39).

Les dessins au crayon et à la craie sont à la fois descriptifs et dynamiques, fruits d'un tour de main souple et maîtrisé, et expression de l'admiration de John pour les œuvres sur papier de Giambattista Tiepolo, peintre vénitien du XVIIIe siècle. John était en quête d'une manière propre de modeler les formes au-delà d'une simple reproduction. Quand, en 2007, à près de 80 ans, il a dessiné les bâtiments, le pont et le canal qui bordent une petite place à côté de l'église San Francesco della Vigna (fig. 14), il a eu l'impression d'y être enfin parvenu, et l'idée l'a rempli de joie. Les traits sont plus rares, l'ombrage est plus présent, chaque marque de crayon évoque un coup de pinceau, et les zones sombres et lumineuses rappellent une peinture sur papier (fig. 15).

John aimait le dessin en soi, et aucune raison n'explique que certains croquis sont devenus des aquarelles et d'autres non, ni pourquoi il lui arrivait de retourner dans un lieu déjà exploité pour y peindre une nouvelle aquarelle. L'aquarelle aura d'ailleurs toujours été son moyen d'expression préféré, et je pense que cette prédilection, qui se manifestait surtout à Venise, va de pair avec son retour à la figuration au milieu des années 1980, après 15 ans environ d'une production plus abstraite (fig. 23). S'il restait fidèle à l'essentiel du sujet, la palette, par moments assez proche de la réalité, était aussi en grande partie le fruit de son imagination. La longue pratique de l'abstraction lui avait donné l'aisance nécessaire pour rendre Venise dans des couleurs et une lumière qui lui étaient propres, sans porter atteinte à son authenticité (fig. 40 et 41).

C'est à l'intérieur que John peignait ses aquarelles, dans nos cuisines vénitiennes où le mélange de lumière artificielle et de lumière naturelle de l'après-midi n'était pas si loin de l'éclairage de son atelier montréalais. À cela, une seule exception : au printemps 1996, quand nous avons pris nos quartiers dans un ancien casinò, un petit palazzo ayant appartenu jadis à une branche de la dynastie des Habsbourg, puis devenu un centre

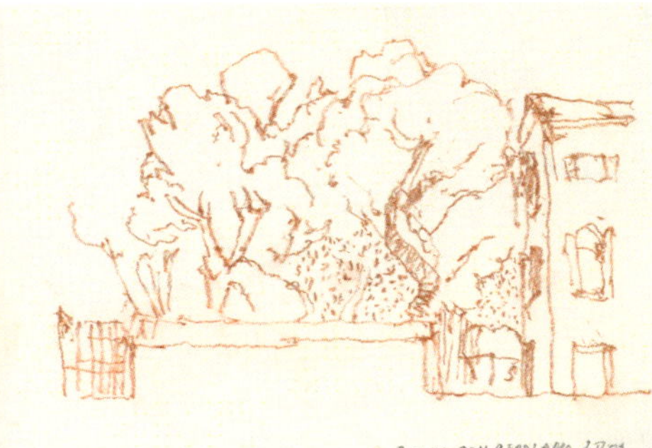

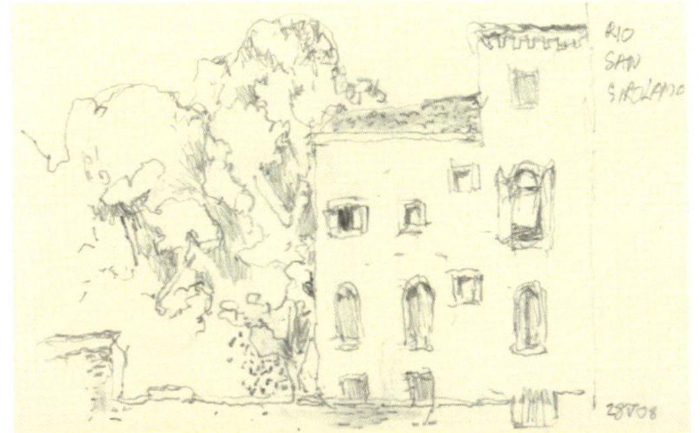

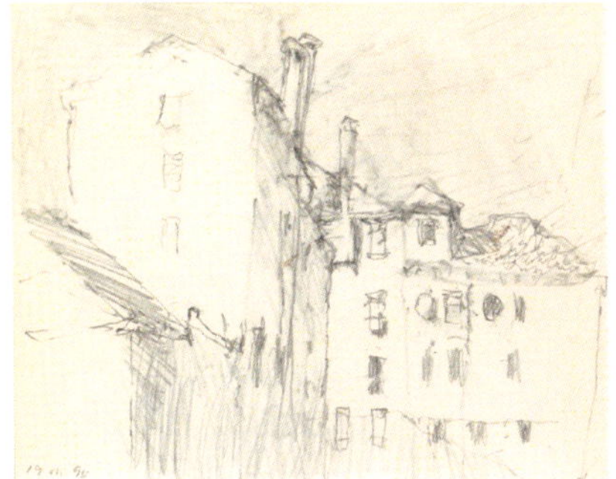

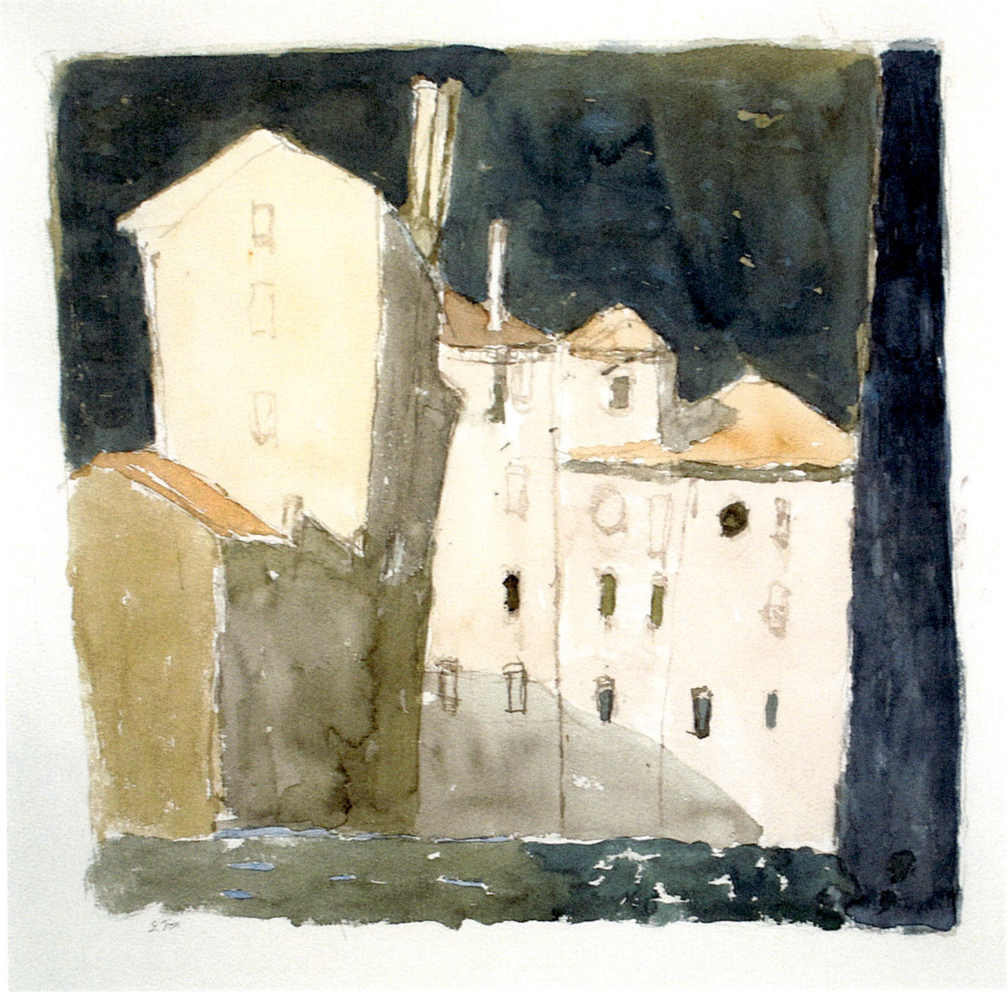

(clockwise from top left |
à partir de la gauche ci-dessus)

36. *Rio di San Girolamo (Rio Ca' Moro at San Girolamo)*, 2 May 2003 | 2 mai 2003

37. *Rio di San Girolamo (Rio Ca' Moro at San Girolamo)*, 28 May 2008 | 28 mai 2008

38. *Venice Houses*, 19 December 1995 | 19 décembre 1995

39. *Venice Houses*, 1993

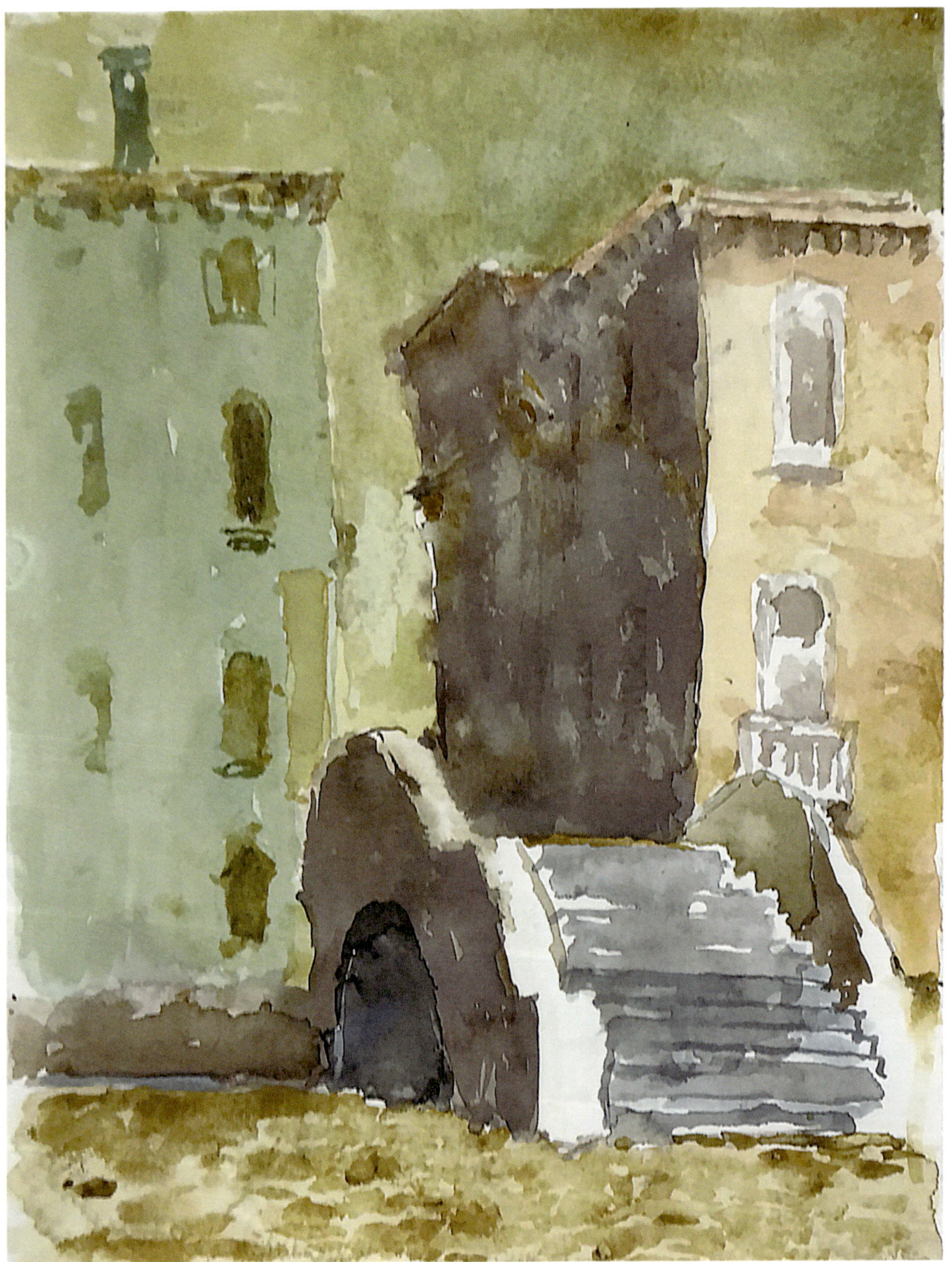

40. *Bridge at the Campo and Rio dei Gesuiti*, 2002

(opposite | ci-contre)
41. *Rio Ca' Moro at San Girolamo II*, 2008

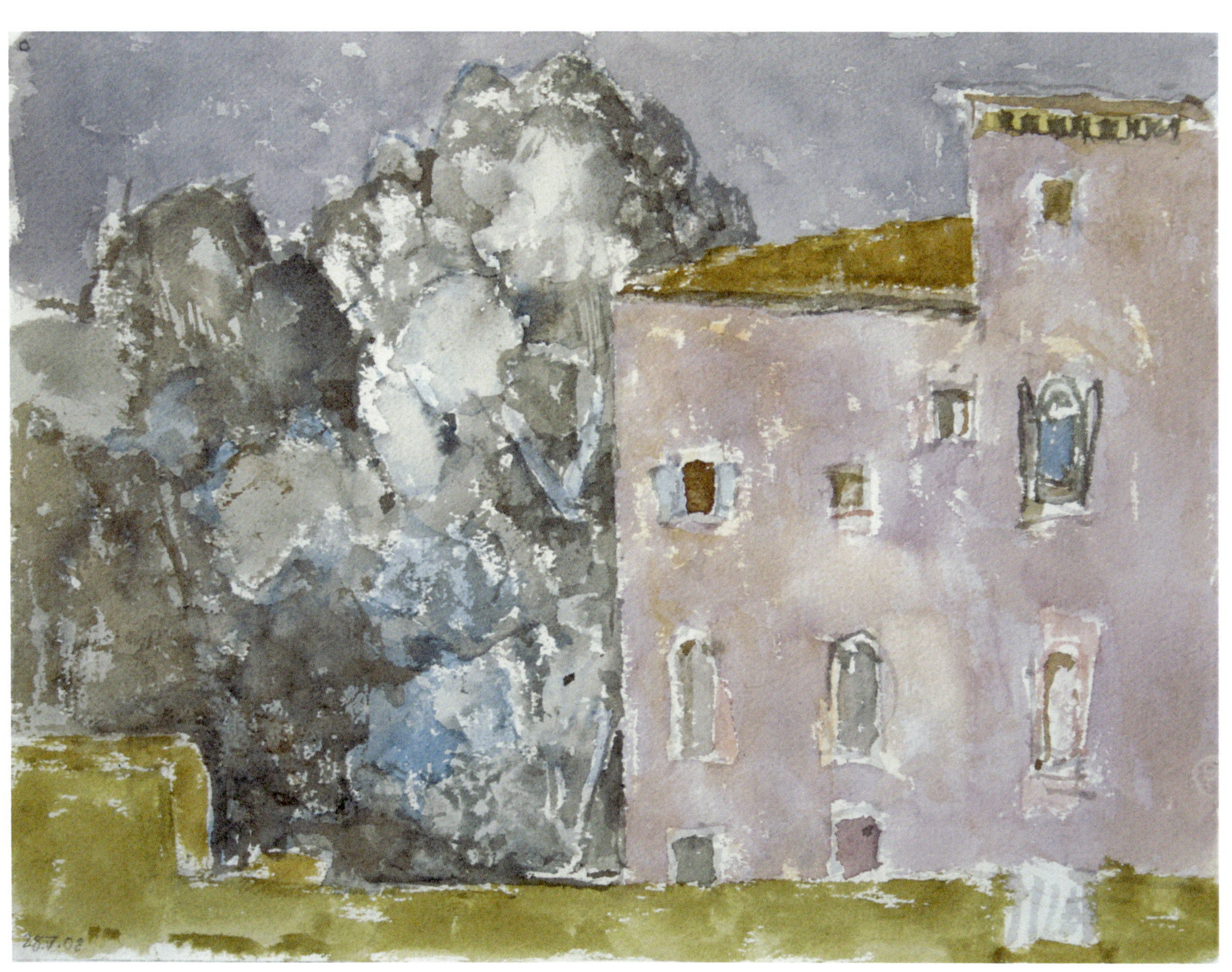

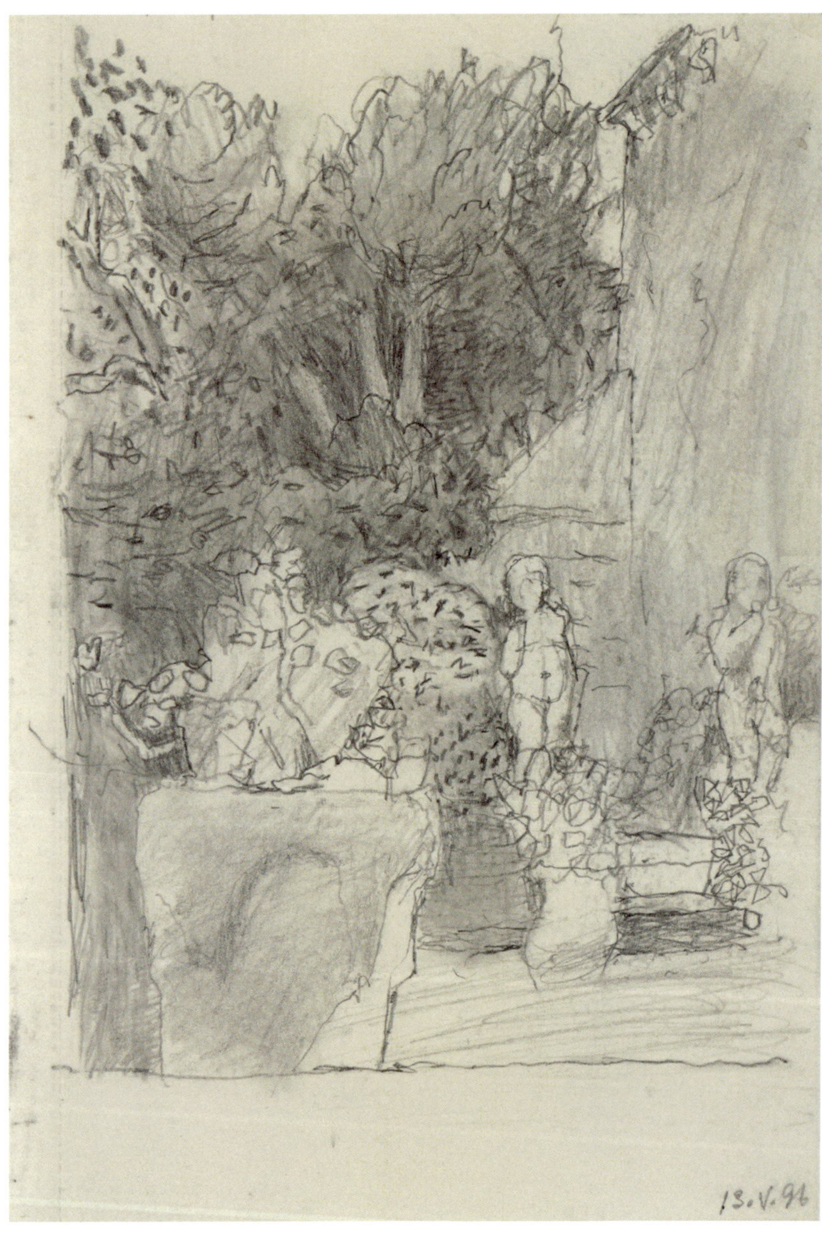

42. *Habsburg Garden*, 13 May 1996 | 13 mai 1996

(opposite | ci-contre)
43. *Habsburg Garden*, 1997

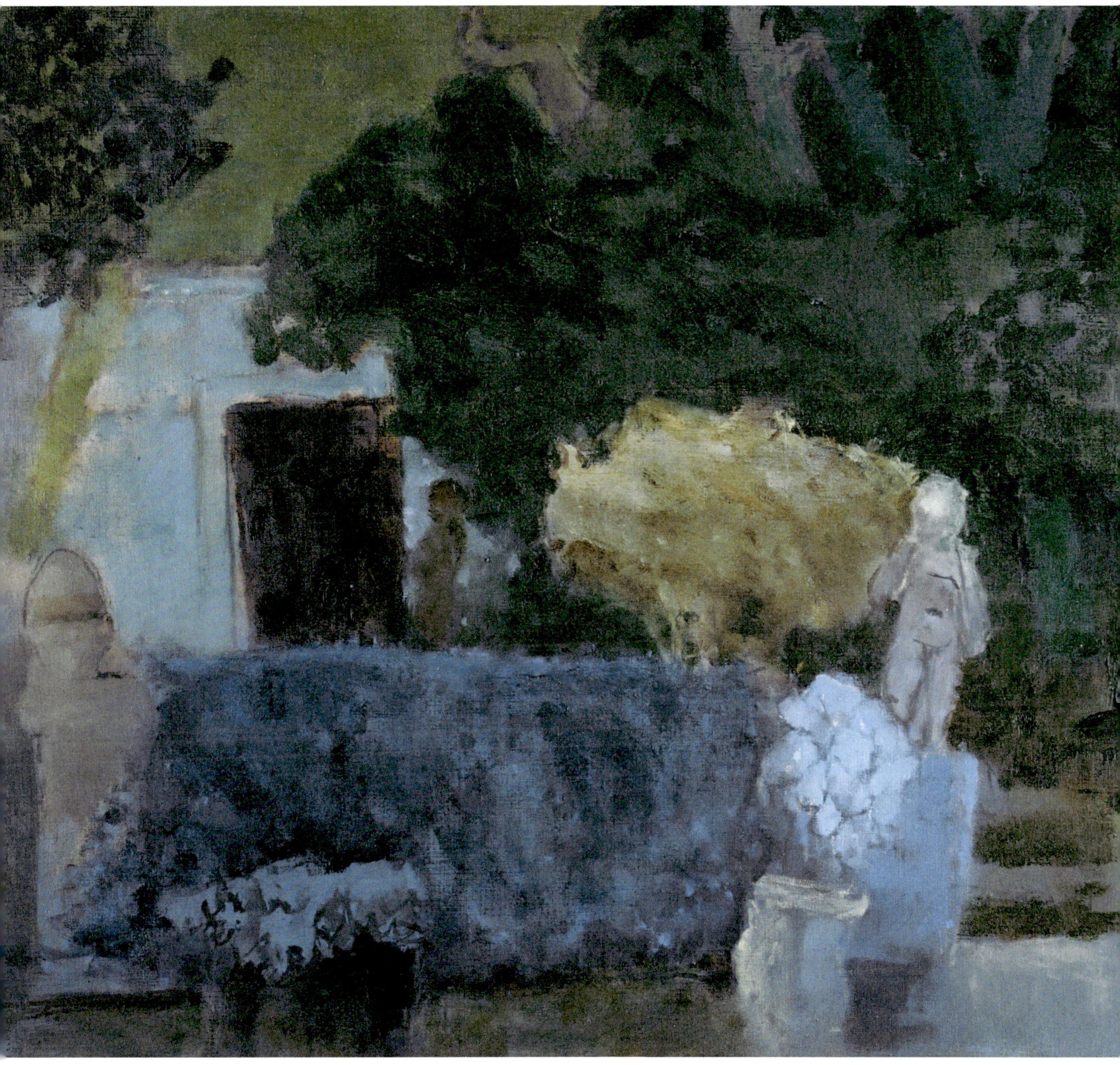

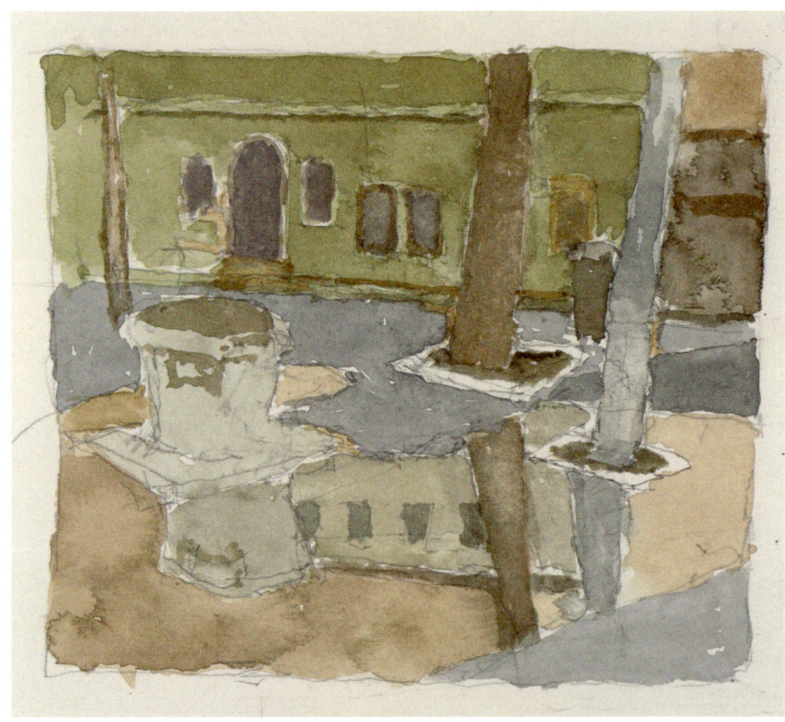

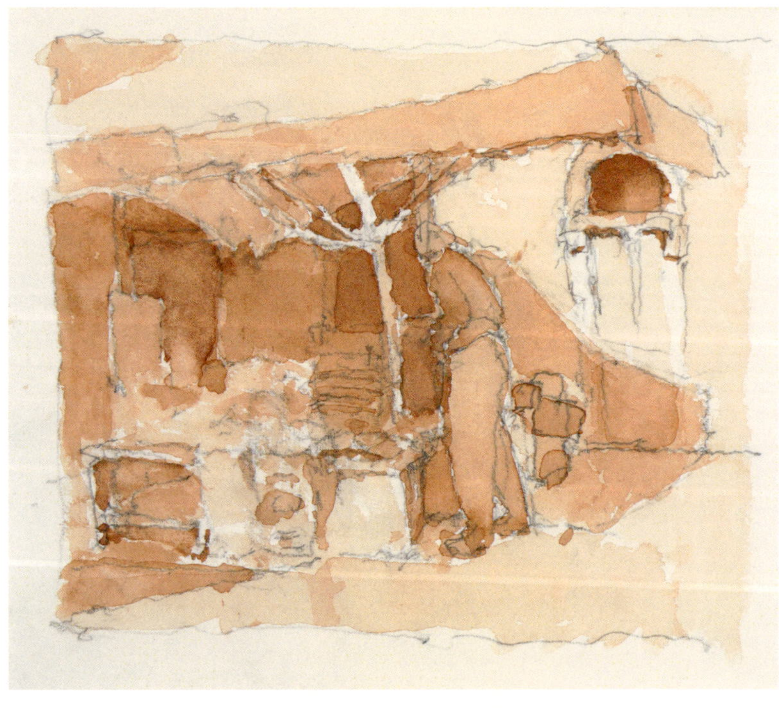

44. *Campo Ghetto Nuovo,*1993

45. *Campo Santa Margherita,* 2004

musical dédié au romantisme français. Comme l'édifice était précédé d'une cour ceinte de hauts murs, John s'installait volontiers à l'extérieur pour dessiner et peindre, sous les néfliers et le regard exclusif des *putti* replets qui bordaient le jardin Renaissance (fig. 42 et 43). Où qu'il soit, il travaillait à ses aquarelles en consultant les croquis du jour ou ceux des semaines ou des jours antérieurs (fig. 44 et 46). Il n'éprouvait pas le besoin de rapporter ses anciens carnets, dont sa mémoire prodigieuse retenait le contenu.

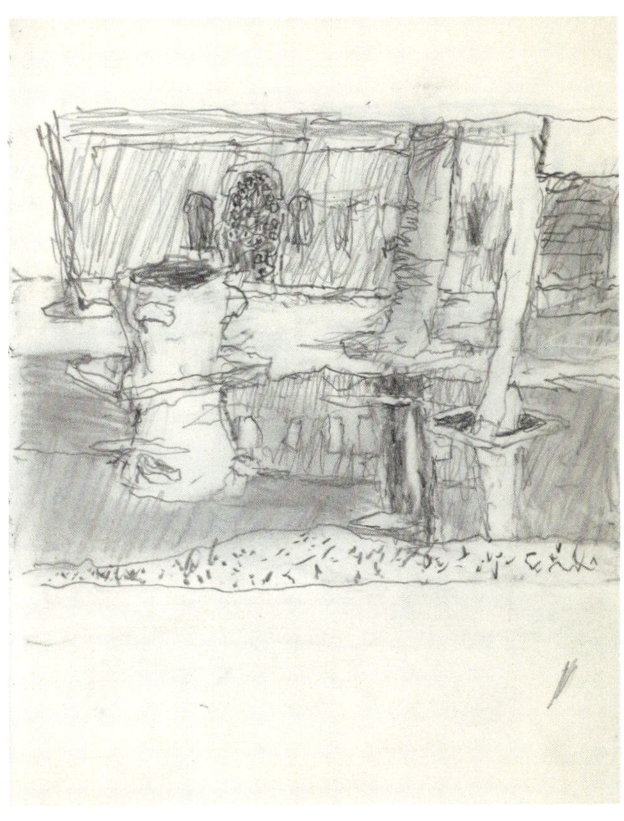

46. *Campo Ghetto Nuovo*, 1993

Il lui arrivait de faire plus d'une aquarelle en un après-midi et d'y retravailler les jours suivants, ou de revenir sur d'autres, exécutées depuis notre arrivée, pour y apporter ce qui lui semblait être des changements essentiels. Les aquarelles vénitiennes présentent un spectre chromatique varié, mais 20 % environ sont dominées par le rouge conté. Sur beaucoup, on aperçoit le dessin au crayon sous-jacent (fig. 45). Il a fait à l'occasion deux versions ou plus d'un même sujet, dans des couleurs très différentes (fig. 47 et 48) ou dans des nuances plus subtiles ou plus appuyées d'une même couleur. Dans les premiers temps, il achetait sur place du papier Fabriano d'un magasin d'État (fig. 25 et 34), mais la fermeture de ce commerce et la disparition progressive d'autres fournisseurs, à Venise, l'ont finalement contraint à emporter de Montréal son papier et ses tubes d'aquarelle Winsor & Newton.

À la veille de chaque retour à Montréal, John examinait une à une ses aquarelles d'un œil plus que critique et n'hésitait pas à réduire en lambeaux celles qui le décevaient, en m'annonçant du reste que d'autres subiraient vraisemblablement le même sort dans son atelier. Je ne saurais dire combien ont disparu de la sorte, parce que je quittais l'appartement, incrédule et exaspérée, jusqu'à la fin de la purge (fig. 55). Les survivantes, placées en sûreté dans un portfolio de sa fabrication, montaient à bord de l'avion.

La peinture à l'huile est une technique un peu encombrante, et il est plus aisé de brosser un croquis à coups de pinceau rapides—la pochade—sur un petit panneau de bois plutôt que sur une toile. Ainsi, grâce aux dimensions plus modestes des panneaux, John pouvait tout voir et représenter d'un coup, un peu comme quand il dessinait dans son carnet. Il travaillait du centre vers l'extérieur, opposant formes et tonalités. Il avait fait des pochades dès ses premiers séjours à Venise (fig. 75) et s'y est remis au printemps 2004, alors qu'il avait loué un petit atelier au bord du large canal de Cannaregio, près de notre appartement du Ghetto Nuovissimo (frontispice). L'atelier, qui a conservé pendant des semaines les relents de fréquentes inondations, a fait partie de ses principaux sujets (fig. 22) et de ceux des dessins et aquarelles préalables. Fait également important, John a continué à peindre sur panneau de bois de retour à Montréal, cet été-là, en privilégiant toutefois les personnages.

Les toiles de John qui figurent Venise ont été exécutées à Montréal et sont de trois types. Un premier groupe est directement issu d'aquarelles et de dessins exécutés sur place. Il y a cependant une grande différence entre les premières œuvres et les œuvres plus tardives. En effet, les toiles initiales s'inscrivent dans un espace modulé par l'architecture, alors qu'ensuite, l'espace définira l'architecture (fig. 51 et 56). Si l'image est fidèle au lieu, elle est transformée par la richesse tonale de l'huile sur la toile de lin et par les sensations que génère la réinvention de la couleur et de la lumière dans l'atelier de Montréal. Ainsi, *Habsburg Garden* (fig. 43), peinte en 1997, regorge de bleus et de verts somptueux qu'on ne retrouve pas dans les aquarelles réalisées sur place. Dans

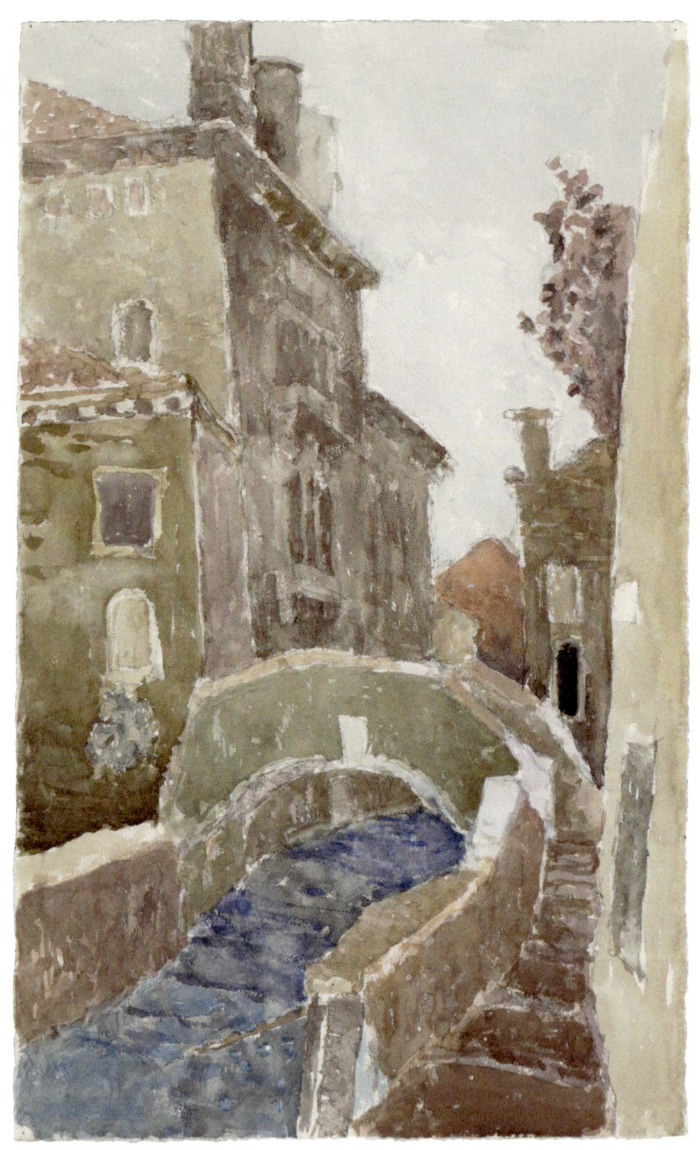

47. *Ponte delle Tette, Rio San Cassiano I*, 1998

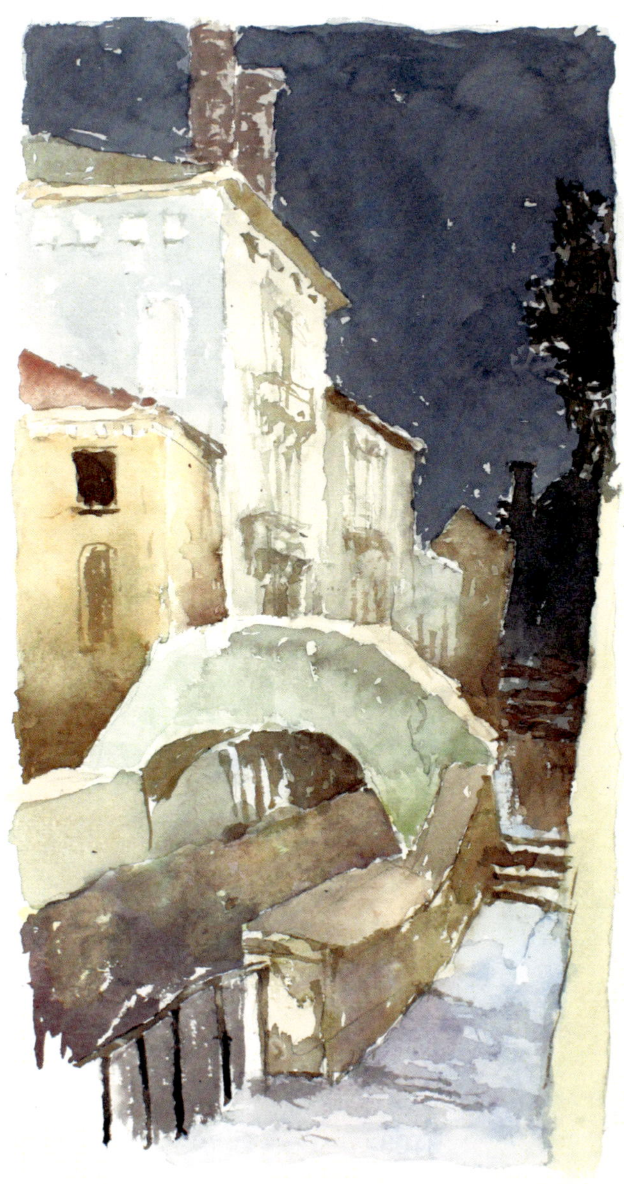

48. *Ponte delle Tette, Rio San Cassiano II*, 1998

son propre atelier, loin de Venise, John se sentait libre de se concentrer sur des manières de peindre plutôt que sur des manières de voir. Les toiles du deuxième groupe sont certes inspirées par la cité lagunaire, mais le rendu est issu de l'imagination de John (fig. 68). On en trouve des références dans ses croquis et ses aquarelles, mais elles sont nées de ses souvenirs et de son inventivité. Plus difficile à définir, le troisième groupe, enfin, est formé d'acryliques et d'huiles sur toile non figuratives, fruits de vues et de sensations proposées par Venise. C'est le cas, par exemple, de *Inch by Ounce* (fig. 23), peinte en 1979, qui se trouve au Musée des beaux-arts Beaverbrook. Le tableau évoque les bâtiments de pierre décrépits qui abondent dans la lagune. Les lignes et les formes suggèrent à la fois des vestiges d'architecture ancienne et des graffitis contemporains qui composent une sorte de carte de la ville flottante (fig. 24). Ses œuvres abstraites ont également été pour lui un moyen de réinventer la ville après son retour à la figuration.

L'intérêt de John pour l'estampe est né pendant ses études à l'école londonienne de Slade. Des décennies plus tard, alors qu'il se trouve à Montréal et retourne à la figuration, il tirera quelques gravures et monotypes de dessins exécutés à Venise. En 2007, pour ne pas perdre la main, il s'inscrit aux cours hebdomadaires de la Bottega del Tintoretto, sur le canal Sensa, qui borde la maison du Tintoret, près de notre appartement. L'école grand public ne pouvant pas offrir de matériaux de grande qualité, John n'y produit aucune gravure digne d'être exposée. Il y travaillera tout de même avec un maître graveur

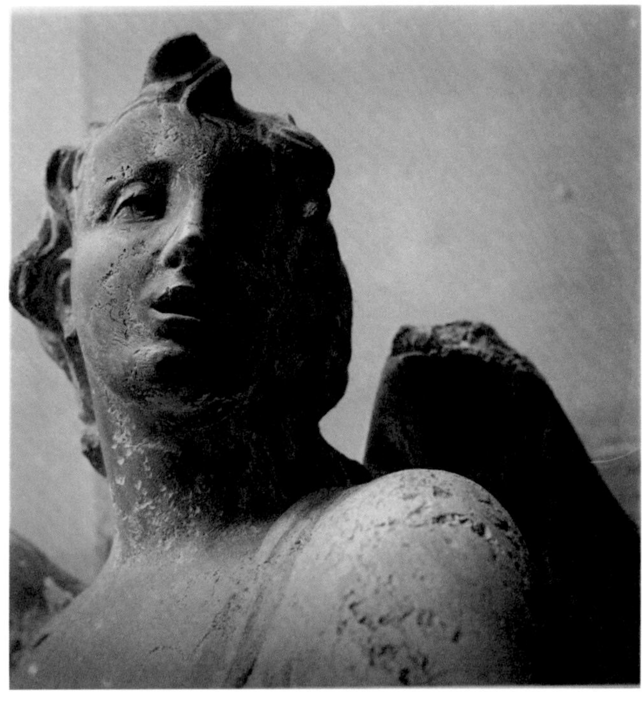

49. *Angel, Church of the Fava, Venice,* undated | sans date

(opposite | ci-contre)
50. *Hotel La Residenza, Campo Bragora, Venice*, c. 1982 | vers 1982

venu de France et pourra expérimenter divers papiers, encres et techniques d'essuyage, et différentes manières de régler une presse à gravure. Les pauses d'après-midi, propices aux conversations légères avec étudiants et professeurs, agrémentées par des vins et des pâtisseries de la région, lui fourniront également l'occasion d'exercer son excellent italien.

C'est aussi armé d'un Leica M3 et d'un *box* Minolta que John a sillonné Venise pendant la plupart de nos séjours, pour le simple plaisir de photographier la ville. Les sujets étaient généralement d'ordre architectural, sans lien avec ses dessins ou ses peintures. De retour à Montréal, longtemps après avoir pris les photographies, il développait la pellicule, toujours en noir et blanc, dans une chambre noire improvisée (fig. 49). Il n'a jamais montré ses images, sauf en 1982, à l'occasion d'une exposition avec d'autres peintres photographes. Son cliché de l'hôtel La Residenza, sur le *campo* Bragora, à l'est de la Piazza San Marco, sera reproduit dans quelques journaux montréalais et lui vaudra des critiques favorables (fig. 50).

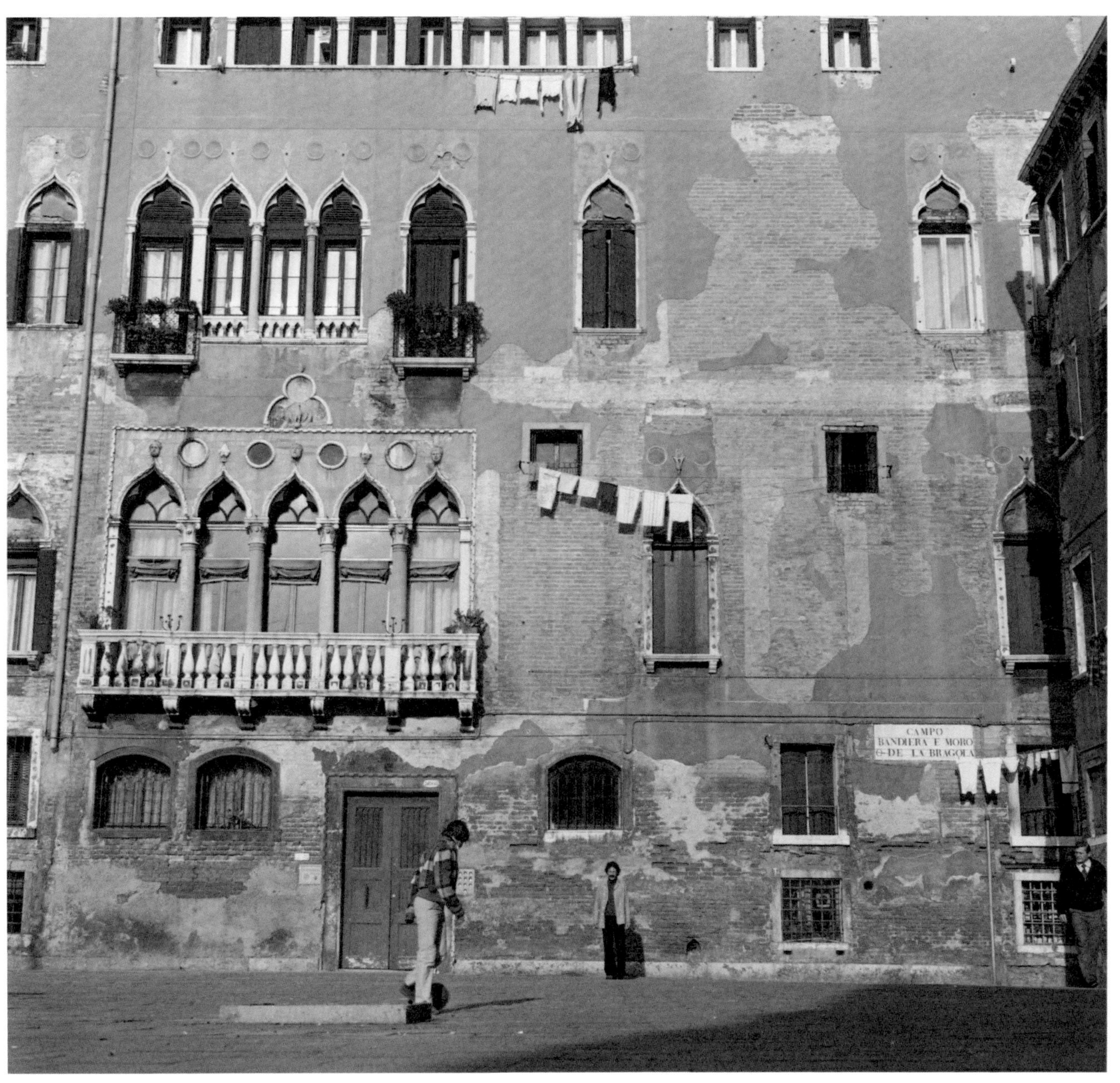
CAMPO
BANDIERA E MORO
O-DE LA BRAGOLA

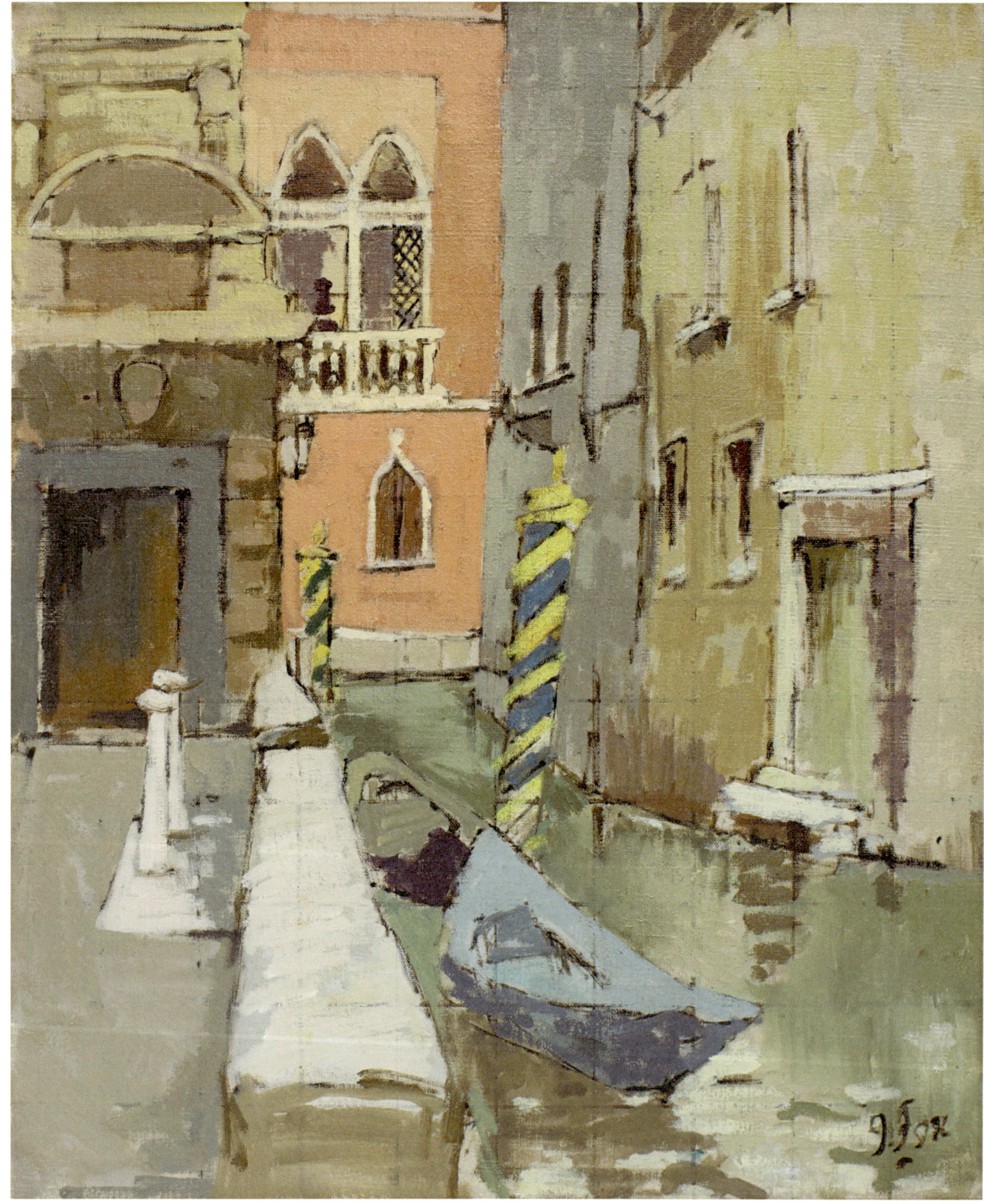

Des manières de voir Venise

Venise est une ville de contradictions : des siècles de styles architecturaux se disputent un même espace, l'eau débouche en clapotant dans des canaux de transport, des canaux et des trottoirs sans direction apparente dessinent secrètement son histoire 17 fois centenaire. Venise est aussi un objet, modelé par une lumière directe et reflétée, des couleurs vives ou douces, des formes géométriques et organiques, des espaces ouverts ou clos. Comme l'écrivit James McNeill Whistler à sa mère, un jour de printemps : « Cette ville fabuleuse [a été] créée [...] exprès pour les peintres[5]. »

Le *sestiere* de Cannaregio aura toujours conservé tout son attrait pour John, avec ses canaux qui bordent des voies résidentielles et des jardins confidentiels qui déversent leur feuillage par-dessus de hauts murs. Il dessinait aussi volontiers les rues modestes du Castello, ainsi que des *sestieri* Santa Croce et de San Polo, même si nous n'y habitions plus. C'est en partie la recherche sur les bâtiments des confréries que je devais faire pour mon cours sur le patronage artistique à Venise pendant la Renaissance qui a orienté nos promenades loin de San Marco. Ces excursions qui passaient habituellement par de nombreuses églises, plus riches en peintures et en sculptures que les musées, nous ont permis de voir la ville sous un angle très différent. Cima, Titien, le Tintoret, Véronèse, Lotto, Tiepolo et Piazzetta ne sont que quelques-uns des peintres vénitiens qui avaient la faveur de John. Il aimait tout autant les sculptures des Lombardi, Sansovino, Rizzi ainsi que les œuvres d'artistes inconnus — sculptures et bas-reliefs — qui ornent l'intérieur et l'extérieur des édifices de Venise. Cette admiration était nourrie par de fréquentes relectures de l'ouvrage classique d'Adrian Stokes intitulé *Venice: An Aspect of Art* (publié en français par les éditions Le Promeneur, en 1997, dans une traduction de Marie-France Du Roy-Lévi, sous le titre *Venise*).

Dès ses premiers séjours dans la Sérénissime, John a dessiné et aquarellé ce que j'appellerais des vues de canaux. Il a d'abord été fasciné par les grandes voies d'eau, comme le montrent deux œuvres sur panneau de bois et une toile représentant le Grand Canal depuis le pont de l'Accademia, vers Piazza San Marco (fig. 75). Une autre vue, depuis sa chambre à la pension La Calcina (1964), reproduite sur un panneau de bois et quelques toiles, représente le quai des Zattere, le Canal de la Giudecca et l'église du Redentore (fig. 35). Bientôt, les quelque 175 canaux intérieurs allaient attiser davantage sa curiosité. Il était particulièrement impressionné par le fait que chaque *rio* semble déterminer

51. *Canal and Boats [Rio della Verona]*, 1957

l'architecture environnante et que l'eau module la couleur des édifices en reflétant la lumière du ciel sur les façades. Certaines vues sont cernées d'édifices. C'est le cas notamment d'une huile de 1957 représentant le *rio* della Verona (fig. 51) ainsi que de la toile figurant le *rio* Sant' Angelo (fig. 20) exposée au Musée des beaux-arts Beaverbrook et réalisée après son séjour de 1963. Dans une aquarelle de 2007 intitulée *Rio San Daniele* (fig. 60), la géométrie réaliste laisse place aux rondeurs, bien que les formes inclinées nous renvoient aux bateaux du tableau du Beaverbrook. Un dessin et une aquarelle appelés *Rio Madonna dell' Orto* (fig. 28 et 52), exécutés la même année et représentant un canal des alentours de notre appartement, montrent une rare embarcation de travail appelée *sandolo*. Les deux aquarelles sont enveloppées de la chaleur sensuelle et de l'air limpide des premiers jours d'été qui ont donné tant de cachet à notre séjour sur le canal Misericordia.

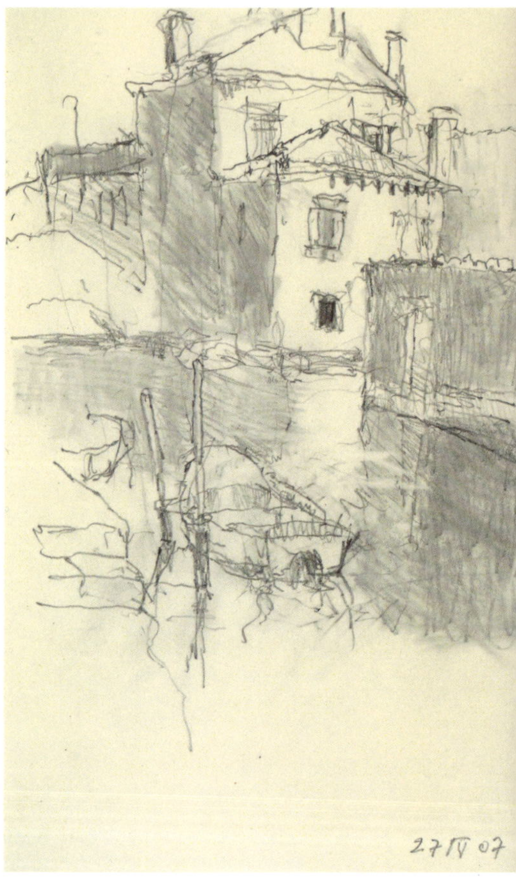

52. *Rio Madonna dell' Orto*, 27 April 2007 | 27 avril 2007

Venise a entre autres odonymes particuliers la *fondamenta*, soit une voie qui longe un canal (*rio*), souvent d'un seul côté. John a fait de nombreux dessins des *fondamente* près de notre appartement. On y voit le canal et les murs de brique ou de pierre des bâtiments, les portes qui donnent sur les voies navigables, plus quelques arbres ou un jardin sur l'autre rive. Dans *Rio Sant' Alvise* (fig. 57), peinte en 1998, les pavés nous situent dans un des lieux favoris de John. Le canal et l'architecture présentent l'angularité caractéristique de son travail. Dans *Rio Madonna dell' Orto* (même année, fig. 6 et 7), l'absence des pavés rend le tableau plus intime. La même sensation se dégage de l'aquarelle rehaussée de rouge conté (fig. 59), où figurent un jardin et le restaurant favori de John, sur une rue étroite le long du *rio* della Sensa. Déjà, le motif de l'eau et des murs se voyait dans un dessin et l'aquarelle de grandes dimensions qui représentent un quai de Burano, sur le rivage de l'île opposé à Venise (fig. 21). Comme Burano n'avait pas beaucoup de distractions à offrir au cours des deux mois que nous y avons passés, John a beaucoup, beaucoup dessiné. Le décor décrépit de ce dessin contraste fortement avec les rues pittoresques que l'on associe généralement à Burano. Lui fait écho, à Venise, ce *Canal Grande* de 1993 (fig. 53), avec vue sur le *palazzo* Balbi, dont la placidité, fort bien exprimée par le pinceau de John, tranche sur l'atmosphère générale de la ville.

John a aussi dessiné des bâtiments depuis le côté opposé du canal, sans toutefois représenter l'eau ni indiquer autrement la distance qui le séparait du sujet. C'est ce qui explique les tonalités différentes du *rio* Trapolin, ou l'on voit le mur d'enceinte, le jardin et le clocher de l'église Santa Fosca (fig. 78). Ses nombreux dessins du lieu (fig. 11) marquaient les promenades qui nous y menaient régulièrement et qui comportaient également une pause dans l'unique *caffè* du canal. Les deux boutiques situées près de l'église, sur le *rio terra* della Maddalena (fig. 30), sont un sujet très rare dans l'œuvre de John. Il n'aimait pas cette large rue et faisait volontiers de longs détours pour éviter la foule qui s'y pressait. Aucun indice ne permet d'identifier le lieu, et seule la tache sombre au pied des marches signale les méandres inhabituels d'un canal. Le point de vue signifie que l'artiste se trouvait sur le *campo* où se dresse l'église de la Maddalena, sur l'autre rive du canal. La forte compression de l'espace est habilement camouflée.

Mais revenons à l'aquarelle du *rio* Madonna dell' Orto de 2004 (fig. 4 et 29), à cette fenêtre vétuste (maintenant rénovée) et à ce *sottoportego* (passage couvert), humbles sujets auxquels John a redonné leurs lettres de noblesse grâce à la palette opulente et à la lumière joyeuse que lui inspirait la *venezianità*. Parmi ses dernières aquarelles (fig. 41 et 58) figurent deux images aux tonalités différentes du *rio* Ca' Moro, à l'extrémité ouest du canal sur lequel donnait notre appartement de Cannaregio. Cette double représentation d'une même vue, à laquelle s'ajoute une œuvre sur papier, n'est pas sans rappeler les natures mortes aux bouteilles et aux bols de l'artiste italien Giorgio Morandi, et montre bien à quel point la répétition révèle la manière d'un peintre. Certes, la lumière et les couleurs différentes confèrent une nette autonomie à chacune de ces aquarelles, mais toutes deux sont à la fois figuratives et abstraites, bien que John n'ait fait aucune distinction entre ces deux approches.

53. *Canal Grande*, 1993

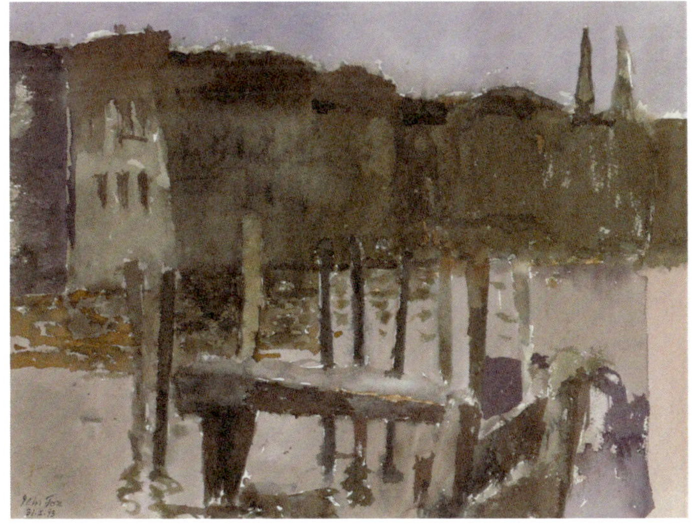

Dès son premier périple vénitien, John a aussi été séduit par les squares ou *campi* qui sont disséminés dans toute la ville, sont bordés d'une église, de maisons, de cafés et de commerces, et font à la fois office de larges parvis et d'espaces sociaux. Témoin ce marché de l'aquarelle intitulée *Campo Santa Margherita* (fig. 45), situé près de notre restaurant favori. Parmi les *campi* de toutes formes et de toutes tailles, John avait un faible pour ceux, plutôt rares, que quelques bancs et bouquets d'arbres transformaient en une oasis où il pouvait s'installer et dessiner en paix tout ce qu'il trouvait digne de son crayon. Nous sommes rapidement devenus des habitués du *campo* San Giacomo dell' Orio (fig. 3), relativement proche du marché du Rialto, peu fréquenté par les touristes, mais grouillant de Vénitiens de tous âges. Après notre installation dans Cannaregio, sur l'autre rive du Grand Canal, John a consacré beaucoup de temps, seul ou avec moi, à dessiner le *campo* dei Gesuiti, qui ouvre sur la lagune du nord (figs. 8 et 9). Les quelques arbres qui croissent à l'extrémité la plus étroite du *campo*, au sud, et les bancs peints en rouge forment un contraste saisissant avec les *palazzi* que l'on voit sur d'autres aquarelles et qui se dressent de l'autre côté d'un canal invisible (fig. 79). Les détails qui distinguent entre eux les tableaux des Gesuiti tiennent notamment à l'endroit où John s'installait et à la lumière particulière du cœur de l'hiver ou des débuts de l'été, qui déterminent leurs coloris et leur caractère.

John a beaucoup peint le canal Sant' Alvise. Il adorait le *campo* adjacent pour son caractère typiquement vénitien. Ce sont même la paix et le bien-être qui s'en dégagent qui sont le réel sujet d'une aquarelle et d'un dessin réalisés vers la fin de sa vie. On aperçoit un coin de l'église de Sant' Alvise, le couvent qui se dressait devant son banc préféré et une haute maison sur l'autre rive (fig. 72 et 73). À noter également ses dessins et une aquarelle d'une grande douceur du Ghetto Nuovo (fig. 44 et 46), près duquel se trouvait notre logement dans Cannaregio. Le plaisir de la vie à Venise tenait pour beaucoup à la joie d'emprunter des chemins peu fréquentés par les touristes. C'est d'ailleurs en traversant le *campo* Santa Ternità, dans l'est de Castello, que John a découvert l'entrée et le jardin du *palazzo* Soranzo.

Une toile de 2003 (fig. 62) et plusieurs aquarelles (fig. 61) et dessins réalisés en deux années consécutives révèlent l'attrait irrésistible qu'ont exercé sur John les formes et les surfaces des bâtiments si différents des autres autour de ce square pourtant si ordinaire. Une autre toile de la même année, intitulée *Campiello della Madonna* (fig. 63) et représentant un petit square situé à mi-chemin entre notre appartement et le Rialto, est l'aboutissement de nombreux croquis (fig. 1) ainsi que d'aquarelles peintes dans les mêmes tons rouges. Dans chaque cas, John a inversé l'échelle relative des bâtiments et des alentours pour en faire des lieux intimes, comme pour se les approprier.

Venise compte 400 ponts, et depuis presque chaque square, au moins deux franchissent un canal adjacent. Pourtant, les aquarelles et les dessins du *campo* dei Gesuiti, l'un de ses sujets favoris, font tout juste allusion aux marches du principal pont qui y mène. L'ouvrage devient en revanche le sujet indéniable d'une aquarelle de 2002 (fig. 40), exécutée depuis l'extrémité du square opposée à celle où John travaillait habituellement. Il se tenait en effet près d'un mur de l'ancien monastère des Gesuiti. L'aquarelle est très fidèle au dessin antérieur. Comme d'habitude, les différences tiennent au matériel : crayon et peinture. Un autre pont, plus petit, occupe le centre d'une aquarelle de 2004. C'est celui qui jouxte la *fondamenta* Moro (fig. 69) et mène au couvent des Servi depuis le *campo* San Marziale, lui aussi près de notre appartement. (De fait, rien n'est jamais très loin, à Venise !) Les angles donnés au pont, aux murs et à la porte correspondent à la vue que John en avait en s'adossant au mur de la *fondamenta* – qu'on ne voit donc pas sur le tableau. Avant d'habiter dans le Ghetto Nuovissimo, nous avons logé à quelques reprises sur le *campiello* Albrizzi, près du marché du Rialto. À l'hiver 1998-1999, John a peint deux aquarelles du *ponte* delle Tette (fig. 47 et 48), jadis rendu célèbre par les prostituées qui y battaient le pavé, derrière le *palazzo* Albrizzi. Ces deux aquarelles sont issues notamment d'un dessin (fig. 31) dont le cadre crayonné suggère que John avait immédiatement vu la possibilité d'en tirer un tableau. La répétition du sujet souligne à quel point les changements d'échelle, la couleur et la lumière produisent des images très différentes, comme Giorgio Morandi l'a amplement prouvé.

John a bien peu dessiné l'extérieur des quelque 140 églises de Venise, mais il en franchissait régulièrement les portes pour dessiner. Au plaisir d'y découvrir des merveilles artistiques et architecturales s'ajoutaient la chaleur que les épais murs de pierre y maintenaient en hiver, comme la fraîcheur en été, mais également la possibilité de déambuler dans l'édifice ou de s'y asseoir pour dessiner sans être dérangé ni même remarqué. Malgré son peu de goût pour les édifices très ornementés de la ville, John était étonnamment attiré par le plus fameux de tous : la basilique San Marco (fig. 70). Séduit par le mariage de la sculpture et de l'architecture qui semblent y projeter des arabesques de leur propre volonté, il a souvent dessiné dans différentes perspectives une vue du maître-autel depuis l'avant de l'allée proche du transept nord. Par ailleurs, une petite huile sur bois de 2004 (fig. 64 et 67) donne une idée des dimensions impressionnantes de l'église des Carmini, tandis qu'un dessin modeste, préalable à une toile inachevée, privilégie un autel latéral et l'escalier en colimaçon qui mène à la chaire (fig. 65). Les carnets de

John regorgent de ces dessins qui mettent en valeur l'architecture intérieure des églises et, souvent, leur décor sculptural. Des dessins de petits objets cultuels, comme cet encensoir et ce chandelier aperçus dans un coin de l'église des Gesuiti, sont aisément devenus, en 1993, des natures mortes dédiées à la forme et à l'espace (fig. 66).

Les nombreux croquis de nos intérieurs vénitiens successifs n'étaient en général qu'un passe-temps. Certains représentent le petit atelier loué au printemps 2004. Une huile sur bois transforme en abstraction géométrique quelques meubles et la porte au grillage en fer forgé ouverte sur le canal Cannaregio (fig. 22). Rappel des inondations fréquentes, l'humidité conférait un caractère nettement vénitien au local, mais était peu propice au travail artistique. John y passait donc son temps à lire les livres d'art et les catalogues d'exposition abandonnés par ses prédécesseurs. L'aquarelle du cloître de San Pietro di Castello, première basilique de Venise avant San Marco, est aussi, en quelque sorte, la représentation d'un intérieur. De fait, dans le dessin et l'aquarelle de 2007 (fig. 71), les vêtements mis à sécher aux fenêtres des appartements qui dominent l'arcade transforment le petit cloître ancien en un espace domestique.

Le nom des voies piétonnières de Venise indique à la fois leurs dimensions et leur emplacement. Les déambulations de John donnent la mesure de sa fascination pour les tenants et les aboutissants d'une *calle* (rue) ou d'un *ramo* (petite voie transversale). À quelques pas du *rio* della Sensa, par exemple, John est parvenu un jour au *ramo* dei Muti et à l'un des derniers *squeri* de la ville, ces chantiers où l'on construit les gondoles. Au fil des ans, il a beaucoup dessiné cette voie étroite, au crayon et à la sanguine, depuis le pont du *squero* ou un mur. Dans des œuvres de 2003 (fig. 5 et 56), l'architecture du *ramo* est réduite à des formes simples ou altérées, aux limites de l'abstraction. Présence inhabituelle dans ses tableaux vénitiens : une fillette, presque au centre, aussi discrète et attentive à ce qui l'entoure que l'était John. Les espaces piétonniers sont nombreux à fuir vers un *sottoportego*, ces passages anciens ménagés sous un édifice et coiffés d'un toit plat ou d'une arche, qui débouchent sur une rue, un *campo* ou, comme dans ces diverses représentations du *sottoportego* Mosto (fig. 2, 12 et 13), sur le Grand Canal, à la hauteur de l'église San Marcuola, près du Ghetto. La perspective, en diagonale, anime ce lieu modeste, tout comme l'angle de vue du peintre avait, quelques années plus tôt, transformé le banc, les édifices et le canal qui bordent l'église excentrée de San Nicolò dei Mendicoli par une géométrie dynamique et un peu déroutante (fig. 74). Ces axes inclinés reviendront dans la toile intitulée *Campo delle Gorne*, qui figure ce square très proche de l'Arsenal du XIIIe siècle, où Venise construisit longtemps ses navires de guerre (fig. 54).

À Montréal, John a exécuté des huiles sur toile de lin qui reconstruisent Venise presque uniquement à partir de ses souvenirs et de son imagination. *Worksite* (fig. 68), par exemple, est un hommage à ces ouvriers qui réparent et restaurent incessamment la ville à peine évoquée par le cadre blanc de la fenêtre, dans le coin supérieur droit. La dernière œuvre issue de l'atelier de John est *Palazzo da Silva* (fig. 76), une huile sur toile peinte en 2007 pour souligner notre 25e anniversaire de mariage. Le décor est à peu près celui du séjour de notre appartement du Ghetto Nuovissimo. Le mobilier et la fenêtre sont conformes à la réalité, mais le rouge sombre du mur est une allusion à la couleur si typique de l'art et de l'architecture de Venise. John s'y représente à la fois sous les traits du jeune homme qu'il était à son premier séjour dans la ville et sous ceux du vieillard qui s'y trouvait, sans le savoir, pour l'avant-dernière fois. Le regard direct qui nous unit est le reflet d'une vie extraordinairement enrichie par tout ce temps passé dans le paradis des villes, et illuminée par l'éclat infini de Venise.

NOTES

1. Les confréries de Venise, ou *scuole*, étaient des associations caritatives formées de laïcs, qui veillaient au bien-être social, matériel et religieux de leurs membres. Il pouvait s'agir de guildes, de regroupement de personnes qui ne résidaient pas à Venise ou d'organismes voués à divers rites ou saints catholiques. La plupart se réunissaient dans des salles modestes, mais certaines possédaient de grands immeubles décorés d'œuvres d'art. C'était le cas, notamment, des six *Scuole Grande*.
2. Les cendres de John sont inhumées au cimetière de San Michele, à Venise. Je retourne presque chaque année à Venise depuis 2008. J'ai consacré beaucoup de ces visites à la rédaction de mon livre intitulé *James Wilson Morrice: Paintings and Drawings of Venice*, publié à Stuttgart par arnoldsche Art Publishers à la fin de 2023.
3. L'expression est de John Ruskin, critique d'art britannique, qui a écrit dans son journal, le 6 mai 1841 : [traduction] « Dieu merci, je viens d'arriver ! C'est le paradis des villes. » Voir également l'article sur la peinture vénitienne plus tardive de John Fox dans le contexte de l'œuvre montréalais, dans Sandra Paikowsky et coll., *Refiguration*, Montréal, Centre des arts visuels, Galerie McClure, 2010.
4. Les œuvres non figuratives de John sont l'objet de l'ouvrage de Liz Wylie et coll., intitulé *John Fox. Abstractions*, Montréal, Battat Contemporary, 2012, et de Sandra Paikowsky, *John Fox Abstractions*, Bloomfield, Ontario, Oeno Gallery, 2015.
5. Lettre de James McNeill Whistler à Anna Matilda Whistler, mars ou mai 1880 [ici en traduction]. Charles Lang Freer Papers, Freer Gallery of Art and Arthur M. Sackler Gallery Archives, Smithsonian Institution, Washington, D.C.

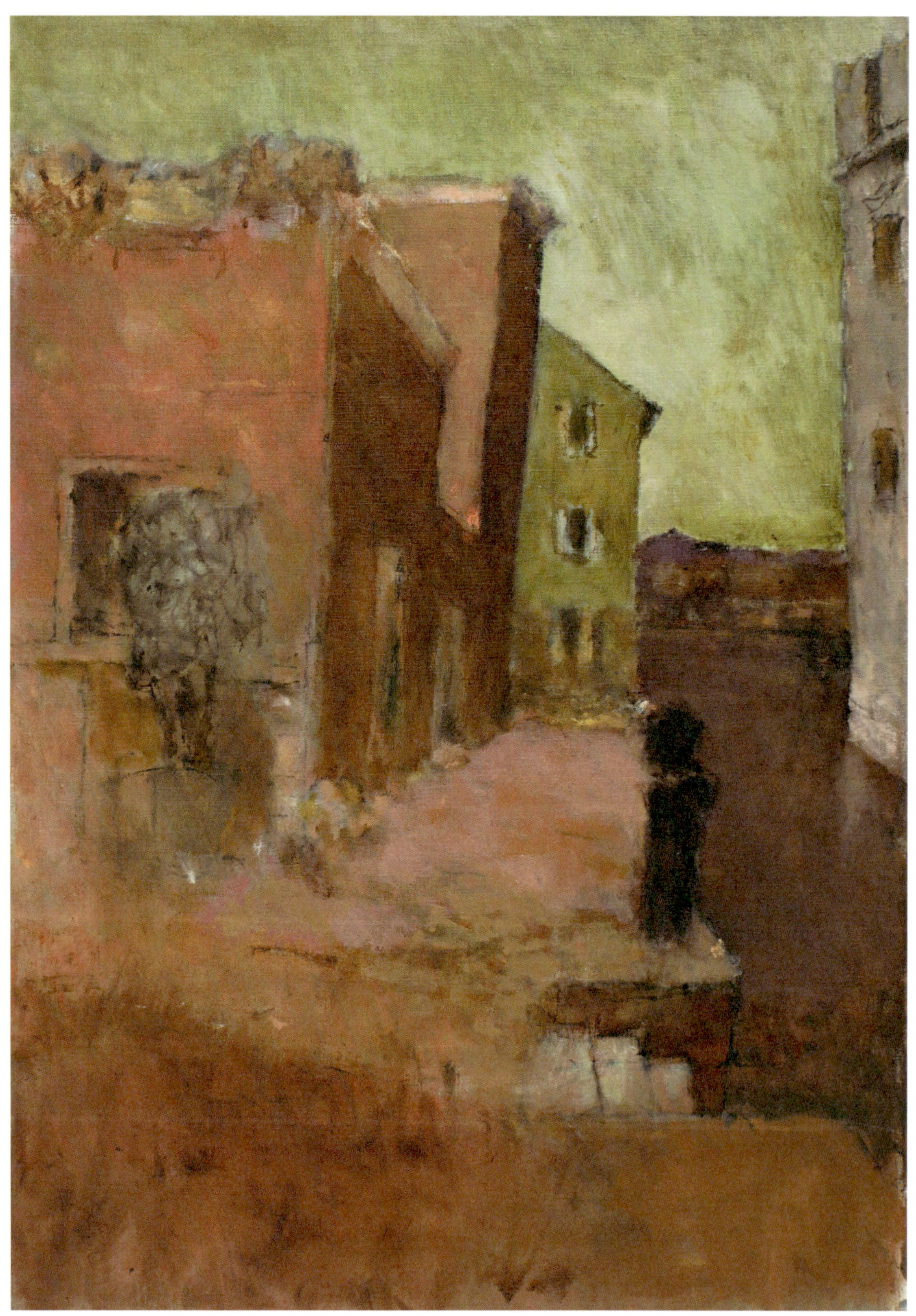

Colour/tone/touch
The Venice Works of John Fox

VICTORIA LEBLANC

There is no model. There is only colour. —Cézanne

To speak of colour in the Venice works of John Fox is to acknowledge the artworks' most consistent and enduring allure. The artist was a master of colour, of its sensuality, of the subtlest shifts in tonality that could anchor at the same time a work's structure, poetry, and meaning. It is through colour that John Fox captures his encounter with the seen world and translates it into the language of art.

Over a period of more than fifty years (1953–2008) the artist returned again and again to Venice. From the late 1970s on, he and his partner, art historian Sandra Paikowsky (fig. 55), spent between several weeks and two months annually in the city built on mudbanks, floating in the sea. The painter's aesthetic was formed by Venice, both the specific ambiance and physicality of the place, and the Venetian masters who revolutionized the very act of painting. Indeed, it is the works of Tiepolo, Tintoretto, and above all Titian that enamoured and trained John Fox's eye.

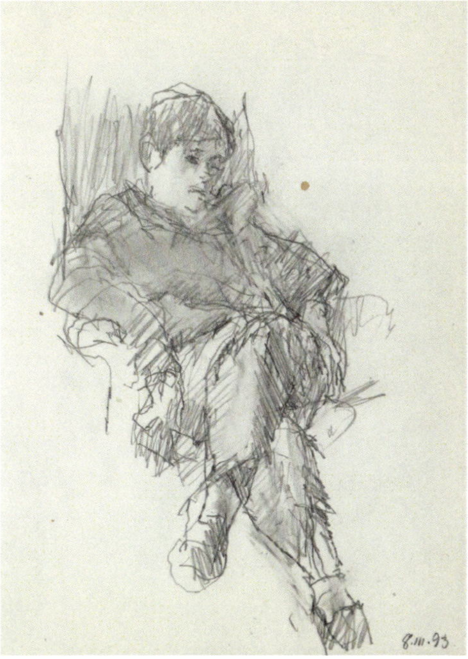

The Venetian influence can be seen in every aspect of his approach to colour. It is reflected in his use of colour rather than drawing to construct a painting's composition and to model form—a key tenet of sixteenth-century Venetian painting.

(opposite | ci-contre)
54. *Campo delle Gorne*, 2003

(right | à droite)
55. *Sandra in Venice*,
8 March 1993 | 8 mars 1993

It is reflected in Fox's subtle manipulation of tonality, of which Titian was the early master. Lastly, it is revealed in the way colour is laid down. Fox builds up the rhythm and texture of his surface through a layering and interweaving of daubs of colour—what the Venetians termed *macchie* or spots—an approach that captures the ever-shifting play of reflections on the city's canals and buildings. The technique had also marked Titian's late style, not only rendering the unique aura of the city but highlighting the artist's hand at work. Similarly, Fox's sensitive and quietly expressive brush marks make palpable his presence and establish the poetic tenor of each work.

The Palette

John Fox's palette was specific and minimal: burnt sienna, brown madder, rose quinacridone, indanthrene blue, yellow ochre. For oil, add raw umber, cobalt, titanium white. Perhaps black, though the artist preferred to mix his own; the same for tertiary hues. While he never ceased to experiment, adding others as needed, it is with this palette of colours that the artist found the intensity and subtlety to shape his vision.

The first three hues reflect the luminous colour of Venice itself, the iron oxide earth of the Veneto region, the baked terracotta bricks and stucco of the buildings, luminous pink in the light, deepening to rust or dark violet in shadow. That burnt sienna was Fox's favourite colour and red conté his favourite drawing tool is not surprising. Variations of the colour appear everywhere as a base note in these works, from the early canvas, *Rialto Fish Market* (fig. 19), to the panel *Interior of the Carmini Church* (fig. 67). Most obviously, the red conté watercolour sketches capture the colour in all its varied intensities, as seen in such works as *Interior, Gesuiti Church* (fig. 66) or *Palazzo Soranzo, Campo San Ternità* (fig. 61).

This earthen red hue is applied as both transparent wash and viscous surface. In the watercolour, *Campo San Giacomo dell' Orio* (fig. 3), a glowing amber ground vibrates through the entire painting, pushing forward from behind to meet the umbers and complementary grey-blue-greens of figure and tree. The picture plane is drenched in this ambient tonality, lending both dynamism and stability to the composition. Here, as in many of the painter's works, colour is transformed into light. The mood of specific hours of day or evening is made tangible through the subtle play of tones.

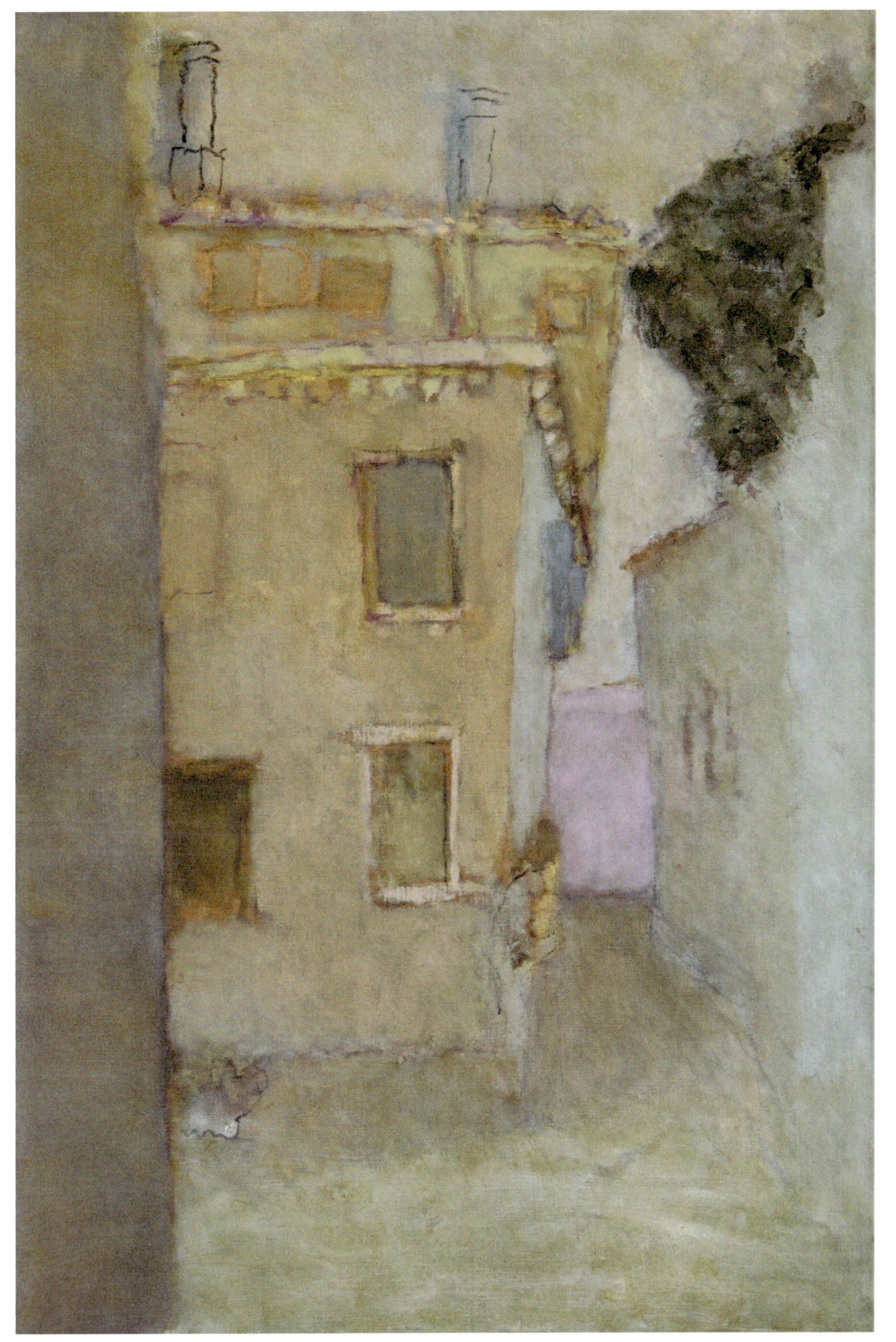

56. *Ramo dei Muti*, 2003

The most viscous and saturated example of Fox's embrace of this native Venetian colour is *Inch by Ounce* (fig. 23). From a series of acrylic abstracts painted in the late 1970s, it is this canvas which most forcefully captures the ubiquitous rose light reflected off old brick and stone facades. The shifting tonalities of pink to rust, woven one atop another, glide across the surface from edge to edge, enveloping the viewer in their layered intricacies. One confronts the canvas as one would an aged Venetian wall (figs. 54, 63).

Place: Line to Colour

The artist drew voraciously in Venice. He knew the city intimately. Sketchbook in hand, he'd set out each morning, strolling through the lesser-known *sestieri* or boroughs—Cannaregio in the northwest or Castello to the east. Unlike most visiting artists, Fox was not in search of famous sites or grand narratives. It was the intimate nondescript spaces that drew his eye, anonymous niches where light, brick, stucco, sky and water met at unpredictable angles (fig. 79). The drawings reveal the artist feeling his way into a place, recording in graceful searching lines the rhythms and sensations of his encounter. One can feel the varied pressure of the hand on the paper, a linear equivalent to the sense of touch he achieves with the brush (figs. 14, 54).

Fox drew on site. To paint, however, with rare exceptions, he preferred the privacy of indoor spaces. His drawings served as *aides-mémoires* as he moved from line into colour. He painted in the afternoon, in later years in the narrow kitchen of their ground-floor Cannaregio apartment, the paper laid flat on the counter, light streaming in from the window over his right shoulder.

Watercolour was his favourite medium. He loved its immediacy, its facility for subtle tonal transitions, its sense of accident and discovery. Fox was intimately attuned to the varied effects of painting on dry, damp, or wet ground; each offered a different mood or pictorial effect. He worked mostly on a dry surface, the white of the paper peeking through the brush marks much like an imprimatura or underpainting, unifying and enlivening the composition (figs. 7, 70). The drier paper surface also encouraged less dilution of colour. So while Fox employed a muted palette, the tonalities maintain their integrity. To this end, Fox also used gum arabic as one would a medium in oil, adding a sense of viscosity to the watercolour as well as extending the drying time. A brush mark could be removed or left as a trace, adding a sense of depth and layeredness to the work.

The earliest Venice watercolours in this exhibition are from the 1990s. Though the planar shapes of walls and building facades endow the works with a certain architectural structure, Fox's colour handling negates any sense of rigid geometry; the tonal harmonies are what ultimately unite the composition. See for instance *At San Nicolò dei Mendicoli Church* (fig. 74) or the minimal *Venice Houses* (fig. 39), whose pale pink building facades vibrate with luminosity while the blue-green surround anchors the light.

In each of these paintings, it is secondary and tertiary tonalities that dominate, either in complementary or analogous hues. Fox carefully calibrates his placement of stronger colour or darker value to balance the composition and lead the eye. In *Ponte delle Tette, Rio San Cassiano I* (fig. 47), the most saturated note of burnt sienna and the black rectangle of window are positioned midway up the vertical incline as if both the canal and adjacent stairs are intended to drop us off precisely here. In a second painting of the canal and bridge, *Ponte delle Tette, Rio San Cassiano II* (fig. 48), the black rectangle of window on the left dialogues with the tree branches pushing into the picture plane from the far right.

57. *Rio Sant' Alvise*, 1998

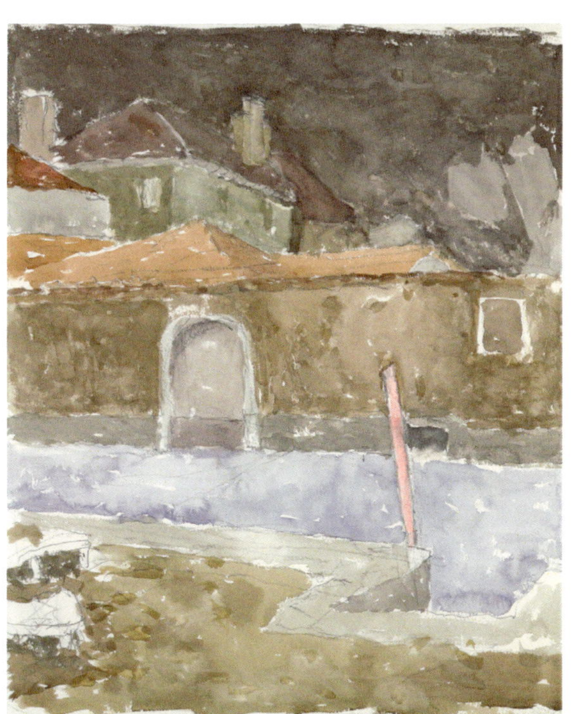

Fox returned repeatedly to certain sites. These compositions often vary only slightly; it is the palette that shifts, as in the two images mentioned above, or, just as frequently, the orchestration of light and dark. We see this for instance in two renderings of Rio Sant' Alvise. While the compositions are almost identical, the subtle shifts in the placement of value change the work's mood. In one version, *Rio Sant' Alvise,* 1998 (fig. 57), the dark tones of the sky and the daub of brilliant pink on the right push forward towards the viewer, augmenting a sense of felt intimacy as well as dynamism. In another version, a grey sky retreats into the distance as the muted tones of the wall balance with other planar elements to create a sense of overall equilibrium and quietude.

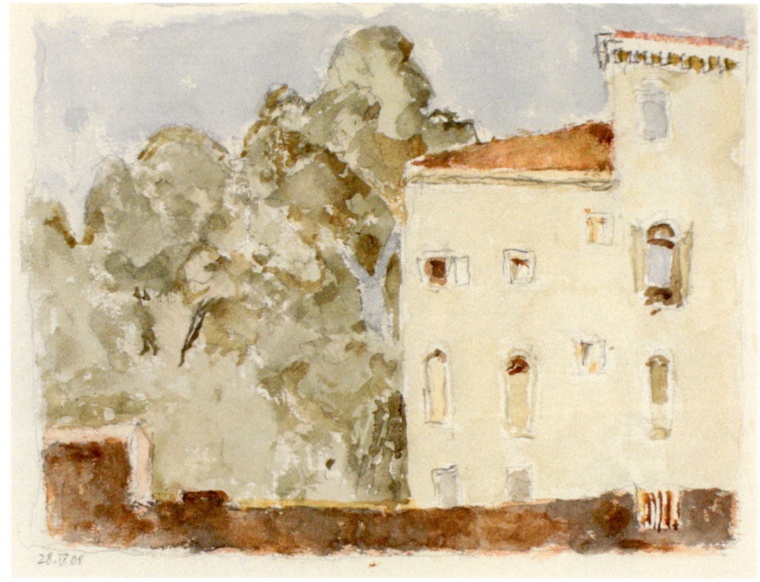

58. *Rio Ca' Moro at San Girolamo I*, 2008

A similar contrast in mood is realized in two versions of *Rio Ca' Moro at San Girolamo* (figs. 41, 58). The composition is repeated: the planar shape of the building contrasts with the loose brush marks of the foliage on the left. Tonal daubs of colour from the foreground wall within each painting respectively anchor roof and windows. However, the differences in colour and value—from an opaque lavender pink to a light sienna on the building façade, or from a brooding to an airy sky—endow each work with its singular poetry. The changes create a different sense of place and our relationship to it.

The Venice watercolours demonstrate Fox's ability to work within the subtlest, most understated tonalities yet still successfully anchor an intensity of both light and shadow. In the 1993 *Canal Grande* (fig. 53), the brush marks on the building façades transition into each other using barely discernable tonal adjustments. In complementary hues, the sombre violet tones of sky and water glide effortlessly into the nuanced umbers. And, despite the muted nature of the raw umber on the façade facing us on the left, it nonetheless establishes, through manipulation of contrasts, a sense of glowing evening light and the distance across the canal. The viewer stands on the edge of the dock, looking.

Fox's mastery of tonality is most tenderly realized in *Rio San Daniele* (fig. 60). The work brings together the intimacy of place with an intimacy of feeling. While it holds true to reality, the rectangular structures are secondary to the layered surface and play of tonalities. The somewhat curved and hesitant angles, as well as the delicate daubs and transitions of colour from slightly more mauve to more ochre, suggest the soft crevices of the human body as much as they do concrete structures. One feels the immediacy and care with which the calibrated tones are laid down.

A similar feeling of intimacy and immediacy is caught in *Sottoportego Mosto* (fig. 13) or *Campiello San Francesco della Vigna* (fig. 15). Moreover, in all three of these watercolours, the pencil lines offer a quiet accompaniment to the brush marks, dialoguing with the subtle tones through which they wander. Drawn lines appear often in Fox's watercolours, less to define shape than to add to the felt experience of place and a sense of the artist's search for its rhythms. The looseness and movement of the pencil lines also contribute to the open, unfinished quality of these works.

In several of the Venice watercolours, the images hover, surrounded on two or more sides by the empty white space of the paper (fig. 70). The emptiness invites the viewer in and also reinforces a sense of the unfinished. The brush marks fray unevenly at the edge of the image, emphasizing the sense of a caught moment, a transient encounter. While this sense of the momentary exists in many of Fox's watercolours, this is particularly true of images that sit off-side, clinging to a paper edge or afloat in the white surround (fig. 66). Along with their quiet play of Venetian reds and siennas and the sense of human touch, they sit on the paper like visual haiku to which one can return again and again to plumb both their meaning and allure.

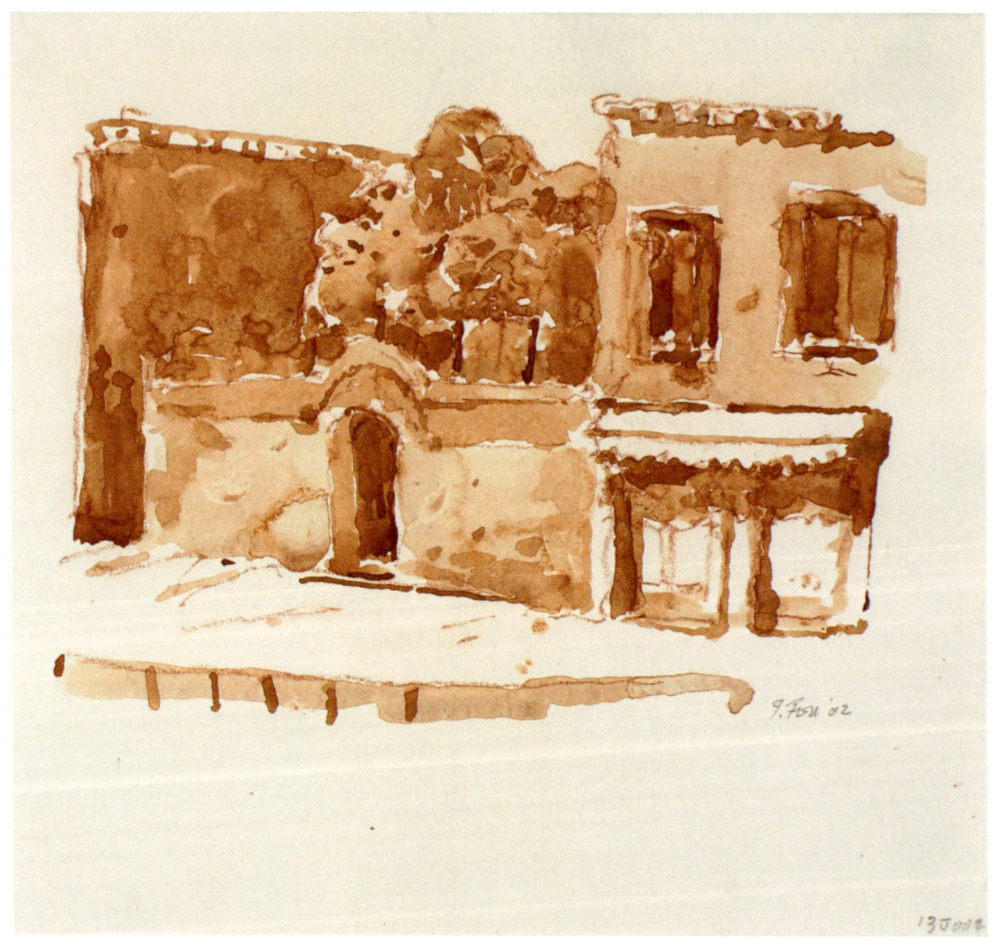

59. *Fondamenta della Sensa*,
2002

(opposite | ci-contre)
60. *Rio San Daniele*,
2007

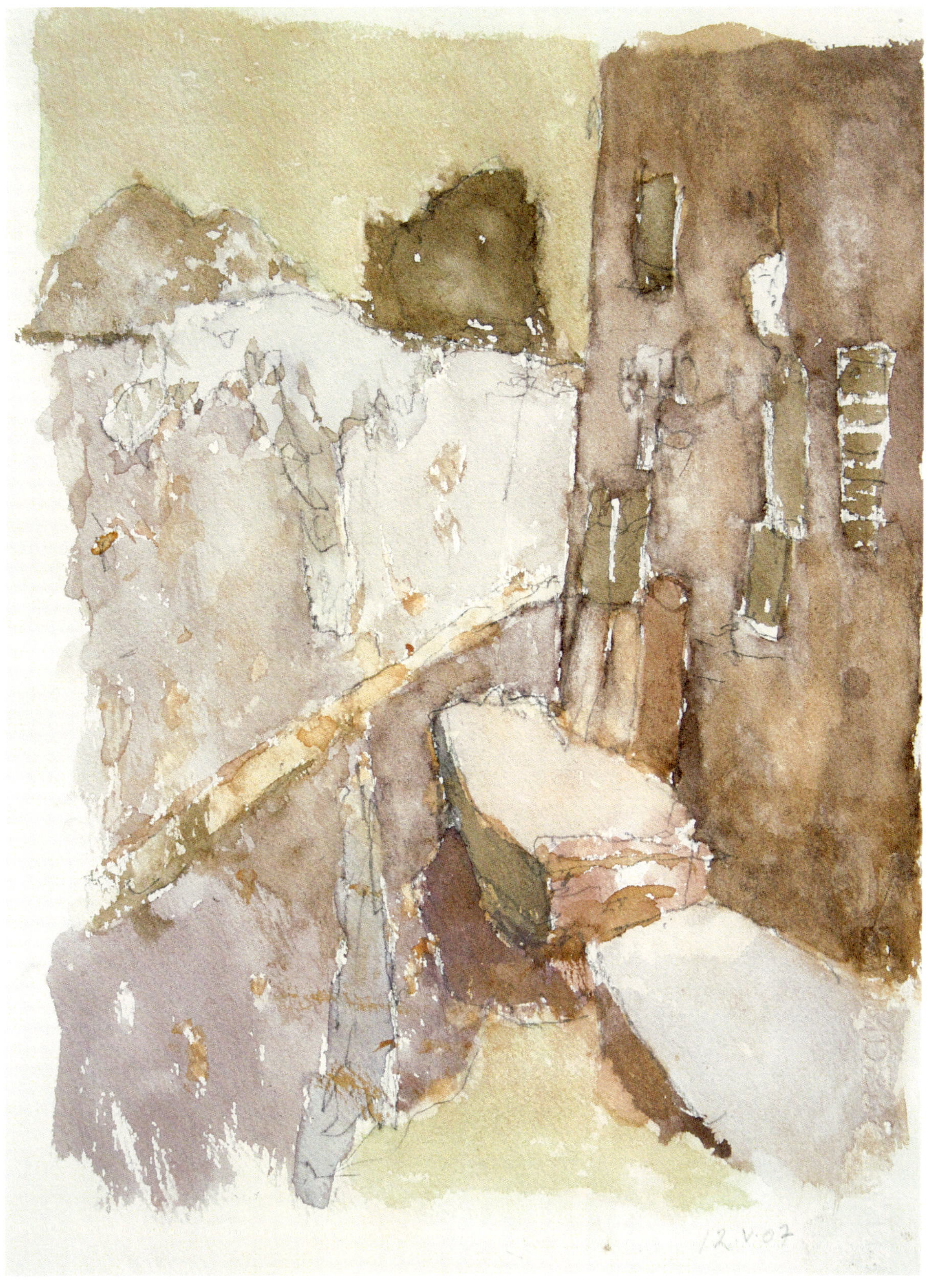
12.V.07

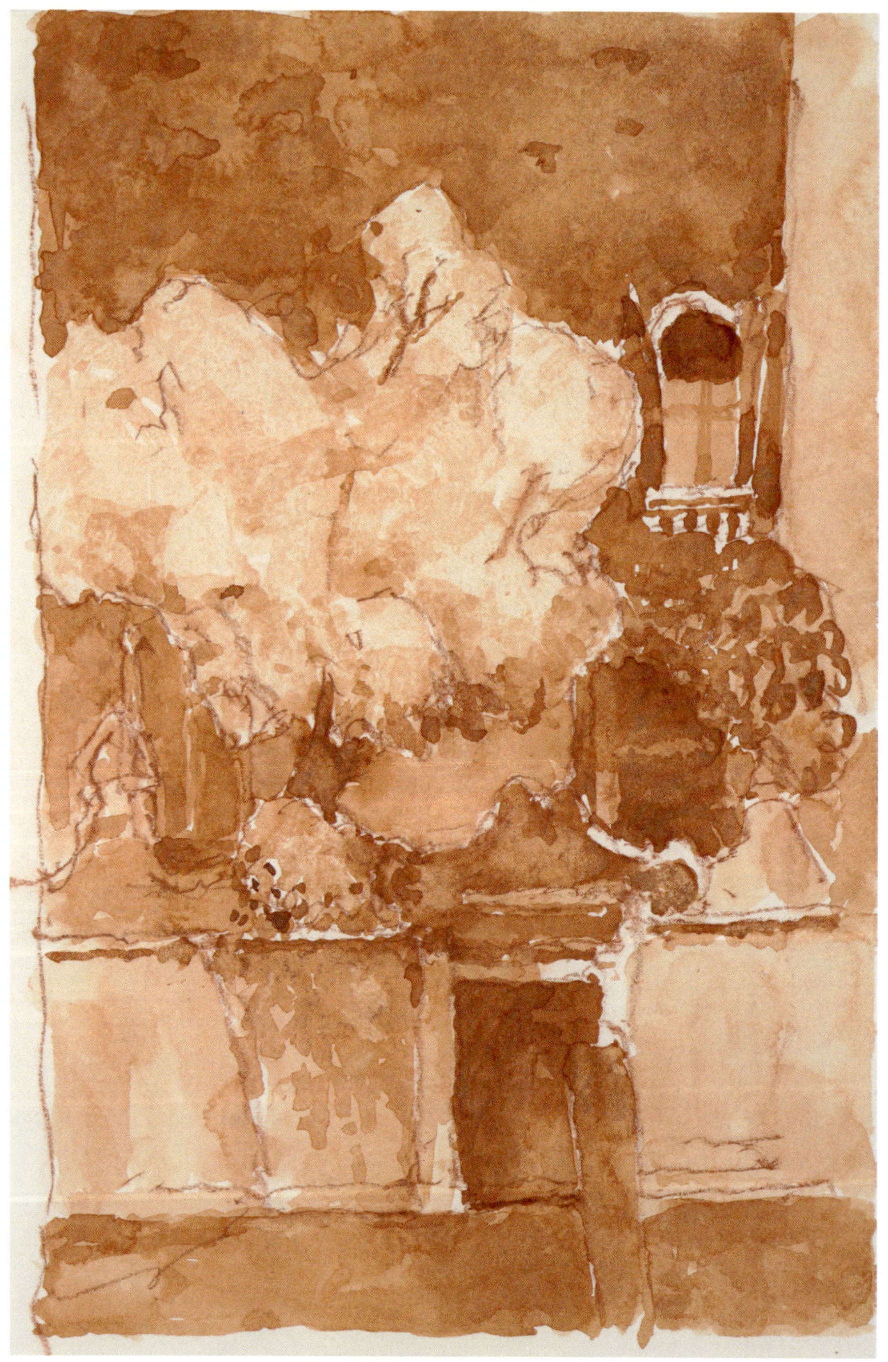

61. *Palazzo Soranzo, Campo Santa Ternità*, 2002

(opposite | ci-contre)
62. *Palazzo Soranzo, Campo Santa Ternità*, 2003

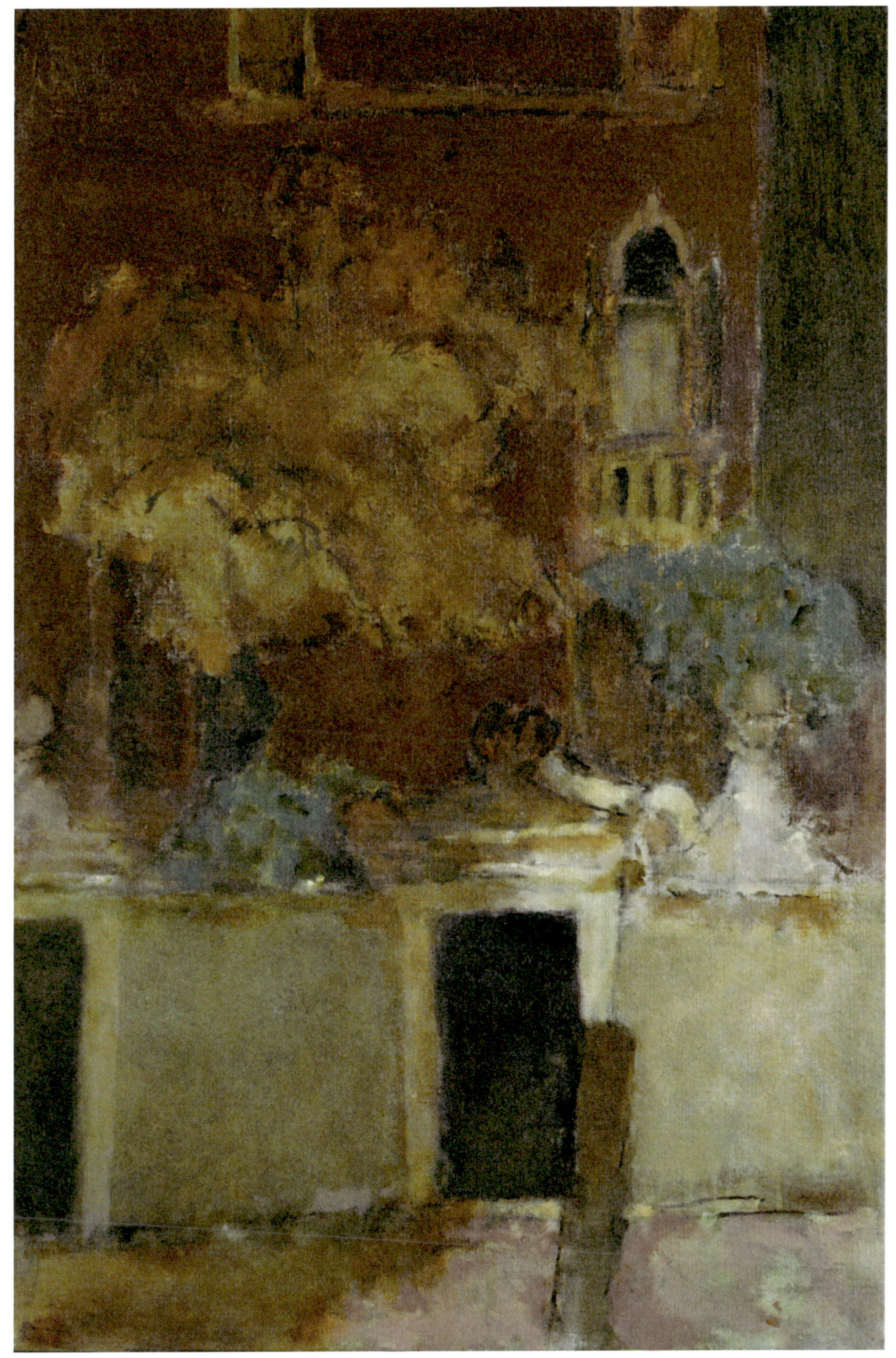

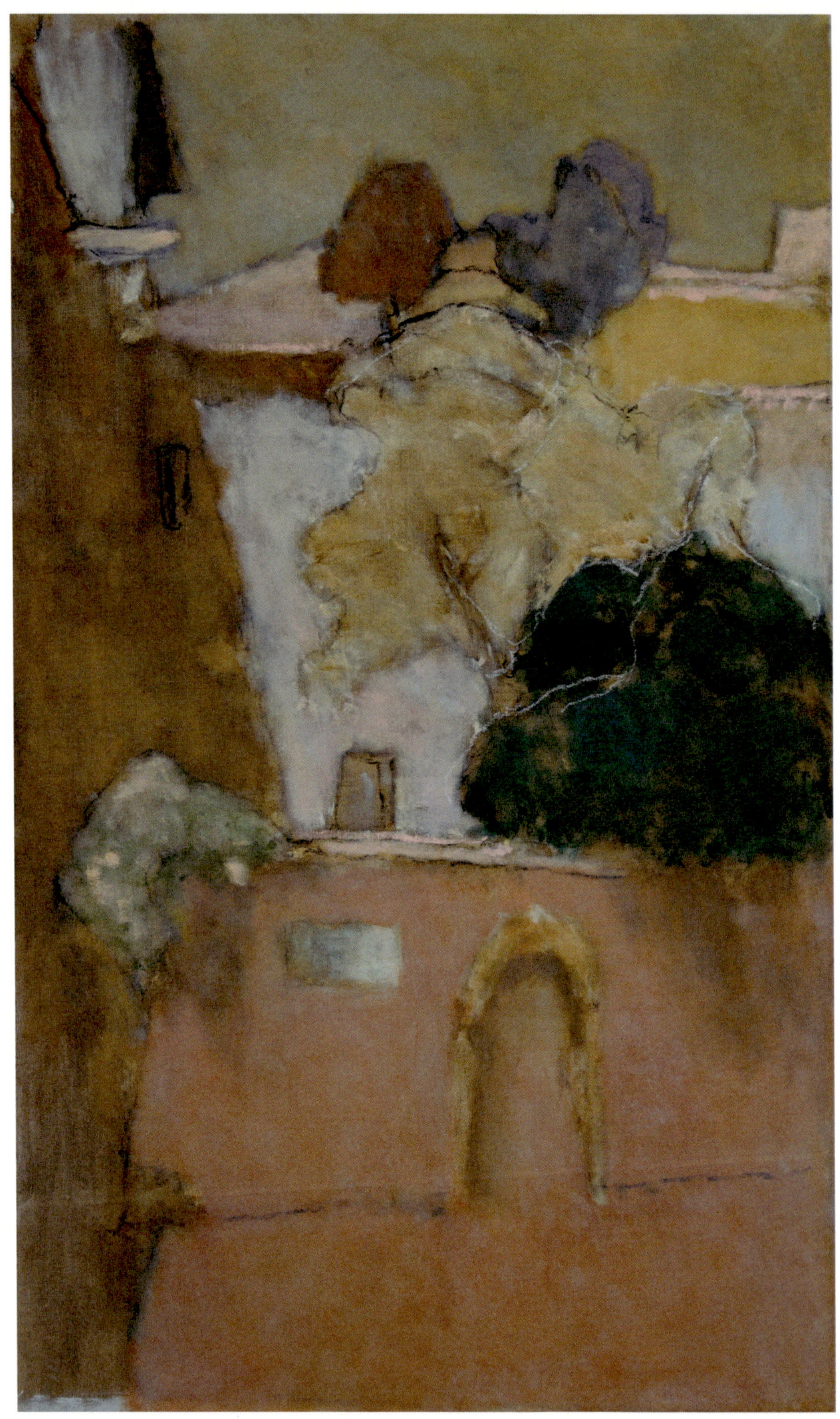

63. *Campiello della Madonna,* 2003

In The Studio: The Oils

Fox's Venetian drawings and watercolors, while standing on their own as independent pieces, often served as touchstones back in his Montreal studio as he reimagined an image in the more viscous medium of oil on linen. What most distinguishes the oils from the watercolours is the layering of colour, beginning with the imprimatura. John Fox was extremely particular about the toning of a painting's ground, constantly experimenting with different proportions of burnt sienna, indanthrene blue and umbers and with different brands of paint, especially with respect to earth tones. He would stumble upon a slightly different nuance and weave it back into the already worked surface, creating a subtle but dynamic figure/ground ambiguity.

While it is difficult to speak categorically of changes in the artist's oeuvre, certain tendencies are evident as we transition from early to late works. For instance, his earliest oil paintings of Venice, from 1956 to 1963, tend to be more architecturally structured, though undertones of shimmering amber pulse through the canvas as in *Interior, Church of the Salute* (fig. 18). The works are also less layered and of a lighter ground. In *Grand Canal Looking Towards the Salute Church* (fig. 75) or *Rialto Fish Market* (fig. 19), the pale yellow underpainting resembles watercolour more than oil.

Many of the later oils carry a mid to dark undertone over which multiple layers of both opaque and transparent paint have been worked in, scraped back, only to be worked in again. A sense of time spent in the process of their making is caught in the finished painting. While the oils are larger than the watercolours, they carry an equal intimacy. This is partly due to the fact that the watercolours take in more distant perspectives, the oils zoom closer in. Compare for example his canvas *Palazzo Soranzo, Campo Santa Ternità* (fig. 62) to the watercolour *Rio Madonna dell' Orto* (fig. 28). However, it is equally the intricate layering and scumbling of colour, teasing the sense of both sight and touch, that urge our engagement.

Fox's use of complementary tonalities to compose a painting is exquisitely illustrated in *Palazzo Soranzo, Campo Santa Ternità*, mentioned above. Here the blue/green and sienna/rose/brown hues are mined for all their subtle iterations of value and positioned strategically throughout the composition to lead the eye from top to bottom, side to side. Similarly, in *Habsburg Garden* (fig. 43), the rhythmic pacing and mapping of shifting tones of blue/green are balanced by the clusters of ochre/sienna. The scumbled brush

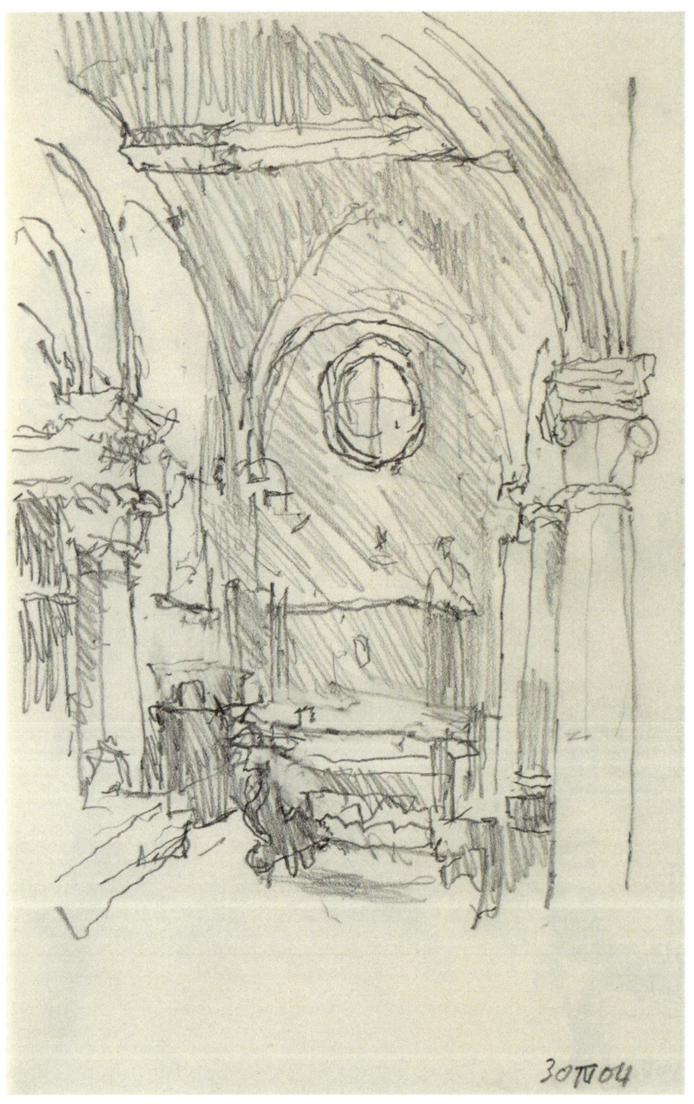

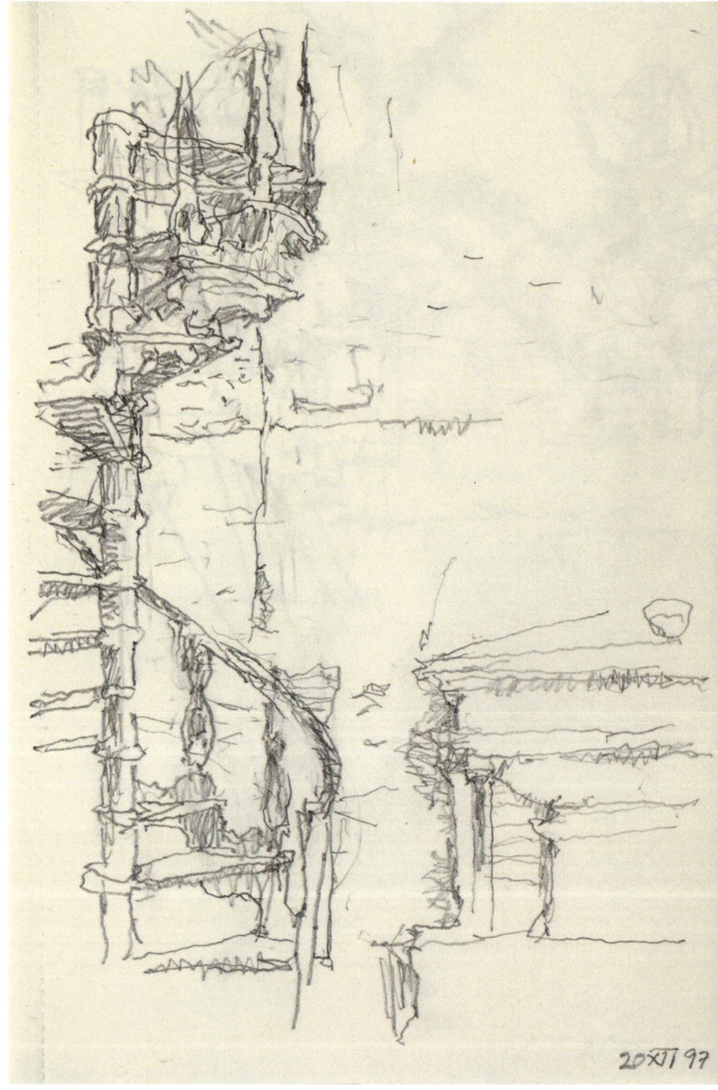

(from left | à partir de la gauche)
64. *Interior, Carmini Church*,
30 April 2004 | 30 avril 2004

65. *Interior, Carmini Church*, 20 December 1997 | 20 décembre 1997

(opposite | ci-contre)
66. *Interior, Gesuiti Church*, 2001

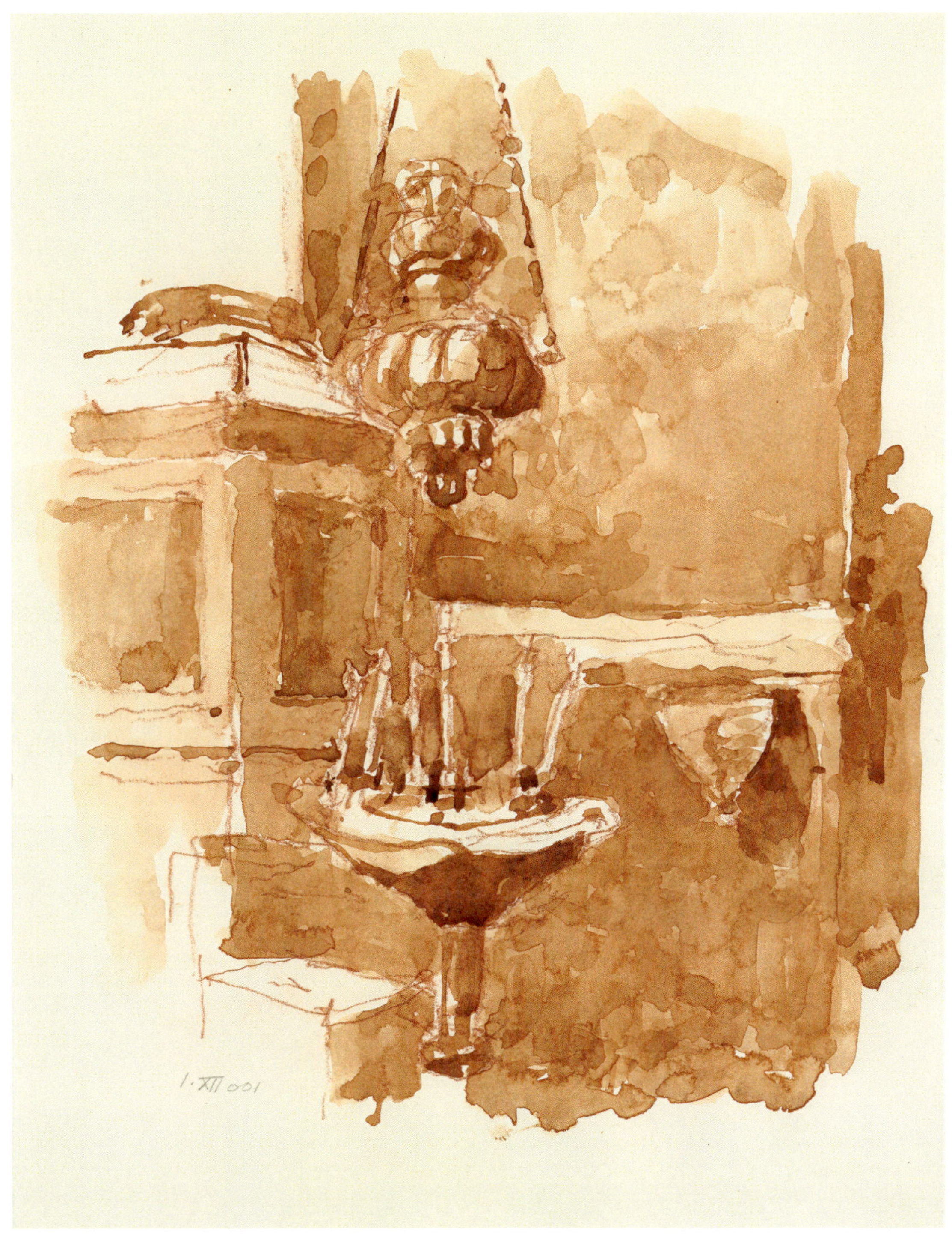
1.XII 001

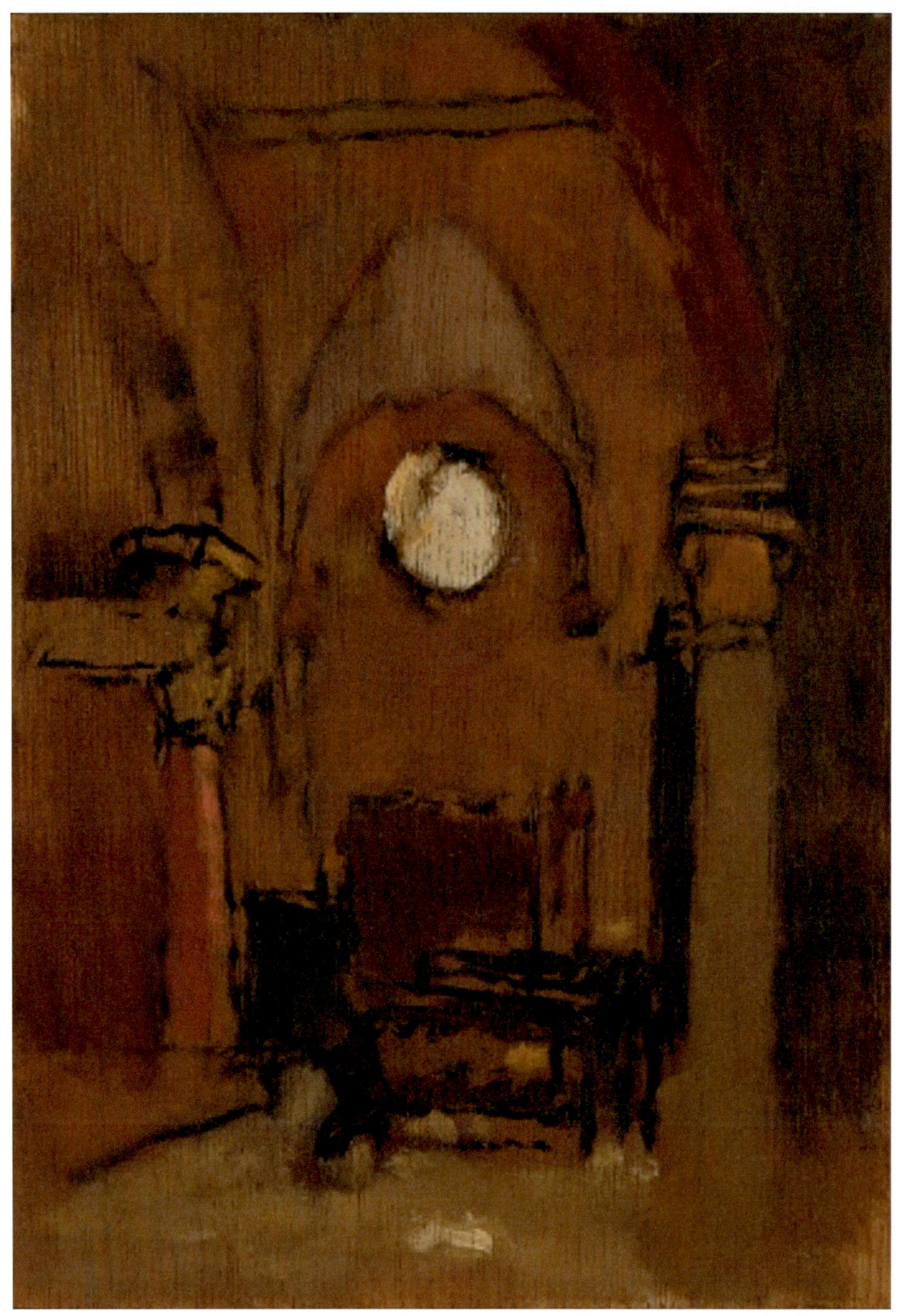

67. *Interior of the Carmini Church,* 2004

marks that define the medlar trees in full bloom play against the planar building façade and door on the left. The layers of colour, darker over light, lighter over dark, intense over subtle, bleed from one form into another. At intervals, the light sienna imprimatura pushes forward. The colour and the method of application carry the meaning of the painting—the artist's felt experience of place, now an invented place of paint.

In both these works, darker values are used strategically to structure the painting but also to extend meaning. The black rectangular doorways that anchor the composition draw us deep into the picture plane as they simultaneously move out towards the viewer. Their frontality speaks directly to us and contributes to the work's sense of openness.

As in the watercolours, Fox introduces more saturated hues sparingly as highlights to enliven or balance the composition. For instance, in *Ramo dei Muti* (fig. 56), the vivid pink rectangle that pushes forward from the far depth of the painting or the bar of cadmium red in the pochade *Interior of the Carmini Church* (fig. 67).

Much has been made of John Fox's break with figuration in the mid-1970s, his production of vibrant abstractions over the ensuing decade, before returning to figuration in 1985. However, the work itself ignores such categorization or divisions. The artist's exploration of colour is constant throughout, as he negotiates between what is observed and what is imagined. *Campiello della Madonna* (fig. 63) is but one example of many. The pencil study (fig. 1) for the canvas renders sensually but accurately the angles of the building, the shadow of foliage, the brilliance of light on the stucco façade. The oil clings only tangentially to realism as Fox bends and alters angles and tonalities to fit the needs of his imagined space. We are unsure where we are as our eye is led from a muted rose foreground to the play of brush work in the recessed middle ground. Here, drawn lines and spots of colour intertwine in lively rhythms, leaving evident the artist's process and touch. A sombre ochre grey hovers above, be it wall or sky, serving to keep us inside the intimate interior space of the painting. The work testifies to Paikowsky's claim that John Fox's unwavering commitment remained "his desire to visualize the necessity of art and his relationship to its inner purpose."[1]

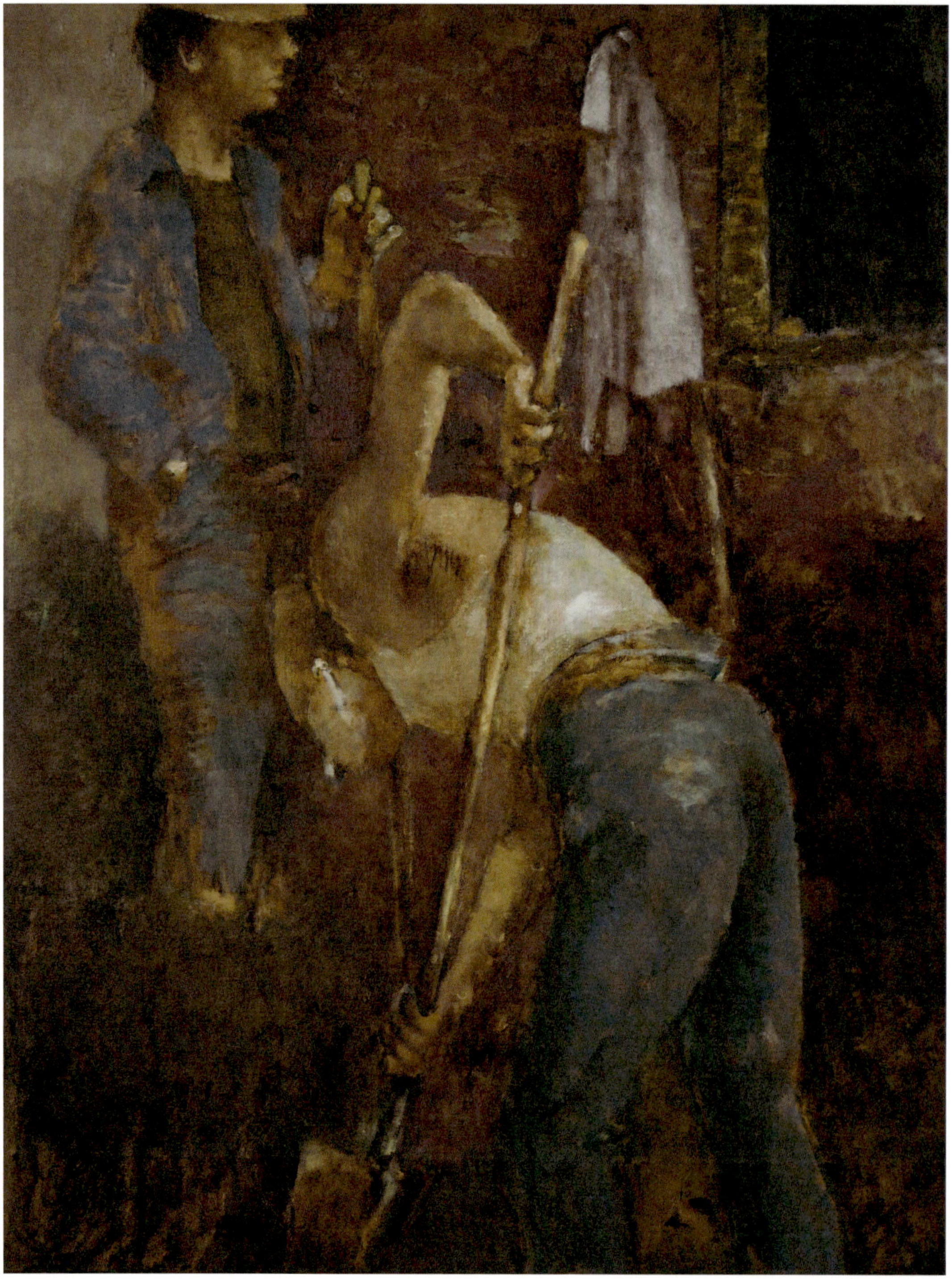

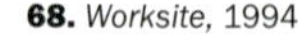

68. *Worksite*, 1994

The Painted Self

Two oils in particular speak to the central role Venice and Venetian colour played in the artist's life.

In *Worksite* (fig. 58), the picture plane is drenched in layers of Venetian red and burnt sienna. The two figures, recognizably workers, long shovels in hand, are roughly defined by a flickering of lighter tones and daubs of blue and green that attempt to clothe them. As with many of Fox's works, the exterior space feels simultaneously interior; the black window edging the upper right of the canvas could as easily be looking out at the world as into a nearby building. One worker gazes intently towards the window, the other physically digs into the earth. The painting speaks metaphorically to the two primary acts of the artist: that of seer, gazing out at the exterior world and that of worker, mining the rich tonalities of earth as paint—here more specifically the iron oxide earth of Venice. Indeed, Fox was not averse to dipping his fingers directly into the paint, applying and spreading it across the surface, underlining his deep visceral engagement with process.

Palazzo da Silva (fig. 76) is one of the artist's largest figurative canvases. Colour moves from dark brown madder to glowing amber—referencing the rich tonalities of Venetian colour Fox has explored throughout his career. As in *Worksite*, the artist appears doubly: as seer looking outward through the window and then inward, in this instance, at the shared Venice life enjoyed with Paikowsky for over three decades. Except for the dark blue shirt of the figure intruding from the right edge of the canvas, the three figures are a mesh of intricate brushwork and subtle shifts of umber, sienna, and red. They are less figures than gatherings of paint, though Fox rides that edge between the figurative and abstract masterfully. Paikowsky also draws attention to the light rectangle on the table which echoes the shape and tonalities of the window but also suggests the colour of raw canvas, serving as "a metaphor for the place of painting in his life."[2]

Colorito

A key tenet of sixteenth-century Venetian painting, as noted earlier, was the use of colour as the predominant means of composing a painting. However, the Venetian term *colorito*, used to define this approach, also implies the use of colour towards sensual, expressive ends.

The paintings of John Fox are characterized by a quiet, yet palpable sensuality. First is the colour itself, the warm, inviting earthiness of the palette, the muted secondary hues whose tonal ranges carry both light and dark, and all the in-betweens in poetic measure (figs. 3, 69). Moreover, the recurring iterations of rose or burnt sienna, dominant in so many of these works, subtly echo the tones of the human body.

It is also in the pressure and placement of brush marks—the touch of the artist's hand—that an underlying sensuality is anchored. Fox's mark making is far from a grand gesture, or expressive flourish. There are "no easy licks," to use Paikowsky's phrase.[3] Rather, his marks carry a quiet expressiveness and emotion. They are paced and considered, creating an effect at once serene, intimate, and sensual.

It is through the gathering of these elements of colour, tone, and touch that we are invited to linger in John Fox's paintings of Venice, to experience the felt encounter of his imagined world.

NOTES

1 Sandra Paikowsky, *Refiguration* (Montreal, Visual Arts Centre and McClure Gallery, 2010), 11.

2 Ibid, 60.

3 Sandra Paikowsky, in conversation with the author, Montreal, May 2024.

(opposite | ci-contre)
69. *Moro Bridge at the Servi Convent*, 2004

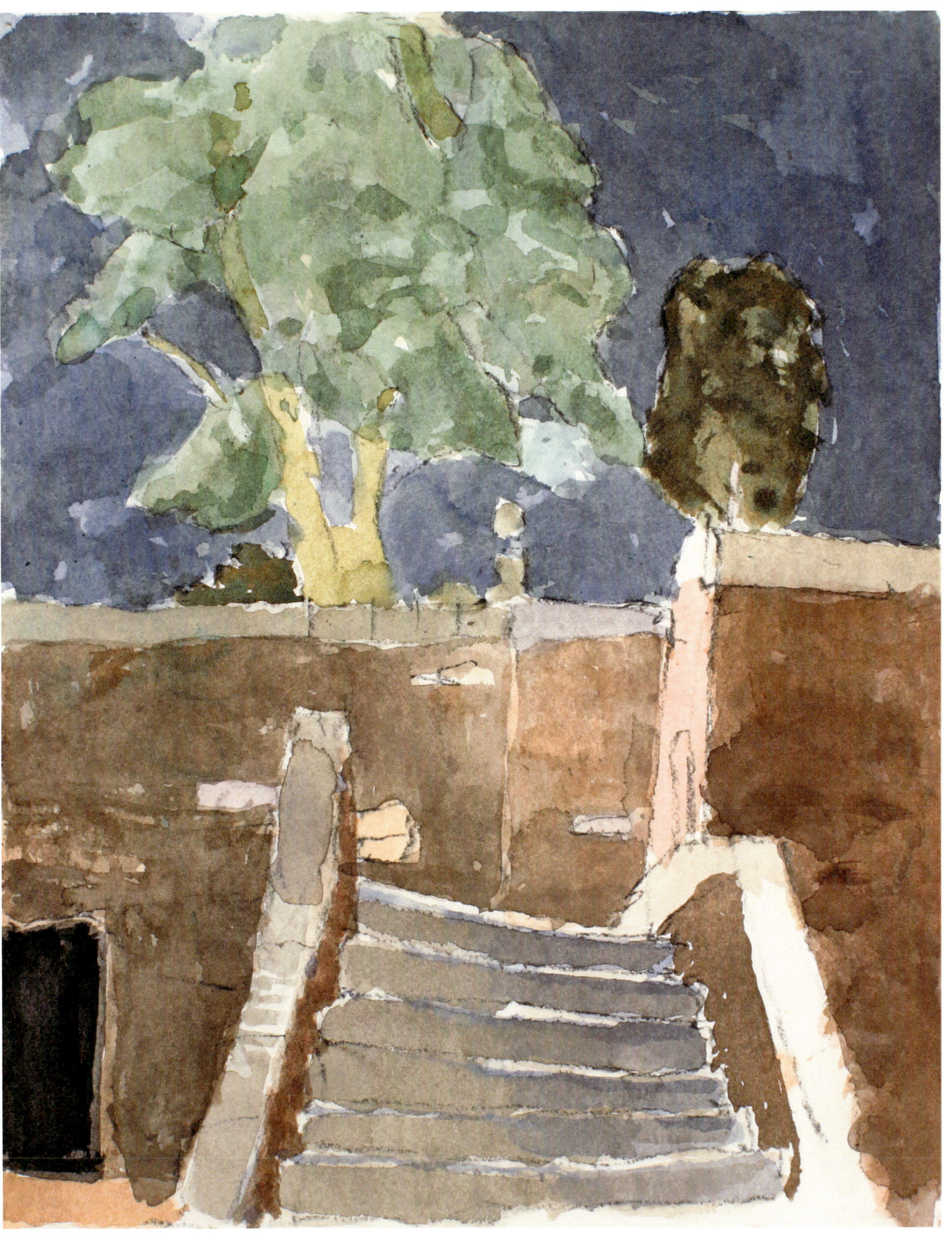

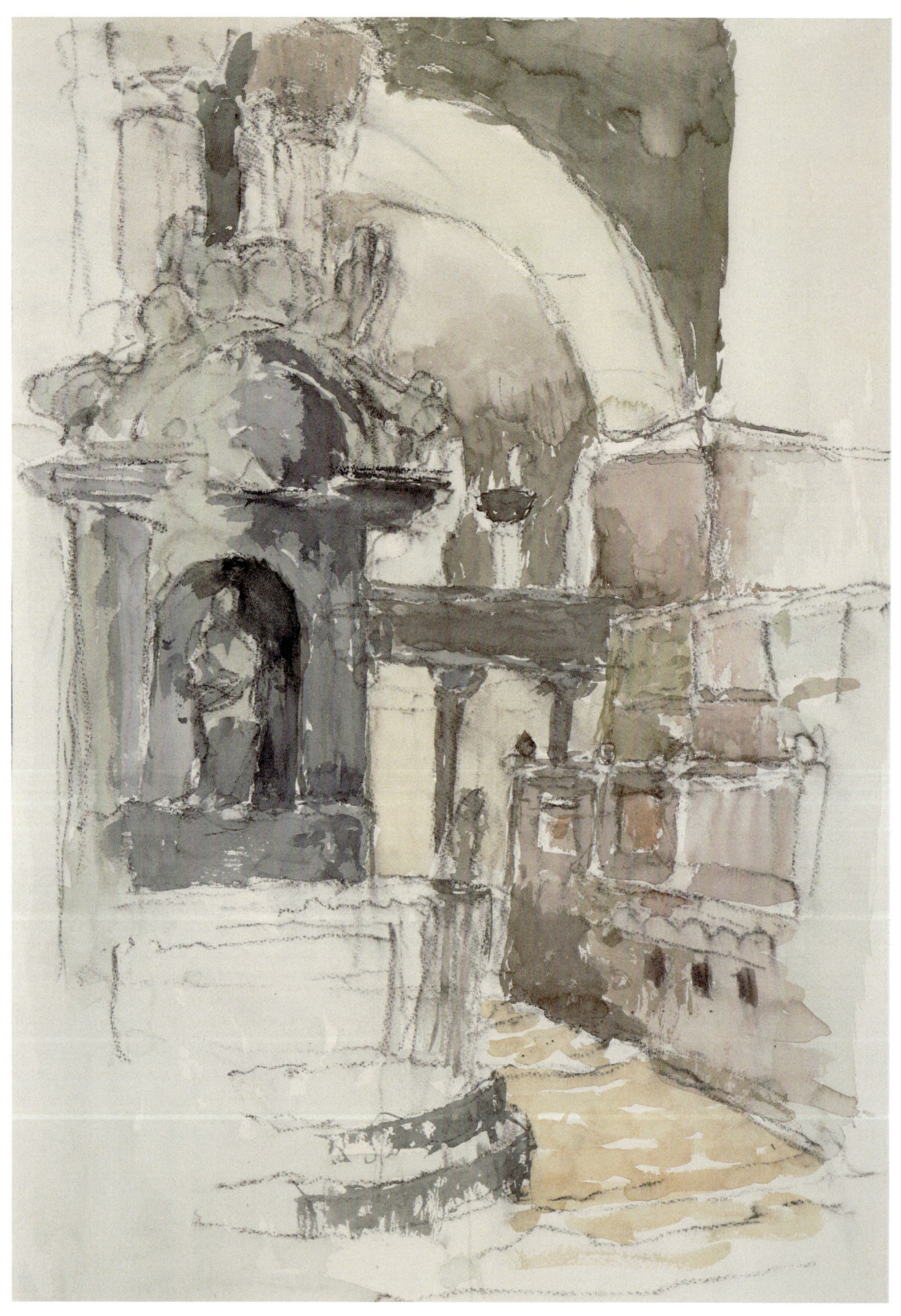

70. *Interior, Basilica San Marco,* 1998

Couleur, tonalité, geste
Les œuvres vénitiennes de John Fox

VICTORIA LEBLANC

Il n'y a pas de modèle, il n'y a que de la couleur. — Cézanne

Parler de la couleur dans les œuvres vénitiennes de John Fox, c'est aller au cœur de ce qui fait leur charme indéfectible. John Fox était un maître de la couleur ; il se servait d'elle, de sa sensualité et de ses fluctuations comme d'un pivot autour duquel se greffent à la fois la structure, la poésie et la signification de l'œuvre. C'est, chez lui, par le prisme de la couleur que se touchent la réalité vue et le langage de l'art.

Pendant plus de 50 ans (1953–2008), l'artiste retournera fidèlement à Venise, y faisant avec sa compagne, l'historienne de l'art Sandra Paikowsky (fig. 55), des séjours annuels de quelques semaines à deux mois à partir de la fin des années 1970. Son esthétisme fut façonné à la fois par l'ambiance unique et par la réalité matérielle de cette ville bâtie sur des bancs de vase et baignant dans la mer autant que par les maîtres vénitiens qui ont révolutionné la peinture : les œuvres de Tiepolo, du Tintoret et surtout de Titien ont indéniablement séduit et formé John Fox.

Cette influence se voit dans tous les aspects du traitement de la couleur chez Fox, à commencer par sa manière de la privilégier — plutôt que le dessin — pour composer un tableau et créer ses formes, approche caractéristique de la peinture vénitienne du XVIe siècle. Notons aussi son usage subtil de la tonalité, inauguré en maître par Titien. Soulignons enfin, dans la même veine, l'art de poser la couleur. En effet, Fox crée un rythme et une texture par la superposition ou le tuilage de taches de couleur — les fameuses *macchie*, comme on les appelait à Venise — évoquant le chatoiement perpétuel des reflets de la lumière sur les canaux et les bâtiments de la ville. On reconnaît ici encore la technique du dernier Titien, qui non seulement rend ainsi l'aura particulière de la ville, mais illustre aussi la main de l'artiste à l'œuvre. De même, les coups de pinceau sensibles et doucement expressifs de Fox rendent palpable sa présence et assoient la teneur poétique de chaque œuvre.

LA PALETTE

John Fox avait une palette minimaliste : terre de Sienne brûlée, brun de garance, rose quinacridone, bleu d'indanthrène, ocre jaune. Pour l'huile, on peut ajouter terre d'ombre naturelle, bleu de cobalt et blanc de titane. Et peut-être le noir, que l'artiste préférait toutefois concocter lui-même ; idem pour les couleurs tertiaires. Certes, Fox ne s'est jamais privé d'explorer, mais c'est dans cette zone qu'il a trouvé l'intensité et la subtilité de sa vision.

Les trois premières teintes évoquent la lumière de la ville elle-même, la terre d'oxyde de fer de la Vénétie, le stuc et les briques de terre cuite, le rose radieux de la lumière contrastant avec le rouille ou le violet foncé des ombres. Rien de surprenant à ce que le terre de Sienne brûlée ait été la couleur préférée de Fox, et la sanguine, son instrument de prédilection. C'est d'ailleurs cette palette qui colore toutes ses œuvres, depuis *Rialto Fish Market*, l'une de ses premières toiles (fig. 19), jusqu'au panneau *Interior of the Carmini Church* (fig. 67). Le rouge conté des croquis et des aquarelles en exprime les infinies déclinaisons, comme on le voit par exemple dans *Interior, Gesuiti Church* (fig. 66) ou *Palazzo Soranzo, Campo Santa Ternità* (fig. 61).

Ce rouge terre sert autant au lavis transparent qu'à l'empâtement. Dans l'aquarelle *Campo San Giacomo dell' Orio* (fig. 3), un fond ambre luisant imprègne l'ensemble et se heurte aux terre d'ombre et aux gris-bleu-vert complémentaires des silhouettes et de l'arbre. Tout le tableau baigne dans cette tonalité, ce qui lui confère à la fois dynamisme et stabilité. Comme dans tant d'autres œuvres du peintre, ici, plus de couleur, que de la lumière. Et la subtile palette chromatique découvre l'ambiance propre à l'heure du jour.

C'est dans *Inch by Ounce* (fig. 23), une acrylique s'inscrivant dans une série d'abstraits de la fin des années 1970, que Fox se livre avec le plus d'ardeur à la saturation et à l'empâtement de cette couleur typiquement vénitienne. Cette œuvre capture en effet avec une vigueur inégalée la lumière rose omniprésente des vieilles façades de brique et de pierre. Le spectateur est emporté par des vagues diaprées du rose au rouille, qui se fondent les unes dans les autres, d'un côté à l'autre de la toile. On la contemple et on se retrouve devant un vieux mur vénitien (fig. 54 et 63).

(opposite | ci-contre)
71. *Cloister, San Pietro di Castello*, 2007

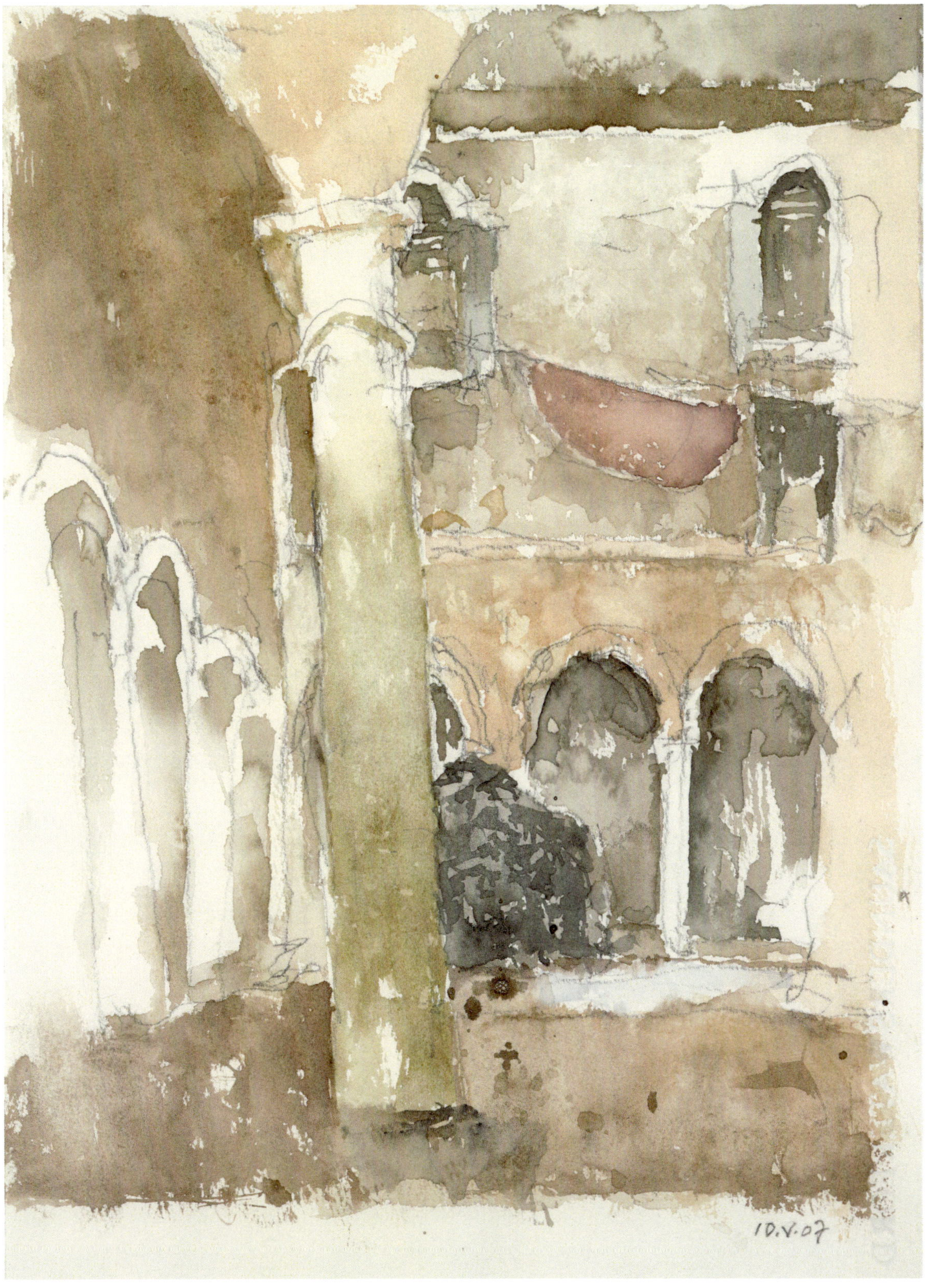
10.V.07

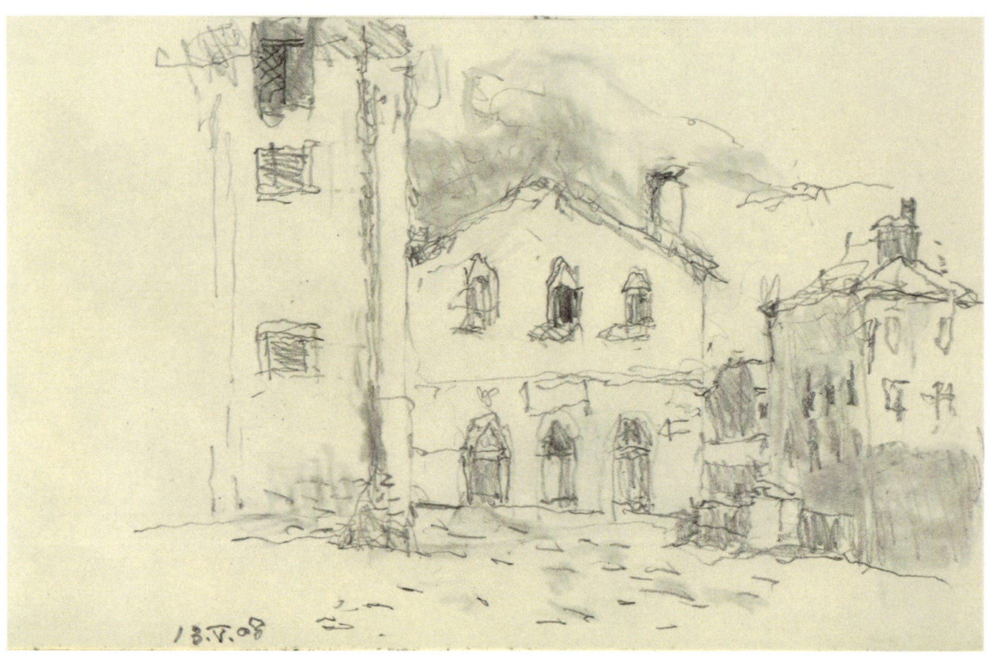

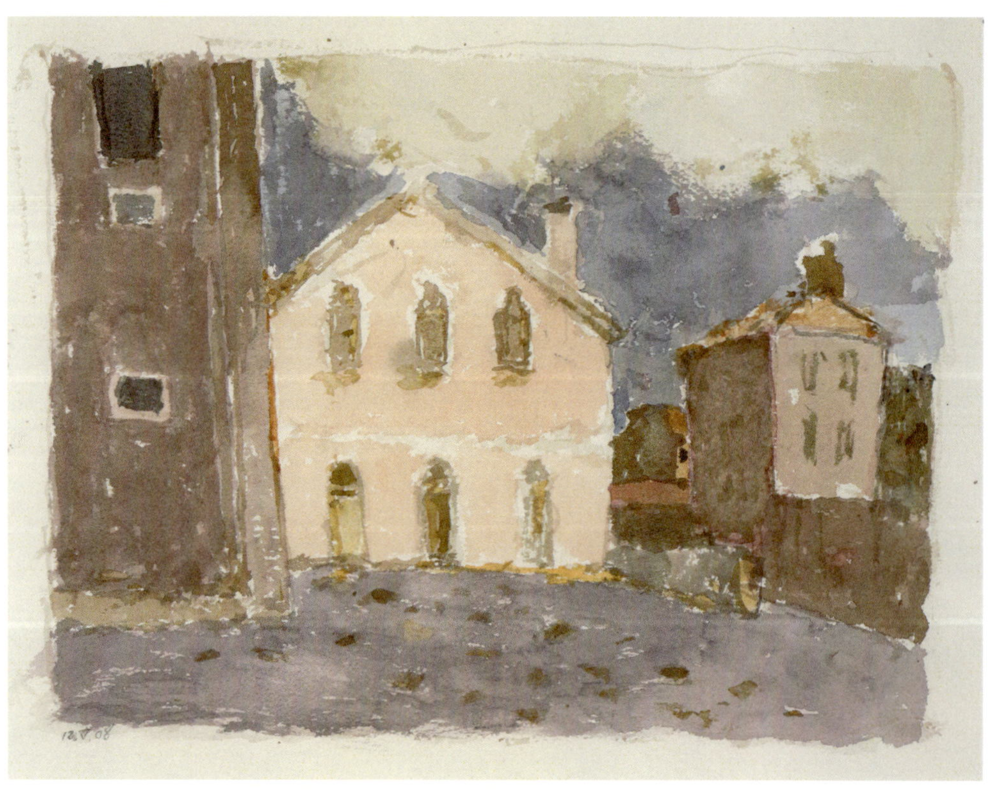

72. *Campo Sant' Alvise*
13 May 2008 | 13 mai 2008

73. *Campo Sant' Alvise*, 2008

SUR LE MOTIF : DE LA LIGNE À LA COULEUR

John Fox n'en avait jamais assez de dessiner à Venise, qu'il connaissait intimement. Chaque matin, carnet en main, il se lançait à l'assaut des *sestieri* (quartiers) les moins connus pour y flâner : Cannaregio, dans le nord-ouest, Castello, dans l'est. Contrairement à la plupart des artistes étrangers, il ne cherchait ni les grands sites ni les grandes histoires. Ce qui attirait son œil, c'étaient les espaces intimes et vierges, les recoins anonymes où la lumière, la brique, le stuc, le ciel et l'eau se marient sous des angles imprévisibles (fig. 79). L'artiste révèle, par son dessin, comment il se taille une place dans l'intimité de l'endroit; sa ligne gracieuse nous fait vivre le rythme et le ressenti de sa découverte du lieu. On sent la pression variable de la main sur le papier, semblable à la sensation tactile qu'il obtient avec le pinceau (fig. 14 et 54).

Fox dessinait sur le motif. Pour la peinture, toutefois, à de rares exceptions près, il préférait l'intimité de l'intérieur. Ses dessins lui servaient d'aide-mémoire pour passer du trait à la couleur. Il peignait l'après-midi : durant les dernières années, c'était dans la cuisine exiguë du rez-de-chaussée de l'appartement de Cannaregio, où il étendait son papier sur le comptoir, devant la fenêtre par où entrait la lumière, au-dessus de son épaule droite.

L'aquarelle était son médium favori. Il aimait son caractère immédiat et la manière dont les couleurs y évoluent de façon fluide et parfois imprévisible. Fox savait parfaitement comment travailler sur les apprêts secs, humides ou mouillés, chacun donnant un effet pictural ou une ambiance caractéristiques. Il privilégiait le sec, laissant le blanc du papier affleurer à travers les traits de pinceau telle une *imprimatura* ou une sous-couche, ce qui unifiait et dynamisait la composition (fig. 7 et 70). Les surfaces sèches, de surcroît, limitent la dilution, en sorte que chaque teinte de la palette de l'artiste, même tempérée, garde son intégrité. Fox employait d'ailleurs de la gomme arabique comme on incorpore parfois un médium dans une peinture à l'huile, pour ajouter une certaine viscosité à l'aquarelle et ralentir le séchage. Il lui arrivait aussi d'effacer un trait de pinceau ou d'en laisser une trace pour donner de la profondeur et du relief.

Les plus anciennes aquarelles de l'exposition datent des années 1990. Bien que la forme plane des murs et des bâtiments dotent les œuvres d'une certaine structure architecturale, le traitement de la couleur élimine toute rigidité géométrique, et les harmonies tonales unissent la composition. On le voit par exemple dans *At San Nicolò dei Mendicoli Church* (fig. 74) et dans la minimaliste *Venice Houses* (fig. 39), où les façades roses rayonnent d'une lumière emprisonnée par le contour bleu-vert.

Dans chacune de ces peintures, ce sont les tonalités secondaires ou tertiaires qui dominent, par des teintes soit complémentaires soit analogues. Fox est habile à calibrer l'emplacement des couleurs fortes ou des teintes foncées pour équilibrer la composition et diriger le regard. Dans *Ponte delle Tette, Rio San Cassiano I* (fig. 47), la note la plus saturée de terre de Sienne brûlée et le rectangle noir de la fenêtre sont situés à mi-chemin de l'inclinaison verticale, comme si le canal et l'escalier nous y menaient directement, de conserve. Dans *Ponte delle Tette, Rio San Cassiano II* (fig. 48), la fenêtre noire, à gauche, entre en dialogue avec les branches d'arbre qui surgissent de la droite.

L'artiste revenait souvent sur les mêmes lieux. D'une fois à l'autre, la composition ne changeait guère : il jouait plutôt de la couleur – comme on le voit dans ces deux images – et parfois du clair-obscur. Comparons maintenant deux évocations du *rio* Sant' Alvise. La composition est presque identique, mais le déplacement subtil des valeurs crée une atmosphère différente. Dans *Rio Sant' Alvise* (fig. 57), les tons foncés du ciel et le bloc rose clair sur la droite créent un mouvement vers le spectateur qui accroît à la fois le dynamisme et la sensation d'intimité. Dans la seconde, le ciel gris en retrait et les tons feutrés du mur qui font contrepoids aux autres composantes planes procurent une sensation générale de quiétude et d'équilibre.

On observe le même phénomène avec deux versions de *Rio Ca' Moro at San Girolamo* (fig. 41 et 58). Les deux affichent la même composition : les murs lisses, à droite, s'opposent aux coups de pinceau du feuillage à gauche, tandis que les couleurs épaisses du muret au premier plan servent d'assise au toit et aux fenêtres. Mais les différences de couleurs et de valeurs – façade rose lavande opaque dans un cas, ocre brun pâle dans l'autre, ciel chargé dans un cas, serein dans l'autre – confèrent à chaque version sa poésie propre. D'où une impression d'ailleurs ou d'un autre rapport avec un même lieu.

Les aquarelles de Venise nous montrent un artiste habile à jouer avec les tonalités les plus subtiles et les plus discrètes tout en exploitant vigoureusement les contrastes d'ombre et de lumière. Dans le *Canal Grande* (fig. 53), les coups de pinceau sur les façades fusionnent en variations de tonalités à peine perceptibles, tandis que les violets sombres du ciel et de l'eau, en couleurs complémentaires, se fondent naturellement dans les nuances de terre de Sienne. Quant à la façade qui nous regarde sur la gauche, malgré la discrétion

74. *At San Nicolò dei Mendicoli Church*, 2000

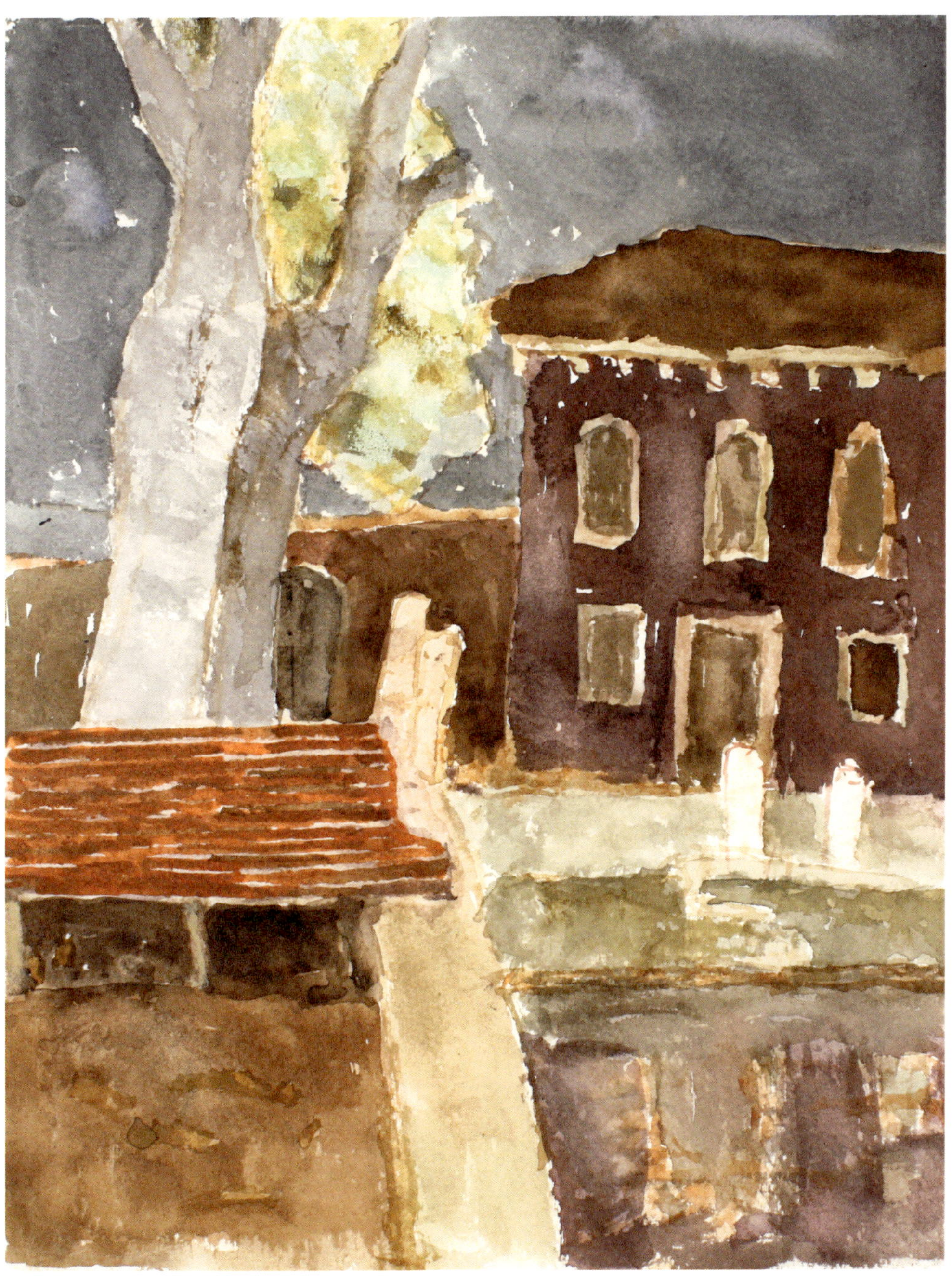

de sa terre d'ombre, elle nous fait apprécier, par un jeu de contrastes, les lueurs du soir et la largeur du canal qui nous en sépare. Nous contemplons le tout depuis le quai.

C'est dans *Rio San Daniele* (fig. 60) que la maîtrise tonale de Fox se manifeste avec le plus de tendresse. L'œuvre allie l'intimité du lieu à l'intimité du sentiment. Elle reste fidèle à la réalité, mais la structure que lui apportent les formes rectangulaires s'efface au profit du tuilage et du jeu des tons. Les angles incertains et les délicats coups de pinceau en couches épaisses, de même que les transitions du mauve à l'ocre, évoquent aussi bien les rides humaines que les lézardes du béton. On sent ici l'amour et l'immédiateté avec lesquels l'artiste a couché ses tons calibrés.

Intimité et immédiateté sont également les maîtres mots pour décrire *Sottoportego Mosto* (fig. 13) ou encore *Campiello San Francesco della Vigna* (fig. 15). Ajoutons que, dans ces trois aquarelles, les traits de crayon accompagnent doucement les coups de pinceau, dialoguant avec les tons subtils qu'ils traversent. Les traits de crayon apparaissent souvent dans les aquarelles de Fox, où elles servent moins à définir des contours qu'à communiquer l'expérience du lieu et la quête du rythme. La souplesse et le mouvement des traits de crayon contribuent à l'impression d'avoir devant soi un tableau ouvert, inachevé.

Dans plus d'une aquarelle de Venise, l'image nage entre des espaces vides (fig. 70) qui invitent le spectateur et accentuent cette sensation d'inachèvement. Les coups de pinceau se perdent au petit bonheur dans les marges, donnant l'impression d'une scène croquée en vitesse, d'une rencontre éphémère. Cette sensation de fugacité, fréquente, ressort particulièrement dans les images décentrées, qui semblent accrochées au bord de la feuille ou flottent dans un pourtour blanc (fig. 66). Par le chatoiement tranquille des rouges vénitiens et des terres de Sienne ainsi que par la sensation tactile qui s'en dégage, les images s'offrent à nous, sur le papier, comme des haïkus auxquels on revient sans cesse pour en découvrir chaque fois davantage le charme et la profondeur.

75. *Grand Canal Looking Towards the Salute Church,* 1963

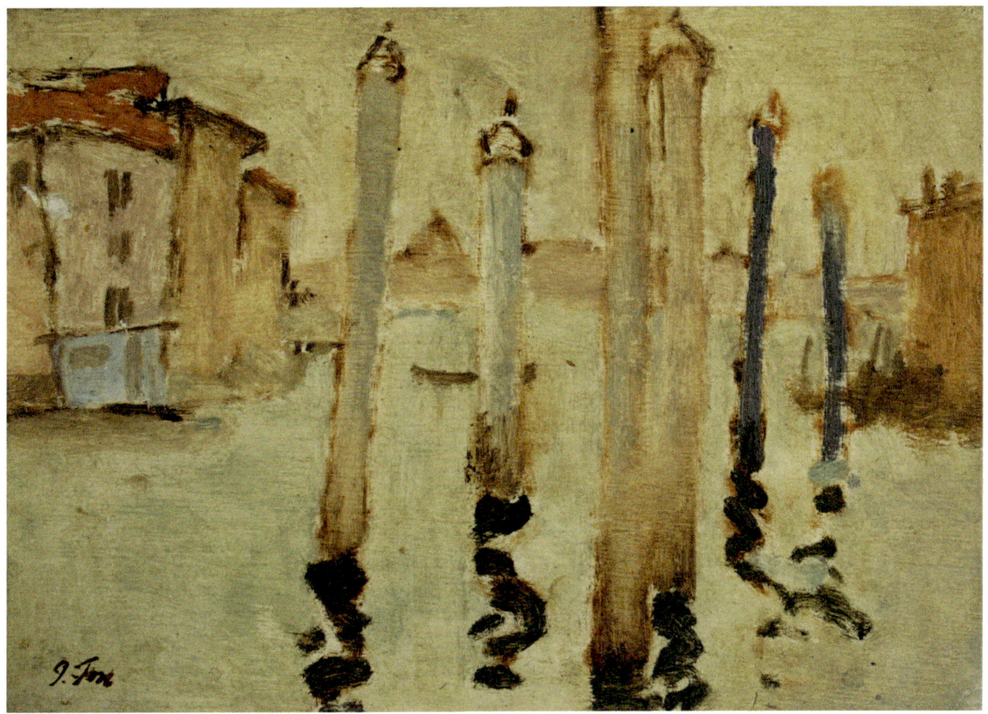

EN ATELIER : LES HUILES

Les dessins et les aquarelles de Fox, tout en ayant leur existence propre, servaient souvent d'aide-mémoire à l'artiste qui, de retour à son atelier de Montréal, reprenait une scène, cette fois à l'huile et sur toile de lin. Or, outre la viscosité, ce qui distingue le plus l'huile de l'aquarelle, ce sont les couches, à commencer par l'*imprimatura*. Très pointilleux sur le ton de la sous-couche, John Fox expérimentait en permanence différentes proportions de terre de Sienne brûlée, de bleu d'indanthrène et de terre d'ombre ainsi que différentes marques de peinture, surtout pour les tons de terre. S'il découvrait une nuance, si ténue soit-elle, il la réintégrait dans sa surface finie, ce qui conférait une ambiguïté subtile mais dynamique entre le fond et le sujet.

Si tout l'œuvre de Fox affiche indéniablement une certaine uniformité, on n'en constate pas moins une évolution entre le début et la fin de son parcours. Par exemple, ses premières huiles de Venise (1956-1963) sont généralement plus architecturées, malgré les pulsations de chatoiements ambrés qui animent la toile, par exemple dans *Interior, Church of the Salute* (fig. 18). Les couches y sont aussi moins nombreuses, et les fonds plus clairs. Dans *Grand Canal Looking Towards the Salute Church* (fig. 75) ou *Rialto Fish Market* (fig. 19), la sous-couche jaune pâle évoque davantage l'aquarelle que l'huile.

Bon nombre des huiles ultérieures jouent dans des tons de base moyens à foncés, recouverts de couches multiples de peinture opaque ou transparente appliquées, grattées, puis réappliquées. On sent, en contemplant le résultat, tout le temps consacré à ce travail. Plus grandes que les aquarelles, les huiles n'en relèvent pas moins du registre intime, car là où l'aquarelle convoque une perspective large, l'huile rapproche le sujet. On peut comparer par exemple la toile *Palazzo Soranzo, Campo Santa Ternità* (fig. 62) à l'aquarelle *Rio Madonna dell' Orto* (fig. 28). Dans les deux cas, cependant, c'est l'intrication des couches et du grattage, sollicitant à la fois la vue et le toucher, qui suscite notre engagement.

Par ailleurs, toujours dans *Palazzo Soranzo, Campo Santa Ternità,* on voit un exemple exquis de l'utilisation minutieuse de tons complémentaires. Ici, l'artiste exploite toutes les variations subtiles des teintes bleu-vert et terre de Sienne-rose-brun pour en répartir les valeurs stratégiquement, de manière à conduire l'œil de haut en bas et d'un côté à l'autre. De même, dans *Habsburg Garden* (fig. 43), la rythmique et la distribution des tonalités changeantes de bleu-vert sont contrebalancées par les grappes d'ocre-terre de Sienne. Quant aux coups de pinceau grattés qui définissent les néfliers en fleurs, ils font contraste avec le plan brut du mur et de la porte à gauche. Les couches de couleur, foncées sur pâles, pâles sur foncées, intenses sur subtiles, débordent d'une forme sur l'autre. Ici et là affleure l'*imprimatura* terre de Sienne pâle. La couleur et la manière portent le sens du tableau, soit le ressenti de l'artiste en ce lieu, désormais lieu de peinture inventé.

Dans ces deux œuvres, les valeurs foncées servent à structurer le tableau, mais aussi à enrichir le sens. Les sombres embrasures rectangulaires qui ancrent la composition nous font carrément pénétrer au fond du tableau tout en venant elles-mêmes vers le spectateur. Leur caractère frontal nous interpelle directement et donne une impression d'ouverture.

Comme dans les aquarelles, Fox utilise les tons saturés avec parcimonie pour dynamiser ou équilibrer la composition. Citons par exemple le rectangle rose éclatant qui surgit du fond de *Ramo dei Muti* (fig. 56), ou encore la bande rouge cadmium de la pochade *Interior of the Carmini Church* (fig. 67).

On a fait grand cas de l'abandon de la figuration par Fox au milieu des années 1970, de sa production abstraite exubérante durant la décennie suivante, puis de son retour au figuratif en 1985. Toutefois, l'œuvre global échappe à de telles catégorisations. D'un bout à l'autre de sa production, l'artiste explore la couleur en oscillant entre image et imaginaire. La toile *Campiello della Madonna* (fig. 63) n'est qu'un exemple parmi d'autres. L'étude au crayon (fig. 1) qui l'a précédée reproduit avec sensualité mais précision les angles de l'immeuble, l'ombre du feuillage, la lumière sur le stuc. L'huile ne tient que par un fil au réalisme, l'artiste ayant gauchi les angles et les tonalités en fonction des impératifs de l'espace imaginé. On a du mal à se situer devant ce premier plan rose feutré qui dirige l'œil vers les coups de pinceau du plan intermédiaire, en retrait. Ici, les traits dessinés et les taches de couleur s'entremêlent dans des rythmes vivants, laissant apparaître la manière de l'artiste. Un sombre gris ocre flottant au haut du tableau (mur ou ciel ?) sert à nous garder dans l'espace intérieur intime de la scène. Comme le dit si justement Paikowsky, Fox fut toujours guidé par « son désir de rendre manifeste la nécessité de l'art et sa relation à son but inhérent[1] ».

SE METTRE EN SCÈNE

Deux huiles en particulier témoignent du rôle central que Venise et sa couleur ont joué dans la vie de l'artiste. Le tableau *Worksite* (fig. 68) est saturé de couches de rouge vénitien et de terre de Sienne brûlée. Longue pelle à la main, les deux personnages, manifestement des travailleurs, se démarquent grossièrement par des oscillations de tons clairs et de taches de bleu et de vert ayant vocation à les vêtir. Comme dans bien des œuvres de Fox, extérieur et intérieur se confondent : la fenêtre noire, dans le coin supérieur droit, pourrait donner aussi bien sur la rue ou que sur une pièce. Un des travailleurs, justement, y jette un regard pendant que l'autre s'emploie à creuser. Ce sont les deux postures de l'artiste : celui qui observe le monde et celui qui exploite les riches tonalités de la terre (en l'occurrence l'oxyde de fer vénitien). De fait, Fox n'avait pas peur de plonger les doigts directement dans la peinture pour l'étendre sur la surface, soulignant son engagement viscéral.

Palazzo da Silva (fig. 76) est l'une des plus grandes toiles figuratives de l'artiste. Les couleurs passent du brun garance foncé à l'ambre lumineux, renvoyant sans cesse aux riches tonalités vénitiennes que Fox aura explorées tout au long de sa carrière. Comme dans *Worksite*, l'artiste s'y dédouble : en tant qu'observateur regardant dehors par la fenêtre et en tant que personnage tourné vers l'intérieur, en l'occurrence vers sa vie vénitienne partagée avec Paikowsky pendant plus de trois décennies. Exception faite du bleu foncé habillant le torse du personnage qui surgit à droite, les trois silhouettes résultent d'un canevas serré de coups de pinceau et de subtiles nuances de terre de Sienne, d'ocre brun et de rouges. Ce sont moins des figures humaines que des amas de couleurs, quoique Fox maîtrise parfaitement la fine limite entre art figuratif et art abstrait. Paikowsky met en évidence le rectangle clair sur la table, qui fait écho à la forme et aux tonalités de la fenêtre, mais suggère aussi la couleur de la toile brute, devenant ainsi « une métaphore de la place qu'occupe la peinture dans sa vie[2] ».

COLORITO

Nous avons vu que la peinture vénitienne du XVIe siècle se caractérisait par la prédominance de la couleur comme moyen de composer un tableau. Toutefois, le terme *colorito*, qui désigne cette technique, fait aussi référence à l'exploitation des dimensions sensuelles et expressives de la couleur.

Les peintures de Fox regorgent en effet d'une sensualité tranquille mais palpable. Il y a d'abord les tons terreux qui sautent aux yeux, chauds et invitants, complétés par des teintes secondaires feutrées jouant avec l'ombre et la lumière, avec tous les entre-deux imaginables dans une rythmique poétique (fig. 3 et 69). Sans compter l'omniprésence des roses et des terre de Sienne rappelant les tons de la peau humaine.

C'est aussi dans les marques de pinceau que l'on peut goûter la sensualité de l'artiste. Fox ne faisait pas dans les grands gestes ni dans les fioritures, mais en contemplant sa peinture, on voit le geste précis de sa main. Il n'y a pas de « triomphe facile » chez lui, pour reprendre les mots de Paikowsky[3]. Au contraire, sa manière est porteuse d'une expressivité et d'une émotion tranquilles, rythmée et réfléchie, sereine, intimiste et sensuelle.

C'est à travers ce mariage de la couleur, de la tonalité et du geste que nous sommes invités à nous perdre dans les peintures vénitiennes de John Fox et à vivre la rencontre ressentie de son monde imaginé.

NOTES

1 Sandra Paikowsky, *Refiguration*, Montréal, Centre des arts visuels et Galerie McClure, 2010, p. 11.
2 Ibid., p. 60.
3 Sandra Paikowsky, conversation avec l'autrice, Montréal, mai 2024.

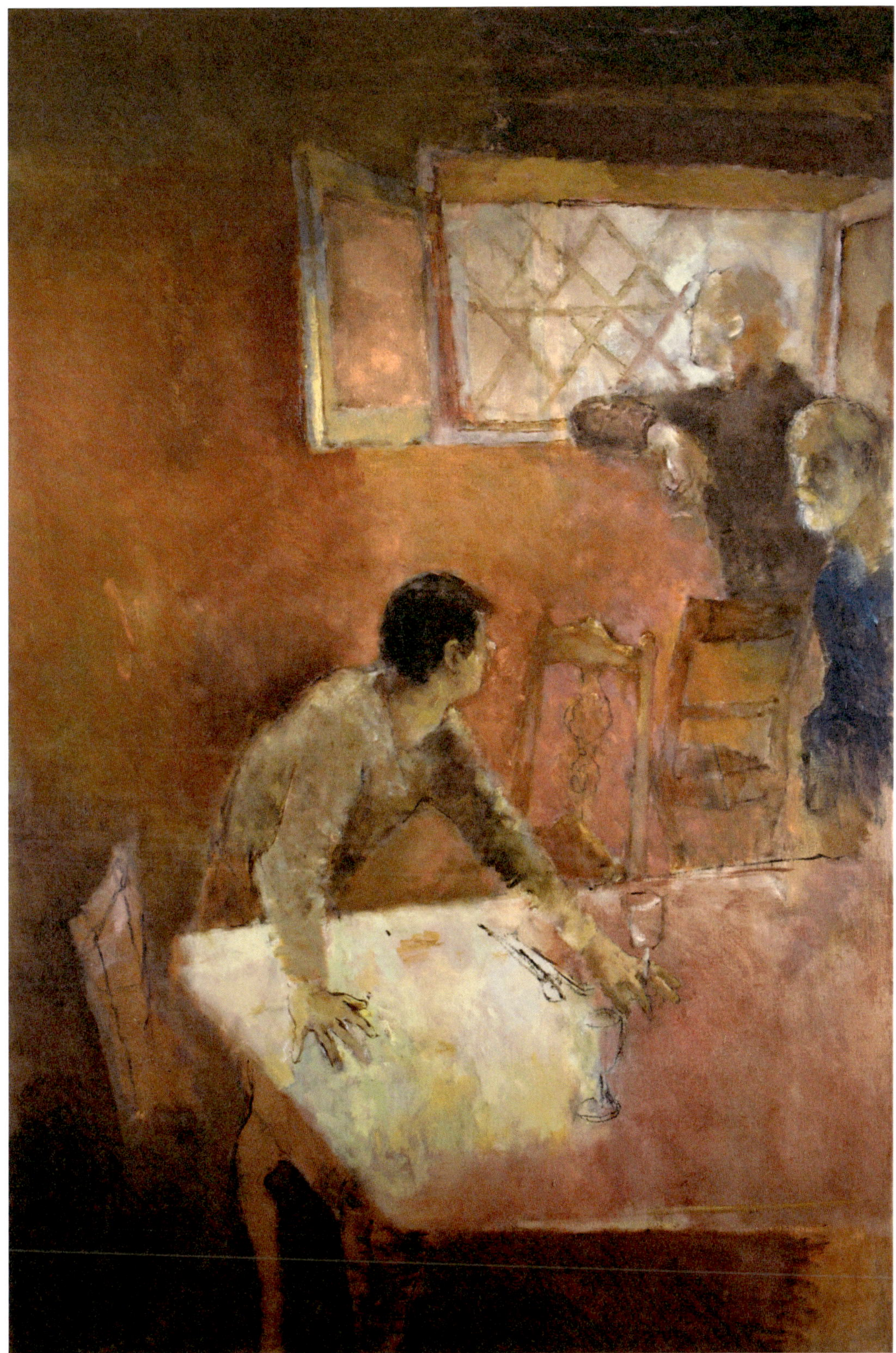

76. *Palazzo da Silva,* 2007

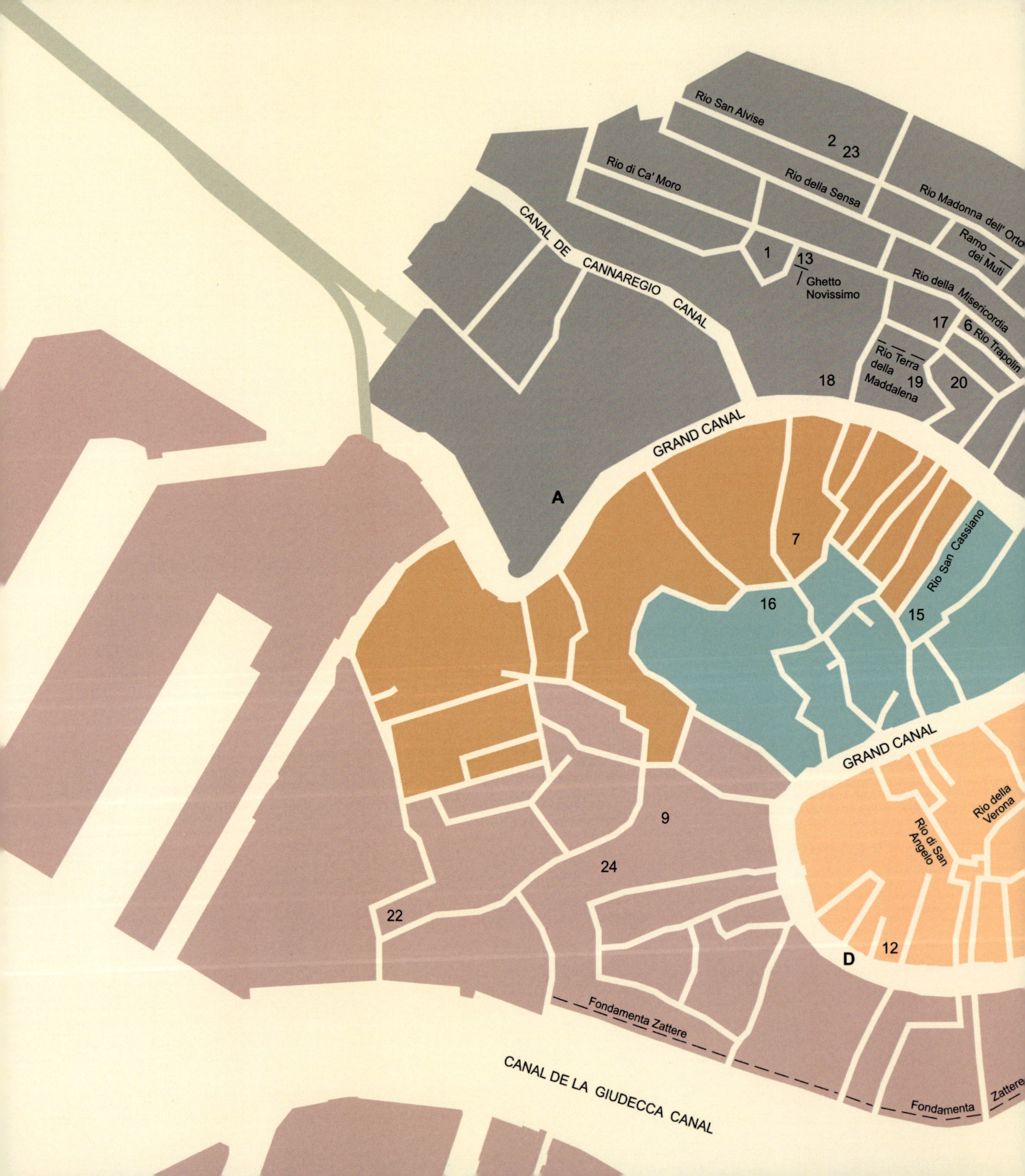
Rio San Alvise
2
23
Rio di Ca' Moro
Rio della Sensa
Rio Madonna dell' Orto
Ramo dei Muti
CANAL DE CANNAREGIO CANAL
1
13
Ghetto Novissimo
Rio della Misericordia
17
6
Rio Trapolin
Rio Terra della Maddalena
19
20
18
GRAND CANAL
A
7
Rio San Cassiano
16
15
GRAND CANAL
Rio della Verona
Rio di San Angelo
9
24
22
12
D
Fondamenta Zattere
CANAL DE LA GIUDECCA CANAL
Fondamenta Zattere

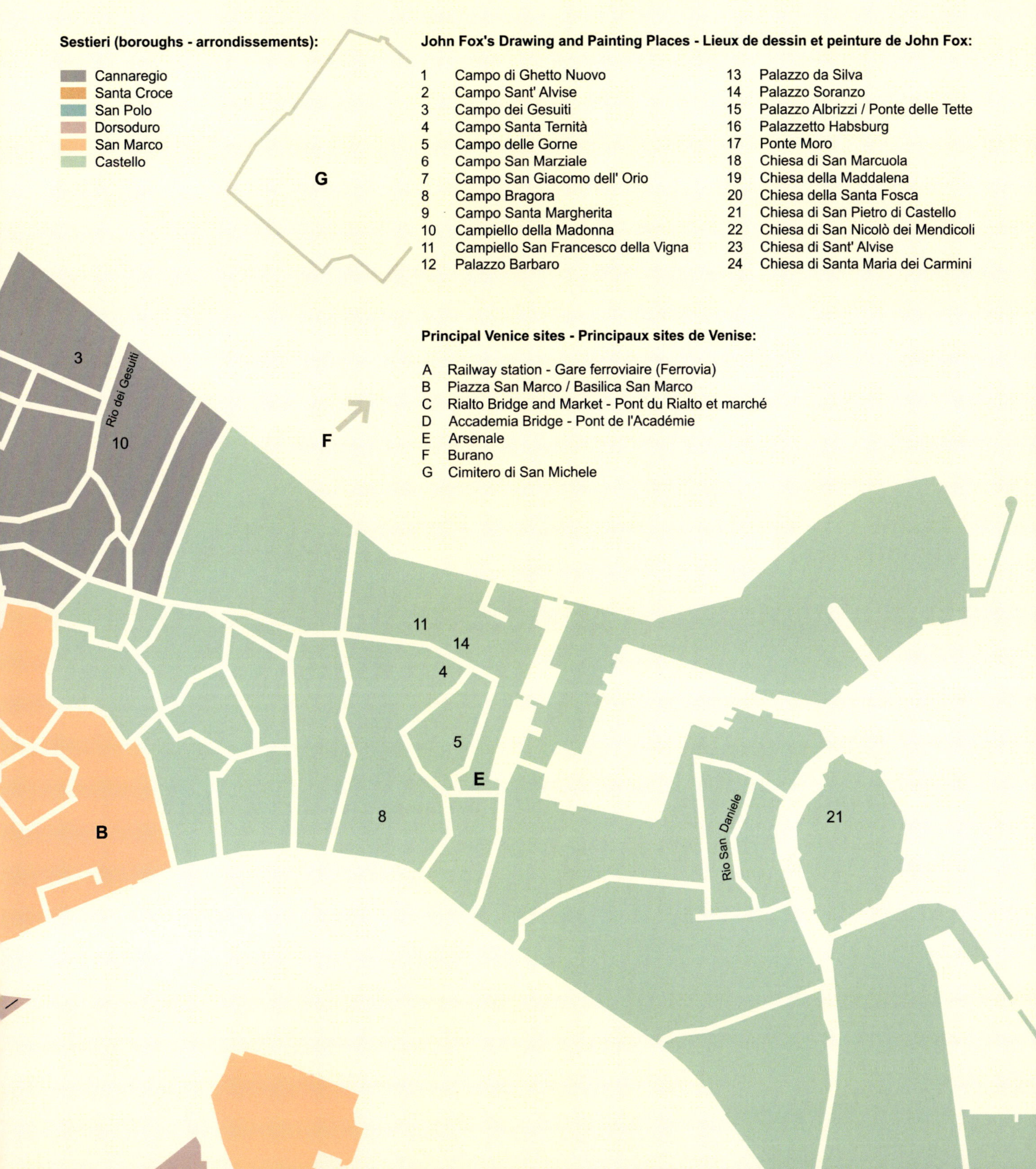

Sestieri (boroughs - arrondissements):
Cannaregio
Santa Croce
San Polo
Dorsoduro
San Marco
Castello
John Fox's Drawing and Painting Places - Lieux de dessin et peinture de John Fox:
1 Campo di Ghetto Nuovo
2 Campo Sant' Alvise
3 Campo dei Gesuiti
4 Campo Santa Ternità
5 Campo delle Gorne
6 Campo San Marziale
7 Campo San Giacomo dell' Orio
8 Campo Bragora
9 Campo Santa Margherita
10 Campiello della Madonna
11 Campiello San Francesco della Vigna
12 Palazzo Barbaro
13 Palazzo da Silva
14 Palazzo Soranzo
15 Palazzo Albrizzi / Ponte delle Tette
16 Palazzetto Habsburg
17 Ponte Moro
18 Chiesa di San Marcuola
19 Chiesa della Maddalena
20 Chiesa della Santa Fosca
21 Chiesa di San Pietro di Castello
22 Chiesa di San Nicolò dei Mendicoli
23 Chiesa di Sant' Alvise
24 Chiesa di Santa Maria dei Carmini
Principal Venice sites - Principaux sites de Venise:
A Railway station - Gare ferroviaire (Ferrovia)
B Piazza San Marco / Basilica San Marco
C Rialto Bridge and Market - Pont du Rialto et marché
D Accademia Bridge - Pont de l'Académie
E Arsenale
F Burano
G Cimitero di San Michele
G
F
3
Rio dei Gesuiti
10
11
14
4
5
E
8
B
Rio San Daniele
21

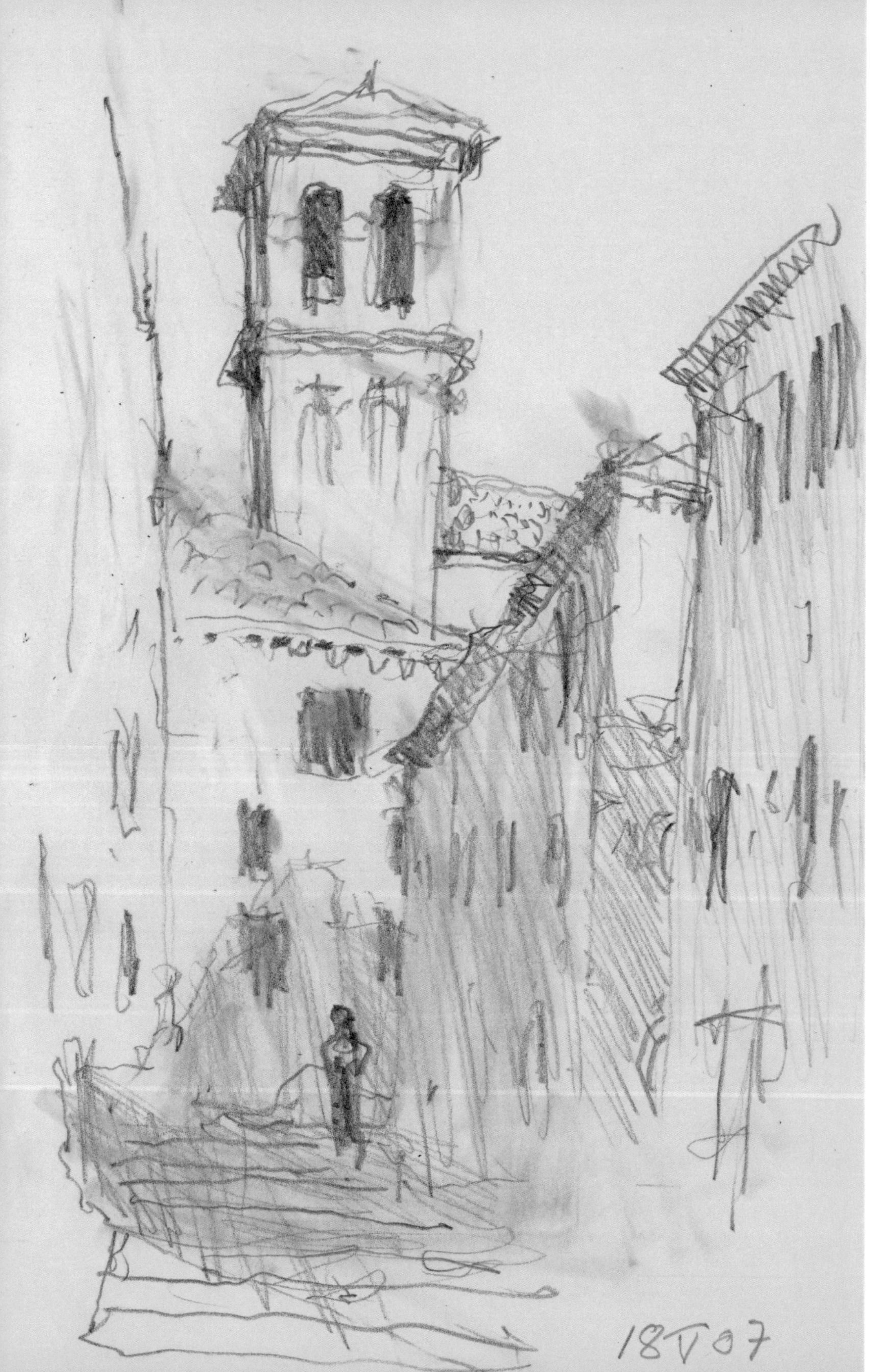

77. *Campanile dei Gesuiti*,
18 May 2007 | 18 mai 2007

Acknowledgements

The authors would like to sincerely thank Victoria Stusiak; Kirbi Pitt and Martie Giefert at Heffel Fine Art; Carlyn Moulton and Matthias Flynn at Oeno Gallery; Jason Paikowsky; Angelica Fox; Sandra Goldie; Kate Marley; Jenny Calder; Philip LeBlanc; Elliot Mann; Pierre-Luc Byham; Cheryl Kyer and Big Brothers Big Sisters of Cornwall and District; Tamara Andrusziewicz and Frederick Lauritzen in Venice, Italy; Alan Sheppard and Julie Scriver at Goose Lane Editions; Laura Kenins for the thorough editing; Ray Cronin, Bernard Doucet, Dawn Steeves, Graeme Kennedy, and Michael Doucet at the Beaverbrook Art Gallery; and all the individuals and institutions who kindly loaned work from their collections.

Remerciements

Les auteurs tiennent à remercier sincèrement Victoria Stusiak ; Kirbi Pitt et Martie Giefert de la Heffel Fine Art ; Carlyn Moulton et Matthias Flynn de l'Oeno Gallery ; Jason Paikowsky ; Angelica Fox ; Sandra Goldie ; Kate Marley ; Jenny Calder ; Philip LeBlanc ; Elliot Mann ; Pierre-Luc Byham ; Cheryl Kyer et l'organisme Big Brothers Big Sisters of Cornwall and District ; Tamara Andrusziewicz et Frederick Lauritzen à Venise, en Italie ; Alan Sheppard et Julie Scriver de Goose Lane Editions ; Laura Kenins pour la révision rigoureuse en anglais ; Ray Cronin, Bernard Doucet, Dawn Steeves, Graeme Kennedy et Michael Doucet du Musée des beaux-arts Beaverbrook ; ainsi que toutes les personnes et institutions ayant gracieusement prêté des œuvres pour l'occasion.

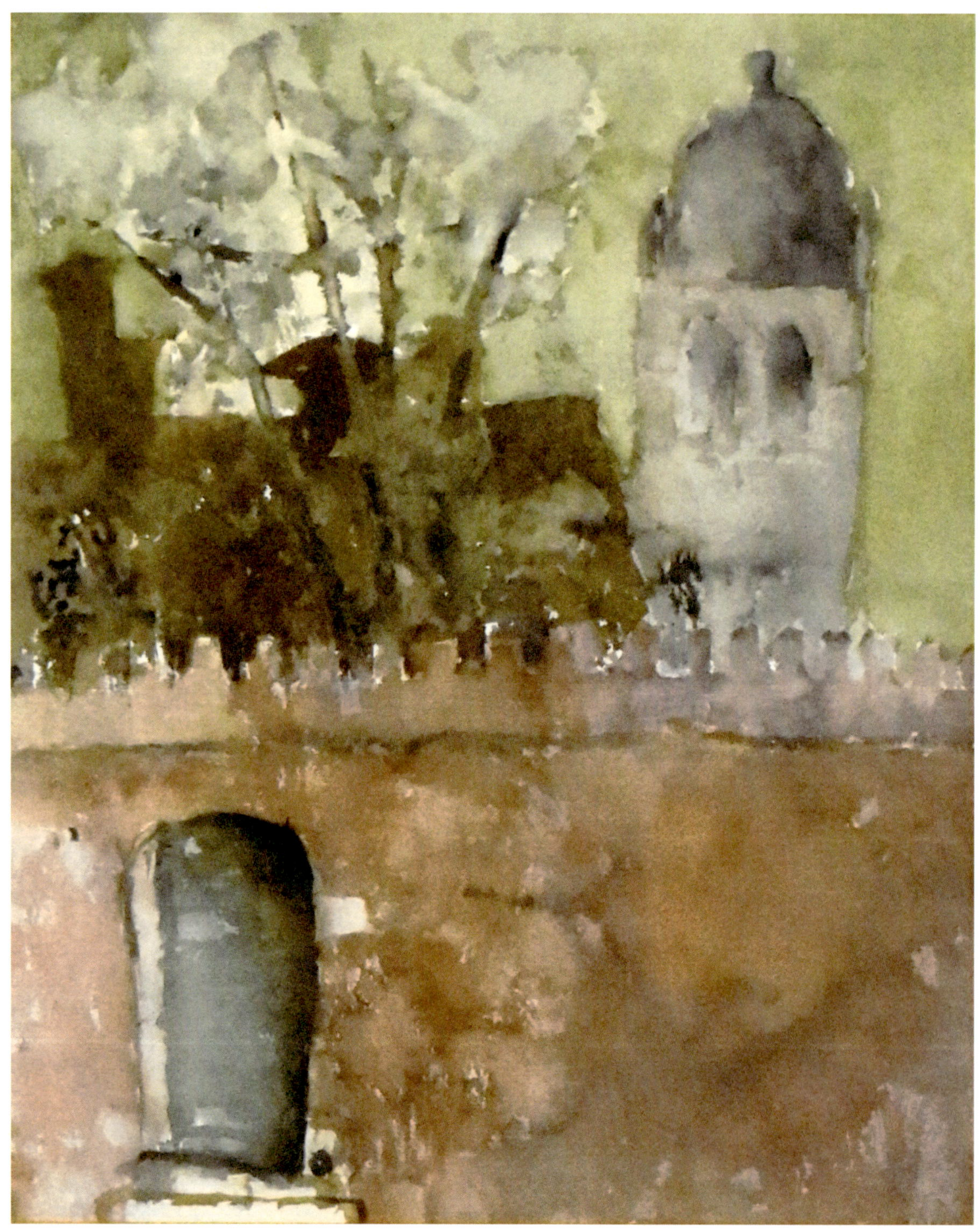

78. *Rio del Trapolin at Santa Fosca Church,* 1993

Artist Biography

Born in Montreal, John Fox (1927–2008) attended McGill University and then enrolled at the École des Beaux-arts de Montréal. Dissatisfied with its academic approach, he attended the Montreal Museum of Fine Arts, School of Art and Design from 1946 to 1949, where he studied under the painter Goodridge Roberts. He later worked for the critic-painter John Lyman in McGill University's Department of Art. In 1952, Fox attended the Slade School of Art, University of London, followed by two years of independent work in Florence and Paris and visits to Venice in the mid-1950s. Returning to Montreal, he began his career as a painter and later as a teacher at the Saidye Bronfman Centre (now the Segal Centre for the Performing Arts) in the 1960s. He subsequently taught as a professor in graduate and undergraduate programs in the Painting and Drawing Department, Faculty of Fine Arts at Concordia University from 1970 until his retirement in 1998.

Fox worked in a variety of media: oil, acrylic, watercolour, gouache, chalk, and graphite. He also made silkscreens, etchings, monotypes, and bronze sculpture. Though his images varied from abstract to representational, he was foremost a colourist, where the materiality of colour and light is a metaphor for objectifying the sensations of the object. His early intimist pictures became abstract images in the early 1970s; he returned to representational imagery fifteen years later. In 1977, he began making annual

Biographie de l'artiste

Né à Montréal, John Fox (1927–2008) fréquente l'Université McGill avant de s'inscrire à l'École des beaux-arts de Montréal. Insatisfait des méthodes pédagogiques de l'institution, il migre à la School of Art and Design du Musée des beaux-arts de Montréal, où il étudiera auprès du peintre Goodridge Roberts de 1946 à 1949. Plus tard, il travaille pour le peintre et critique d'art John Lyman du Department of Art de l'Université McGill. En 1952, on le retrouve à la Slade School of Art de la University of London, d'où il part ensuite pour travailler deux ans de manière autonome à Florence et à Paris, plus quelques visites à Venise au milieu des années 1950. De retour à Montréal, il entame sa carrière de peintre, puis d'enseignant au Saidye Bronfman Centre (aujourd'hui Centre Segal des arts de la scène) dans les années 1960. À partir de 1970, il sera professeur aux programmes de premier cycle et des cycles supérieurs au Département de la peinture et du dessin de la Faculté des beaux-arts de l'Université Concordia jusqu'à sa retraite en 1998.

Fox a travaillé avec plusieurs matières : huile, acrylique, aquarelle, gouache, craie, graphite. Il s'est adonné par ailleurs à la sérigraphie, à l'eau-forte, au monotype et à la sculpture en bronze. Ayant exploité aussi bien le figuratif que l'abstrait, il est d'abord un coloriste pour qui la couleur et la lumière matérialisent les sensations inspirées par l'objet. Après ses premières scènes intimistes, il se lance dans l'abstraction au début des années 1970, pour une période de 15 ans qui se conclura par un retour à la figuration. C'est en 1977 qu'il

trips to Venice until his death there in 2008. Both his abstract and representational painting were deeply influenced by the light and colour of Venetian art and architecture, and especially by the city itself.

John Fox's artwork is held in many private, corporate, and public collections, including the National Gallery of Canada, the Montreal Museum of Fine Arts, the Musée national des beaux-art de Québec, the Art Gallery of Hamilton, the Beaverbrook Art Gallery, and museums and galleries across Canada. This exhibition at the Beaverbrook Art Gallery is the first presentation to exclusively feature his Venetian work.

commence ses voyages annuels à Venise, où il mourra en 2008. Figurative ou abstraite, sa peinture aura toujours été profondément marquée par la lumière et la couleur de l'art et de l'architecture de la Sérénissime, voire par la cité elle-même.

Les œuvres de John Fox sont dispersées dans de nombreuses collections privées, publiques et d'entreprises, dont le Musée des beaux-arts du Canada, le Musée des beaux-arts de Montréal, le Musée national des beaux-arts du Québec, la Art Gallery of Hamilton, le Musée des beaux-arts Beaverbrook et divers autres musées du Canada. Cette exposition, au Musée des beaux-arts Beaverbrook, est la première à présenter exclusivement son œuvre vénitien.

Contributors

VICTORIA LEBLANC is an artist, writer, curator and teacher who has contributed to over 40 publications on Canadian artists. She is a former director of Montreal's Visual Arts Centre and McClure Gallery and was curator of the Gallery at Victoria Hall in Westmount. She has participated in solo and group exhibitions across Canada and is the author of two books of poetry.

JOHN LEROUX, ONB, is an art historian, teacher, retired architect, and the Director of the Marion McCain Institute for Atlantic Canadian Art at the Beaverbrook Art Gallery. He has authored or edited twenty books and contributed to many others. Some of his recent publications include *Peter Powning: A Retrospective* and *Michael Smith: Sea of Change*.

SANDRA PAIKOWSKY, CM, is an art historian, curator, writer, and Professor Emeritus of Art History at Concordia University. She was a longtime director and curator at the Concordia Art Gallery, co-founder and editor/publisher of the *Journal of Canadian Art History*, and co-editor of the McGill-Queen's University Press/Beaverbrook series, *Canadian Foundation Studies in Art History*. She is the author of numerous publications, including *James Wilson Morrice: Paintings and Drawings of Venice*. In 2015, she received the Order of Canada for her contributions to Canadian art history.

Les auteurs

Artiste, autrice, conservatrice et enseignante, VICTORIA LEBLANC a participé à la rédaction de plus de 40 ouvrages sur des artistes canadiens. Elle a été directrice de la Galerie McClure, au Centre des arts visuels de Montréal, et conservatrice de la Galerie du Victoria Hall, à Westmount. Elle a exposé en solo et en groupe dans tout le Canada, en plus de publier deux recueils de poèmes.

Historien de l'art, professeur et architecte retraité, JOHN LEROUX, O.N.-B., est Directeur de l'Institut Marion McCain de l'art du Canada Atlantique au Musée des beaux-arts Beaverbrook. Il a écrit ou dirigé 20 ouvrages et collaboré à de nombreux autres. Parmi ses plus récentes publications, mentionnons *Peter Powning: A Retrospective/Une rétrospective* et *Michael Smith: Sea of change/Mer mouvante*.

SANDRA PAIKOWSKY, CM, est historienne de l'art, conservatrice, autrice et professeure émérite d'histoire de l'art à l'Université Concordia. Longtemps directrice et conservatrice de la galerie d'art de Concordia, elle a cofondé les *Annales d'histoire de l'art canadien*, dont elle a également été rédactrice et éditrice, et a codirigé la série *Canadian Foundation Studies in Art History*, projet conjoint de McGill-Queen's University Press et Beaverbrook. Elle a signé de nombreuses publications, notamment *James Wilson Morrice: Paintings and Drawings of Venice*. En 2015, elle a été investie de l'Ordre du Canada pour sa contribution à l'histoire de l'art canadien.

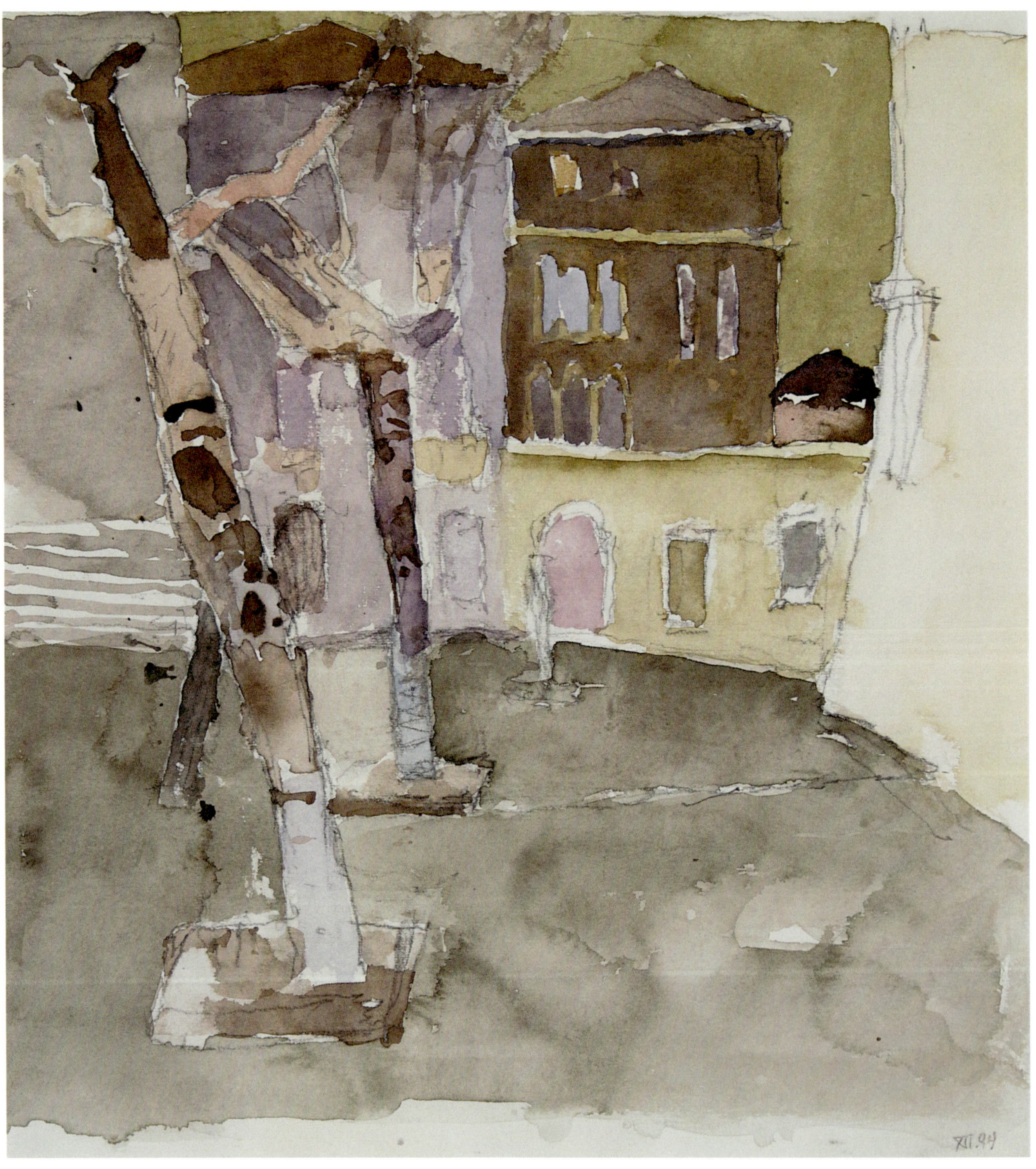
XII.94

List of Works

All works by John Fox, unless otherwise noted.
Sketchbook drawings are collection of Sandra Paikowsky.
Photographs of the artworks are by the Beaverbrook Art Gallery, unless otherwise noted.

John Fox, Venice, 2004 (frontispiece)
Collection of Sandra Paikowsky
Photo: Sandra Paikowsky

Campiello della Madonna, 17 May 2002 (fig. 1)
sketchbook, pencil on paper
15 × 10 cm

Corte Mosto S. Marcuola (Sottoportego Mosto), 2 April 2001 (fig. 2)
sketchbook, pencil on paper
30 × 20 cm

Campo San Giacomo dell' Orio, 2000 (fig. 3)
watercolour and pencil on paper
33 × 33 cm
Collection of Angelica Fox

Window and Sottoportego, Rio Madonna dell' Orto,
25 April 2004 (fig. 4)
sketchbook, pencil on paper
14 × 21 cm

Corte dei Muti, 18 April 2003 (fig. 5)
sketchbook, red conté
21 × 14 cm

Rio della Madonna dell' Orto,
7 May 1998 (fig. 6)
sketchbook, pencil on paper
21 × 14 cm

Rio della Madonna dell' Orto, 1993 (fig. 7)
watercolour and pencil on paper
43 × 38 cm
Private collection

Campo dei Gesuiti, 21 December 1994 (fig. 8)
sketchbook, pencil on paper
20 × 15 cm

Campo dei Gesuiti, 3 May 1998 (fig. 9)
sketchbook, pencil on paper
21 × 14 cm

Bridge on the Rio Santa Fosca,
1 April 2003 (fig. 10)
sketchbook, red conté
21 × 14 cm

Rio Trapolin (at Santa Fosca Church),
10 March 1993 (fig. 11)
sketchbook, pencil on paper
14 × 10 cm

Sottoportego Mosto, 19 May 2006 (fig. 12)
sketchbook, pencil on paper
20 × 13 cm

Sottoportego Mosto, 2003 (fig. 13)
watercolour and pencil on paper
36 × 28 cm
Collection of Irina and Peter Krausz
Photo: Victoria Stusiak

Campiello San Francesco della Vigna,
May 23, 2007 (fig. 14)
sketchbook, pencil on paper
21 × 13 cm

Campiello, San Francesco della Vigna,
2007 (fig. 15)
watercolour and pencil on paper
38 × 28 cm
Private collection

Rialto Bridge, 1956 (fig. 16)
oil on linen
61 × 71 cm
Private collection
Photo: Victoria Stusiak

San Vidal Church and Campo Morosini,
1956 (fig. 17)
sketchbook, pencil on paper
19 × 15 cm

Interior, Church of the Salute, 1956 (fig. 18)
oil on linen
51 × 61 cm
Private collection
Photo: Heffel Fine Art Auction House

Rialto Fish Market, 1964 (fig. 19)
oil on linen
51 × 58 cm
Collection of Jason Paikowsky and Barbara Sauerteig

Canal, Venice [Rio Sant' Angelo], 1964 (fig. 20)
oil on linen
74 × 51 cm
Beaverbrook Art Gallery, Gift of Jack and Joan Craig

Burano, 1992 (fig. 21)
charcoal on paper
51 × 69 cm
Private collection
Photo: Victoria Stusiak

Venice Studio, 2004 (fig. 22)
oil on wood panel
25 × 18 cm
Private collection
Photo: Victoria Stusiak

Inch by Ounce, 1979 (fig. 23)
acrylic on canvas
226 × 168 cm
Beaverbrook Art Gallery, Gift of Sandra Paikowsky

Untitled No. 8308, 1983 (fig. 24)
acrylic and charcoal on paper
71 × 53cm
Private collection
Photo: Victoria Stusiak

79. *Campo dei Gesuiti and Bridge*, 1994

Campo San Angelo, 1984 (fig. 25)
pencil on paper
30 × 23 cm
Collection of Sandra Paikowsky

Caffè Tartaruga, 2008 (fig. 26)
sketchbook, pencil on paper
20 × 13 cm

Interior of the Palazzo Barbaro, 1991 (fig. 27)
oil on linen
124 × 79 cm
Private collection
Photo: Victoria Stusiak

Rio Madonna dell' Orto Towards the Scuola Misericordia, 2007 (fig. 28)
watercolour and pencil on paper
38 × 28 cm
Collection of Shirley MacLeod
Photo: Victoria Stusiak

Window and Sottoportego, Rio Madonna dell' Orto, 2004 (fig. 29)
watercolour on paper
36 × 51 cm
Private collection

Rio Terra della Maddalena, 2006 (fig. 30)
watercolour and pencil on paper
28 × 138 cm
Private collection

Ponte delle Tette, 22 December 1998 (fig. 31)
sketchbook, pencil on paper
21 × 14 cm

Church of the Salute, 1987 (fig. 32)
pencil on paper
24 × 18 cm
Collection of Sandra Paikowsky

Carmine (Sculpture, Carmine Church), 14 March 2001 (fig. 33)
sketchbook, pencil on paper
21 × 14 cm

Rialto Fish Market, c. 1980 (fig. 34)
pencil on paper
30 × 23 cm
Collection of Sandra Paikowsky
Photo: Victoria Stusiak

View of the Zattere and Church of the Redentore, 1964 (fig. 35)
oil on linen
76 × 61 cm
Private collection
Photo: Victoria Stusiak

Rio di San Girolamo (Rio Ca' Moro at San Girolamo), 2 May 2003 (fig. 36)
sketchbook, red conté
21 × 14 cm

Rio di San Girolamo (Rio Ca' Moro at San Girolamo), 28 May 2008 (fig. 37)
sketchbook, pencil on paper
20 × 13 cm

Venice Houses, 19 December 1995 (fig. 38)
sketchbook, pencil on paper
20 × 15 cm

Venice Houses, 1993 (fig. 39)
watercolour on paper
76 × 56 cm
Collection of Lisa Hoffman and Allan Schouela
Photo: Victoria Stusiak

Bridge at the Campo and Rio dei Gesuiti, 2002 (fig. 40)
watercolour on paper
30 × 23 cm
Private collection
Photo: Victoria Stusiak

Rio Ca' Moro at San Girolamo II, 2008 (fig. 41)
watercolour on paper
28 × 38 cm
Collection of Victoria LeBlanc
Photo: Victoria Stusiak

Habsburg Garden, 13 May 1996 (fig. 42)
sketchbook, pencil on paper
21 × 14 cm

Habsburg Garden, 1997 (fig. 43)
oil on linen
64 × 76 cm
Private collection
Photo: Victoria Stusiak

Campo Ghetto Nuovo, 1993 (fig. 44)
watercolour and pencil on paper
28 × 30 cm
Private collection

Campo Santa Margherita, 2004 (fig. 45)
watercolour on paper
25 × 36 cm
Private collection

Campo Ghetto Nuovo, 1993 (fig. 46)
sketchbook, pencil on paper
20 × 15 cm

Ponte delle Tette, Rio San Cassiano I, 1998 (fig. 47)
watercolour and pencil on paper
71 × 43 cm
Private collection

Ponte delle Tette, Rio San Cassiano II, 1998 (fig. 48)
watercolour on paper
56 × 38 cm
Private collection
Photo: Victoria Stusiak

Angel, Church of the Fava, Venice, undated (fig. 49)
silver gelatin print
35 × 33 cm
Printing: John Fox
Collection of Sandra Paikowsky

Hotel La Residenza, Campo Bragora, Venice, c. 1982 (fig. 50)
silver gelatin print
23 × 25 cm
Printing: John Fox
Collection of Sandra Paikowsky

Canal and Boats [Rio della Verona], 1957 (fig. 51)
oil on linen
61 × 50 cm
Private collection
Photo: Stephanie Thomas-Morris

Rio Madonna dell' Orto, 27 April 2007 (fig. 52)
sketchbook, pencil on paper
21 × 13 cm

Canal Grande, 1993 (fig. 53)
watercolour on paper, 31 × 41cm
Collection of Angelica Fox

Campo delle Gorne, 2003 (fig. 54)
oil on linen
112 × 81 cm
Private collection
Photo: Victoria Stusiak

Sandra in Venice, 8 March 1993 (fig. 55)
sketchbook, pencil on paper
20 × 15 cm

Ramo dei Muti, 2003 (fig. 56)
oil on linen
104 × 71 cm
Private collection
Photo: Victoria Stusiak

Rio Sant' Alvise, 1998 (fig. 57)
watercolour and pencil on paper
51 × 41 cm
Private collection

Rio Ca' Moro at San Girolamo I, 2008 (fig. 58)
watercolour on paper
28 × 38 cm
Private collection
Photo: Victoria Stusiak

Fondamenta della Sensa, 2002 (fig. 59)
watercolour and red conté on paper
28 × 38 cm
Collection of Patrick Howlett
Photo: Victoria Stusiak

Rio San Daniele, 2007 (fig. 60)
watercolour and pencil on paper
38 × 28 cm
Private collection
Photo: Victoria Stusiak

Palazzo Soranzo, Campo Santa Ternità, 2002 (fig. 61)
watercolour and red conté on paper
38 × 28 cm
Private collection

Palazzo Soranzo, Campo Santa Ternità, 2003 (fig. 62)
oil on linen
94 × 64 cm
Private collection
Photo: Victoria Stusiak

Campiello della Madonna, 2003 (fig. 63)
oil on linen
107 × 64 cm
Private collection
Photo: Victoria Stusiak

Interior, Carmini Church, 30 April 2004 (fig. 64)
sketchbook, pencil on paper
21 × 14 cm

Interior, Carmini Church, 20 December 1997 (fig. 65)
sketchbook, pencil on paper
21 × 14 cm

Interior, Gesuiti Church, 2001 (fig. 66)
watercolour and red conté on paper
38 × 28 cm
Private collection

Interior of the Carmini Church, 2004 (fig. 67)
oil on wood panel
25 × 17 cm
Musée d'art de Joliette, gift of Sandra Paikowsky

Worksite, 1994 (fig. 68)
oil on linen
122 × 92 cm
Private collection
Photo: Victoria Stusiak

Moro Bridge at the Servi Convent, 2004 (fig. 69)
watercolour and pencil on paper
36 × 28 cm
Collection Rosalind M. Pepall

Interior, Basilica San Marco, 1998 (fig. 70)
watercolour and charcoal on paper
69 × 46 cm
Private collection

Cloister, San Pietro di Castello, 2007 (fig. 71)
watercolour and pencil on paper
38 × 28 cm
Private collection

Campo Sant' Alvise, 13 May 2008 (fig. 72)
sketchbook, pencil on paper
20 × 13 cm

Campo Sant' Alvise, 2008 (fig. 73)
watercolour on paper
28 × 38 cm
Private collection

At San Nicolò dei Mendicoli Church, 2000 (fig. 74)
watercolour on paper
38 × 28 cm
Collection of Caroline Hart and Leopold Plotek
Photo: Victoria Stusiak

Grand Canal Looking Towards the Salute Church, 1963 (fig. 75)
oil on wood panel
18 × 25 cm
Private collection
Photo: Victoria Stusiak

Palazzo da Silva, 2007 (fig. 76)
oil on linen
188 × 122 cm
Collection of Sandra Paikowsky
Photo: Victoria Stusiak

Campanile dei Gesuiti, 18 May 2007 (fig. 77)
sketchbook, pencil on paper
21 × 13 cm

Rio del Trapolin at Santa Fosca Church, 1993 (fig. 78)
watercolour and pencil on paper
46 × 38 cm
Musée des beaux-arts de Sherbrooke
Gift of Luc LaRochelle
Photo: Musée des beaux-arts de Sherbrooke

Campo dei Gesuiti and Bridge, 1994 (fig. 79)
watercolour and pencil on paper
38 × 38 cm
Private collection
Photo: Victoria Stusiak

John Fox painting *Palazzo da Silva* in his Montreal studio in Saint-Henri, Montreal, 2007 (fig. 80)
Collection of Sandra Paikowsky
Photo: Victoria Stusiak

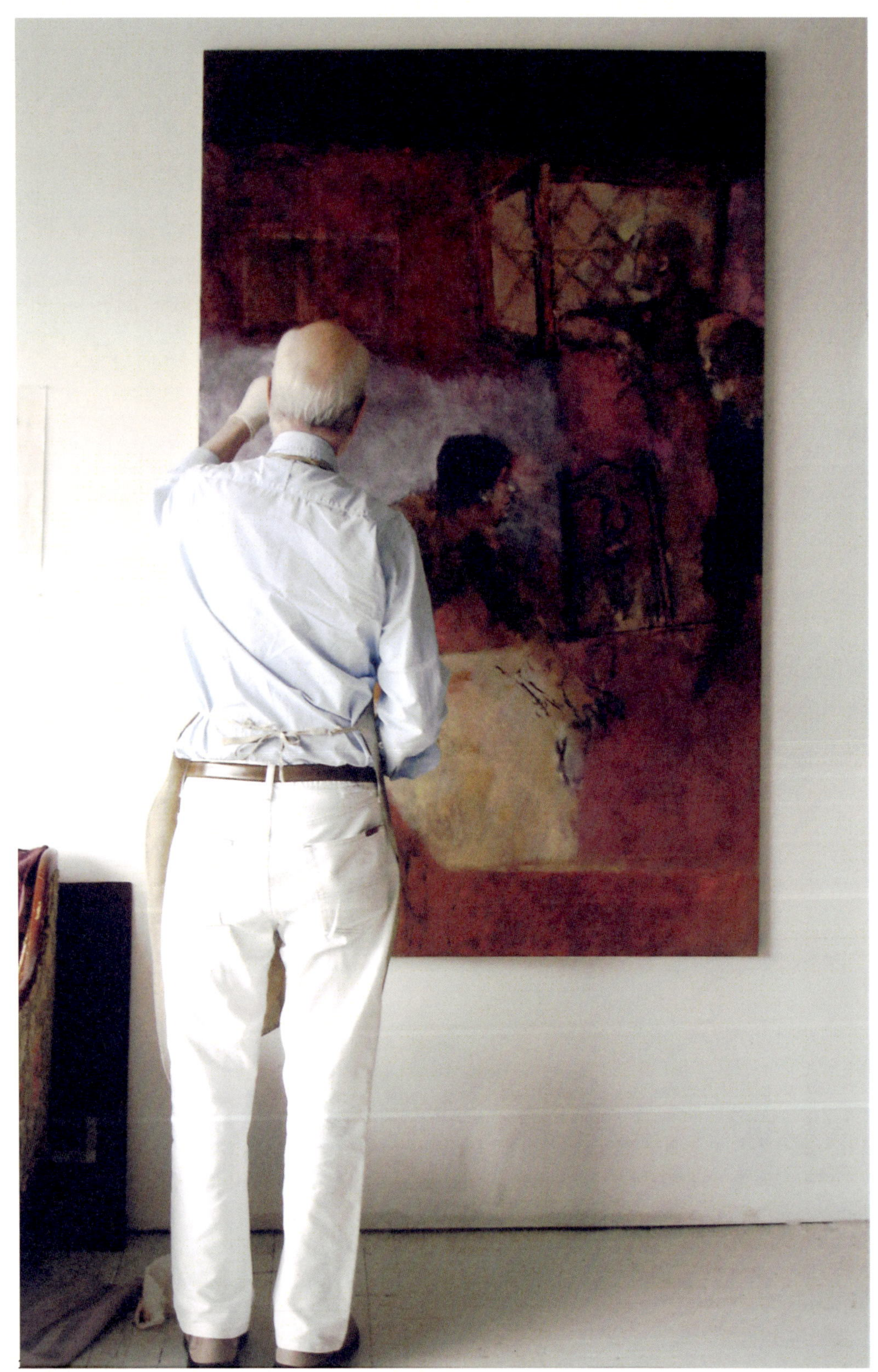

80. John Fox painting *Palazzo da Silva* in his studio in Saint-Henri, Montreal, 2007 | John Fox peint le *Palazzo da Silva* dans son atelier de Saint-Henri, à Montréal, en 2007

Liste des œuvres

À moins d'avis contraire, toutes les œuvres sont de John Fox.
Les dessins des carnets de croquis sont de la collection de Sandra Paikowsky.
À moins d'avis contraire, les photographies sont du Musée des beaux-arts Beaverbrook.

John Fox, Venice, 2004 (frontispice)
Collection Sandra Paikowsky
Photo : Sandra Paikowsky

Campiello della Madonna, 17 mai 2002 (fig. 1)
Carnet, crayon sur papier
15 × 10 cm

Corte Mosto S. Marcuola (Sottoportego Mosto), 2 avril 2001 (fig. 2)
Carnet, crayon sur papier
30 × 20 cm

Campo San Giacomo dell' Orio, 2000 (fig. 3)
Aquarelle et crayon sur papier
33 × 33 cm
Collection Angelica Fox

Window and Sottoportego, Rio Madonna dell' Orto, 25 avril 2004 (fig. 4)
Carnet, crayon sur papier
14 × 21 cm

Corte dei Muti, 18 avril 2003 (fig. 5)
Carnet, rouge conté
21 × 14 cm

Rio della Madonna dell' Orto, 7 mai 1998 (fig. 6)
Carnet, crayon sur papier
21 × 14 cm

Rio della Madonna dell' Orto, 1993 (fig. 7)
Aquarelle et crayon sur papier
43 × 38 cm
Collection privée

Campo dei Gesuiti, 21 décembre 1994 (fig. 8)
Carnet, crayon sur papier
20 × 15 cm

Campo dei Gesuiti, 3 mai 1998 (fig. 9)
Carnet, crayon sur papier
21 × 14 cm

Bridge on the Rio Santa Fosca, 1er avril 2003 (fig. 10)
Carnet, rouge conté
21 × 14 cm

Rio Trapolin (at Santa Fosca Church), 10 mars 1993 (fig. 11)
Carnet, crayon sur papier
14 × 10 cm

Sottoportego Mosto, 19 mai 2006 (fig. 12)
Carnet, crayon sur papier
20 × 13 cm

Sottoportego Mosto, 2003 (fig. 13)
Aquarelle et crayon sur papier
36 × 28 cm
Collection Irina et Peter Krausz
Photo : Victoria Stusiak

Campiello San Francesco della Vigna, 23 mai 2007 (fig. 14)
Carnet, crayon sur papier
21 × 13 cm

Campiello San Francesco della Vigna, 2007 (fig. 15)
Aquarelle et crayon sur papier
38 × 28 cm
Collection privée

Rialto Bridge, 1956 (fig. 16)
Huile sur lin
61 × 71 cm
Collection privée
Photo : Victoria Stusiak

San Vidal Church and Campo Morosini, 1956 (fig. 17)
Carnet, crayon sur papier
19 × 15 cm

Interior, Church of the Salute, 1956 (fig. 18)
Huile sur lin
51 × 61 cm
Collection privée
Photo : Maison de vente aux enchères Heffel

Rialto Fish Market, 1964 (fig. 19)
Huile sur lin
51 × 58 cm
Collection Jason Paikowsky et Barbara Sauerteig

Canal, Venice [Rio Sant' Angelo], 1964 (fig. 20)
Huile sur lin
74 × 51 cm
Musée des beaux-arts Beaverbrook, don de Jack et Joan Craig

Burano, 1992 (fig. 21)
Fusain sur papier
51 × 69 cm
Collection privée
Photo : Victoria Stusiak

Venice Studio, 2004 (fig. 22)
Huile sur panneau de bois
25 × 18 cm
Collection privée
Photo : Victoria Stusiak

Inch by Ounce, 1979 (fig. 23)
Acrylique sur toile
226 × 168 cm
Musée des beaux-arts Beaverbrook, don de Sandra Paikowsky

Untitled No. 8308, 1983 (fig. 24)
Acrylique et fusain sur papier
71 × 53 cm
Collection privée
Photo : Victoria Stusiak

Campo San Angelo, 1984 (fig. 25)
Crayon sur papier
30 × 23 cm
Collection Sandra Paikowsky

Caffè Tartaruga, 2008 (fig. 26)
Carnet, crayon sur papier
20 × 13 cm

Interior of the Palazzo Barbaro, 1991 (fig. 27)
Huile sur lin
124 × 79 cm
Collection privée
Photo : Victoria Stusiak

Rio Madonna dell' Orto Towards the Scuola Misericordia, 2007 (fig. 28)
Aquarelle et crayon sur papier
38 × 28 cm
Collection Shirley MacLeod
Photo : Victoria Stusiak

Window and Sottoportego, Rio Madonna dell' Orto, 2004 (fig. 29)
Aquarelle sur papier
36 × 51 cm
Collection privée

Rio Terra della Maddalena, 2006 (fig. 30)
Aquarelle et crayon sur papier
28 × 138 cm
Collection privée

Ponte delle Tette, 22 décembre 1998 (fig. 31)
Carnet, crayon sur papier
21 × 14 cm

Church of the Salute, 1987 (fig. 32)
Crayon sur papier
24 × 18 cm
Collection Sandra Paikowsky

Carmine (Sculpture, Carmine Church), 14 mars 2001 (fig. 33)
Carnet, crayon sur papier
21 × 14 cm

Rialto Fish Market, vers 1980 (fig. 34)
Crayon sur papier
30 × 23 cm
Collection Sandra Paikowsky
Photo : Victoria Stusiak

View of the Zattere and Church of the Redentore, 1964 (fig. 35)
Huile sur lin
76 × 61 cm
Collection privée
Photo : Victoria Stusiak

Rio di San Girolamo (Rio Ca' Moro at San Girolamo), 2 mai 2003 (fig. 36)
Carnet, rouge conté
21 × 14 cm

Rio di San Girolamo (Rio Ca' Moro at San Girolamo), 28 mai 2008 (fig. 37)
Carnet, crayon sur papier
20 × 13 cm

Venice Houses, 19 décembre 1995 (fig. 38)
Carnet, crayon sur papier
20 × 15 cm

Venice Houses, 1993 (fig. 39)
Aquarelle sur papier
76 × 56 cm
Collection Lisa Hoffman et Allan Schouela
Photo : Victoria Stusiak

Bridge at the Campo and Rio dei Gesuiti, 2002 (fig. 40)
Aquarelle sur papier
30 × 23 cm
Collection privée
Photo : Victoria Stusiak

Rio Ca' Moro at San Girolamo II, 2008 (fig. 41)
Aquarelle sur papier
28 × 38 cm
Collection Victoria LeBlanc
Photo : Victoria Stusiak

Habsburg Garden, 13 mai 1996 (fig. 42)
Carnet, crayon sur papier
21 × 14 cm

Habsburg Garden, 1997 (fig. 43)
Huile sur lin
64 × 76 cm
Collection privée
Photo : Victoria Stusiak

Campo Ghetto Nuovo, 1993 (fig. 44)
Aquarelle et crayon sur papier
28 × 30 cm
Collection privée

Campo Santa Margherita, 2004 (fig. 45)
Aquarelle sur papier
25 × 36 cm
Collection privée

Campo Ghetto Nuovo, 1993 (fig. 46)
Carnet, crayon sur papier
20 × 15 cm

Ponte delle Tette, Rio San Cassiano I, 1998 (fig. 47)
Aquarelle et crayon sur papier
71 × 43 cm
Collection privée

Ponte delle Tette, Rio San Cassiano II, 1998 (fig. 48)
Aquarelle sur papier
56 × 38 cm
Collection privée
Photo : Victoria Stusiak

Angel, Church of the Fava, Venice, sans date (fig. 49)
Tirage à la gélatine argentique
35 × 33 cm
Tirage : John Fox
Collection Sandra Paikowsky

Hotel La Residenza, Campo Bragora, Venice, vers 1982 (fig. 50)
Tirage à la gélatine argentique
23 × 25 cm
Tirage : John Fox
Collection Sandra Paikowsky

Canal and Boats (Rio della Verona), 1957 (fig. 51)
Huile sur lin
61 × 50 cm
Collection privée
Photo : Stephanie Thomas-Morris

Rio Madonna dell' Orto, 27 avril 2007 (fig. 52)
Carnet, crayon sur papier
21 × 13 cm

Canale Grande, 1993 (fig. 53)
Aquarelle sur papier
31 × 41 cm
Collection Angelica Fox

Campo delle Gorne, 2003 (fig. 54)
Huile sur lin
112 × 81 cm
Collection privée
Photo : Victoria Stusiak

Sandra in Venice, 8 mars 1993 (fig. 55)
Carnet, crayon sur papier
20 × 15 cm

Ramo dei Muti, 2003 (fig. 56)
Huile sur lin
104 × 71 cm
Collection privée
Photo : Victoria Stusiak

Rio Sant' Alvise, 1998 (fig. 57)
Aquarelle et crayon sur papier
51 × 41 cm
Collection privée

Rio Ca' Moro at San Girolamo I, 2008 (fig. 58)
Aquarelle sur papier
28 × 38 cm
Collection privée
Photo : Victoria Stusiak

Fondamenta della Sensa, 2002 (fig. 59)
Aquarelle et rouge conté sur papier
28 × 38 cm
Collection Patrick Howlett
Photo : Victoria Stusiak

Rio San Daniele, 2007 (fig. 60)
Aquarelle et crayon sur papier
38 × 28 cm
Collection privée
Photo : Victoria Stusiak

Palazzo Soranzo, Campo Santa Ternità, 2002 (fig. 61)
Aquarelle et rouge conté sur papier
38 × 28 cm
Collection privée

Palazzo Soranzo, Campo Santa Ternità, 2003 (fig. 62)
Huile sur lin
94 × 64 cm
Collection privée
Photo : Victoria Stusiak

Campiello della Madonna, 2003 (fig. 63)
Huile sur lin
107 × 64 cm
Collection privée
Photo : Victoria Stusiak

Interior, Carmini Church, 30 avril 2004 (fig. 64)
Carnet, crayon sur papier
21 × 14 cm

Interior, Carmini Church, 20 décembre 1997 (fig. 65)
Carnet, crayon sur papier
21 × 14 cm

Interior, Gesuiti Church, 2001 (fig. 66)
Aquarelle et rouge conté sur papier
38 × 28 cm
Collection privée

Interior of the Carmini Church, 2004 (fig. 67)
Huile sur panneau de bois
25 × 17 cm
Musée d'art de Joliette, don de Sandra Paikowsky
Photo : Musée d'art de Joliette

Worksite, 1994 (fig. 68)
Huile sur lin
122 × 92 cm
Collection privée
Photo : Victoria Stusiak

Moro Bridge at the Servi Convent, 2004 (fig. 69)
Aquarelle et crayon sur papier
36 × 28 cm
Collection Rosalind M. Pepall

Interior, Basilica San Marco, 1998 (fig. 70)
Aquarelle et fusain sur papier
69 × 46 cm
Collection privée

Cloister, San Pietro di Castello, 2007 (fig. 71)
Aquarelle et crayon sur papier
38 × 28 cm
Collection privée

Campo Sant' Alvise, 13 mai 2008 (fig. 72)
Carnet, crayon sur papier
20 × 13 cm

Campo Sant' Alvise, 2008 (fig. 73)
Aquarelle sur papier
28 × 38 cm
Collection privée

At San Nicolò dei Mendicoli Church, 2000 (fig. 74)
Aquarelle sur papier
38 × 28 cm
Collection Caroline Hart et Leopold Plotek
Photo : Victoria Stusiak

Grand Canal Looking Towards the Salute Church, 1963 (fig. 75)
Huile sur panneau de bois
18 × 25 cm
Collection privée
Photo : Victoria Stusiak

Palazzo da Silva, 2007 (fig. 76)
Huile sur lin
188 × 122 cm
Collection Sandra Paikowsky
Photo : Victoria Stusiak

Campanile dei Gesuiti, 18 mai 2007 (fig. 77)
Carnet, crayon sur papier
21 × 13 cm

Rio del Trapolin at Santa Fosca Church, 1993 (fig. 78)
Aquarelle et crayon sur papier
46 × 38 cm
Musée des beaux-arts de Sherbrooke
Don de Luc LaRochelle
Photo : Musée des beaux-arts de Sherbrooke

Campo dei Gesuiti and Bridge, 1994 (fig. 79)
Aquarelle et crayon sur papier
38 × 38 cm
Collection privée
Photo : Victoria Stusiak

John Fox peint le *Palazzo da Silva* dans son atelier de Saint-Henri, à Montréal, en 2007 (fig. 80)
Collection Sandra Paikowsky
Photo : Victoria Stusiak

Publication coordinated by John Leroux.
Edited by Laura Kenins.
Translated to French by Eve Renaud.
Map by John Leroux and Philip LeBlanc.
Cover and page design by Julie Scriver, Goose Lane Editions.
Cover: *Rio della Madonna dell' Orto*, 1993, watercolour and pencil on paper, 43 × 38 cm. Private collection.
Printed in Canada by HUME Media.
10 9 8 7 6 5 4 3 2 1

Library and Archives Canada Cataloguing in Publication

Title: John Fox : a painter in Venice = un peintre à Venise / Sandra Paikowsky, Victoria LeBlanc, and John Leroux.
Other titles: Painter in Venice | Peintre à Venise | John Fox (2025). | John Fox (2025). French
Names: Paikowsky, Sandra, 1945- writer of added commentary. | LeBlanc, Victoria, 1949- writer of added commentary. | Leroux, John, 1970- writer of added commentary. | Fox, John, 1927-2008. Paintings. Selections. | Beaverbrook Art Gallery, issuing body, host institution.
Description: Catalogue of an exhibition held at the Beaverbrook Art Gallery from July 22 to October 19, 2025. | Includes bibliographical references. | Text in English and French.
Identifiers: Canadiana 20250119765E | ISBN 9781069130501 (softcover)
Subjects: LCSH: Fox, John, 1927-2008—Exhibitions. | LCGFT: Exhibition catalogs.
Classification: LCC ND249.F69 A4 2025 | DDC 759.11074—dc23

Beaverbrook Art Gallery
703 Queen Street
Fredericton, New Brunswick
CANADA E3B 1C4
beaverbrookartgallery.org

Direction de la publication : John Leroux
Révision anglaise : Laura Kenins
Traduction française : Eve Renaud
Révision française : Hélène Ricard
Carte de John Leroux et Philip LeBlanc
Couverture et mise en page : Julie Scriver, Goose Lane Editions
Couverture : *Rio della Madonna dell' Orto*, 1993, aquarelle et crayon sur papier, 43 × 38 cm ; collection privée
Imprimé au Canada par HUME Media
10 9 8 7 6 5 4 3 2 1

Catalogage avant publication de Bibliothèque et Archives Canada

Titre : John Fox : a painter in Venice = un peintre à Venise / Sandra Paikowsky, Victoria LeBlanc et John Leroux.
Autres titres : Painter in Venice | Peintre à Venise | John Fox (2025). | John Fox (2025). Français
Noms : Paikowsky, Sandra, auteur de commentaire ajouté. | LeBlanc, Victoria, 1949- auteur de commentaire ajouté. | Leroux, John, 1970- auteur de commentaire ajouté. | Fox, John, 1927-2008. Peintures. Extraits. | Musée des beaux-arts Beaverbrook, organisme de publication, institution hôte.
Description : Catalogue d'une exposition tenue au Musée des beaux-arts Beaverbrook du 22 juillet au 19 octobre 2025. | Comprend des références bibliographiques. | Texte en anglais et en français.
Identifiants : Canadiana 20250119765F | ISBN 9781069130501 (couverture souple)
Vedettes-matière : RVM : Fox, John, 1927-2008—Expositions. | RVMGF : Catalogues d'exposition.
Classification : LCC ND249.F69 A4 2025 | CDD 759.11074—dc23

Musée des beaux-arts Beaverbrook
703, rue Queen
Fredericton (Nouveau-Brunswick)
CANADA E3B 1C4
beaverbrookartgallery.org